YENAN AND THE GREAT POWERS
The Origins of Chinese Communist Foreign Policy,
1944–1946

Studies of the East Asian Institute
Columbia University

YENAN
and the
GREAT POWERS

*The Origins of Chinese Communist Foreign Policy
1944-1946*

JAMES REARDON-ANDERSON

New York
Columbia University Press
1980

Photo for page iii: "The Yenan Triumvirate: Chou En-lai, Mao Tse-tung, Chu Teh."

Library of Congress Cataloging in Publication Data

Reardon-Anderson, James.
  Yenan and the Great Powers.

  (Studies of the East Asian Institute, Columbia
University)
  Bibliography: p.
  Includes index.
  1. United States—Foreign relations—China.
2. China—Foreign relations—United States. 3. China—
Foreign relations—1912–1949. I. Title. II. Series:
Columbia University. East Asian Institute. Studies.
E183.8.C5R4   327.51'073   79-23343
ISBN 0-231-04784-3

Columbia University Press
New York   Guildford, Surrey

To Kathleen

The East Asian Institute of Columbia University

The East Asian Institute of Columbia University was established in 1949 to prepare graduate students for careers dealing with East Asia, and to aid research and publication on East Asia during the modern period. The faculty of the Institute are grateful to the Ford Foundation and the Rockefeller Foundation for their financial assistance.

The Studies of the East Asian Institute were inaugurated in 1962 to bring to a wider public the results of significant new research on modern and contemporary East Asia.

Contents

Maps

Acknowledgements

This book is the final product of my education at Columbia University, whose East Asian Institute and Morningside campus remain my spiritual home. The faculty, students and staff of the Institute made my years at Columbia worth remembering, and all bear some credit for whatever the reader finds interesting in the pages that follow. The Center for Chinese Studies at the University of Michigan provided friendly shelter during the final stages of the dissertation. The book was completed at Johns Hopkins University's School of Advanced International Studies, where many of my colleagues and students shouted the last hurrahs as I staggered to the finish line. In a world where institutions have a bad name, these three deserve high marks.

Money, in a word, is the fuel for research, and this book represents a small reward to those contributors that have helped me along the way: the Tyng Fellowship of Williams College, the Edward John Noble Fellowship of Columbia's School of International Affairs, the East Asian Institute, and the National Science Foundation.

There is neither time nor space to thank all the people who have played a part in this work. Doak Barnett and Michel Oksenberg were my first teachers in Chinese politics and sparked my interest in this subject. Warren Cohen, Michael Hunt and Andy Nathan read the manuscript in its later stages and provided much needed criticism. Steve Levine managed the affair throughout; his fine hand will be visible to those who know him. Dorothy Borg served as the gray eminence. I have no greater aspiration in writing this book than to add it to the long shelf of fine scholarship Dorothy has inspired.

September 1979   *James Reardon-Anderson*
                                                                       Washington, D.C.

YENAN AND THE GREAT POWERS
The Origins of Chinese Communist Foreign Policy,
1944–1946

Map 1. Provinces of China proper.

Introduction

Nineteen forty-four marks the beginning of contemporary Chinese foreign policy. In that year, changes on the battlefield in China brought Yenan, wartime capital of the Chinese Communist Party (CCP), to the attention of Washington and opened the first chapter of Chinese Communist relations with the great powers. During the 1920s the Communists in China had had close ties to Moscow; but as an instrument of the Comintern they made few decisions on their own, and the leadership of that generation did not survive the breakdown of the First United Front in 1927. During the 1930s the Communists survived and after the Long March prospered in the countryside, where Mao developed a sophisticated "perspective" on foreign affairs; but denied access to the cities and the governmental structure they had few real "relations" with the outside world. Finally, by the end of World War II, a new generation of leaders had taken control of the Party and for the first time they began to shape events on the mainland. Yenan became a factor in the battle for Asia. Confronting the reality of foreign power, the men who would lead the People's Republic of China through its first quarter-century entered the great game of world politics.

The assertion that Chinese Communist foreign policy began in 1944 rests on the notion that circumstances rather than ideas have been the principal force shaping Chinese Communist behavior in international affairs. This study challenges the thesis that Mao's explanation of world politics and their impact on China, borrowed from Lenin and refined in the vacuum of the Chinese countryside during the 1930s, provided a governing framework for the conduct of subsequent Communist foreign policy. Rather, the story begins in the mid-1940s, when the game of dealing with the great powers itself began. Then, ideas meant little, while the hard and stubborn facts of a complex reality meant much.

Although a popular subject for pundits, this first chapter of Chinese Communist foreign relations has received little scholarly attention. The most notable attempts to explain Yenan's foreign policy stress the role of ideology or Mao's "world view."[1] Tang Tsou points out that Yenan's words and deeds "all reflected the Chinese Communist party's ideological and organizational ties with the Soviet Union and its hope for eventual Soviet support." Mao's profession of friendship for the United States was only a "tactical" ploy, a desirable but temporary deferment of the inevitable struggle against capitalism and imperialism which must follow.[2] John Gittings looks down the opposite end of the telescope, stressing Yenan's independence from Moscow and the tactical flexibility of Mao's thought. But Gittings agrees that ideas, specifically Mao's ideas, provide the key to understanding Chinese Communist foreign policy before and after 1949. "Mao's theory of semi-colonialism was the starting point for all the most important strategic concepts of the Chinese revolution," Gittings argues. It "led" Mao to seek American aid in 1945 and to lean to the side of the Soviet Union in 1949. Two decades later, it was "invoked to justify" Nixon's visit to Peking.[3]

Other students of this period have stressed Yenan's pragmatism.[4] In their view, the Chinese Communists had no fixed ideas about international alignments, but were simply trying to get the best deal possible from whoever would help them. John Service, a spokesman for this school then and now, explains: "Essentially, it seemed to me that Mao was treating foreign relations as basically non-ideological. He was thinking in nationalistic Chinese terms; and assuming that most countries (including the Soviet Union *and* the United States) base their foreign policy on national interests."[5]

These works raise the interesting question of what motivated Mao and other policymakers in Yenan in their first attempts to deal with the outside world. They fail to provide an answer, however, because they treat the period of the mid-1940s primarily from the perspective of American foreign policy. None has undertaken a systematic study of the available materials in an attempt to explain what made Yenan tick. That is the purpose of this book.

The story which follows covers the period from the middle of 1944, when the possibility of American aid to the Chinese Communists brought them into world affairs, to the middle of 1946, when the outbreak of civil war froze Yenan into a rigid "anti-imperialist" stance and closed off all foreign-policy options for the next three years. In between, the Communists shifted this way and that, sometimes trying to placate both great powers and win their support, sometimes trying to divide Moscow and Washington along the line of the conflict in China. Most readers will find their thirst for historical detail slaked by the twists and turns of this account. Some may find that it sheds new light on the logic behind Yenan's actions.

The thesis presented here is that in its formative years Chinese Communist foreign policy followed no master plan; rather it was a series of adjustments to the circumstances that entwined and entangled Yenan. At the end of World War II, the Chinese Communists were still insurgents trying to seize power in a poor and backward country. Amidst the chaos of war and the swirl of events, policymakers in Yenan groped their way toward victory. For a time—the period covered in this study—they had to deal with the great powers, the United States and the Soviet Union. But hemmed in on all sides, neither Mao nor anyone else in Yenan was free to apply his grand design. Three factors weighed on their choices in foreign policy.

First, there was the situation in China. Throughout this period, the Chinese were at war, with Japan and with themselves, and this meant that events on the battlefield dominated politics in all areas. For Yenan, the decline of the Nationalist army, the collapse of the Japanese, and the entry of American and Russian forces into China created opportunities for military expansion which would bring quick gains, mostly at the expense of the government in Chungking. Negotiation with the Kuomintang for reforms which might give the Communists a greater role in the government promised no comparable rewards. From the perspective of Yenan, the domestic situation argued for civil war.

Second, this trend was reinforced by the balance of power within the Communist Party itself. After the middle of 1944, Red military commanders began to regroup their forces and press for stepped-up offensive operations. In a movement which was largely militarized to begin with, the generals formed a powerful lobby for armed expansion. On the other side, there were few spokesmen in Yenan for a policy of peaceful reform under the banner of the united front. The Rectification Campaign of the early 1940s had silenced those who favored compromise with the Kuomintang, the urban bourgeoisie, and the foreign supporters of unity in China. Pushed from within and pulled from without, Yenan leaned heavily toward conflict with Chungking.

Third, there were the United States and the Soviet Union. The poverty and disorder of China gave the foreigners a powerful voice in the affairs of that country, and for the most part they used it to promote national unification under the leadership of Chiang Kai-shek. This left the Communists with an unenviable choice. On one hand, they could restrain the urge toward military expansion, offer a peaceful settlement with the Nationalists, and try to lure foreign support away from Chungking toward Yenan. On the other hand, they could advance on the battlefield, seek to divide Moscow and Washington, and invite the Russians to join them in the coming conflict. Alternately, they tried both strategies; ultimately, both failed. Washington refused to play an even-handed role between the two factions in China; Moscow refused to come to the aid of Yenan. In the end, it was the withdrawal of foreign power that freed Chinese on both sides from this unwelcome interference and paved the way toward civil war.

The study of Sino-American relations and the foreign policies of both countries has been marked by a curious irony. The United States emerged from World War II with an overwhelming power in the Far East which alone might have enabled Washington to impose some grand design on the region. Yet the study of American foreign policy has stressed the pulling and hauling of interest groups, the compromise of "bureaucratic politics," the adaptive and incremental nature of policy change. China is a poor, weak country which was devastated by the war. Before 1949 the Communists in China could do little more than respond to sudden and shifting foreign stimuli. Even after taking power, they have never been able to extend their will very far beyond their borders. Yet the study of Chinese Communist foreign policy has stressed the role of ideology and the Maoist "vision" in shaping world affairs.

It is not easy to understand why our scholarship has leaned in this direction. Perhaps we have been the captives of readily available documents, written by the Chinese Communists themselves, which organize the data for us into easily understood categories. Perhaps we have been the captives of our own prejudices: to see Peking either as the villain in an ideological cold war or as the champion of "Chairman Mao's revolutionary line." Whatever the causes, our picture is beginning to change. Several works published in the last few years have begun to describe post-1949 Chinese foreign policy in the full complexity of its conduct and motivation.[6] If internal and external constraints influenced the Communists after they took power, how much more the difficulties of their situation must have weighed on them before! That is the point of this book.

In constructing this narrative, I have relied heavily on two sources. The first is United States government documents: reports by American diplomatic, military, and Office of Strategic Services (OSS) observers in China. Some of these have appeared in previous studies of Sino-American relations; some, particularly the OSS reports, have not. The second is Chinese Communist newspapers: *Chieh Fang Jih Pao* (Liberation Daily), published in Yenan, and *Hsin Hua Jih Pao* (New China Daily) of Chungking. Important articles and editorials from *Hsin Hua Jih Pao* and from other newspapers in Chungking, Shanghai, and Peiping were translated and published by the United States Office of War Information in the *Chinese Press Review*.

Evidence on the military situation is uneven. For the wartime period, events on the Nationalist-Japanese front are described in the official history, *United States Army in World War II*. After the war, American intelligence was good, but limited to select areas. Most useful have been scattered reports by army personnel in

Communist-held cities such as Kalgan, the records of the Marines in north China, and reports by truce teams under the Peiping Headquarters Group. For the most part, information on the Communist fronts comes from Communist sources: newspapers published at the time and military histories published in China since 1949. This study does not include information from Nationalist or Japanese military archives, both of which should tell us more about the situation on the battlefield.

Information on the internal politics of the Chinese Communist Party comes primarily from the attacks made on Mao's rivals during the last thirty years, especially those of the Cultural Revolution. I have gleaned these from the Joint Publications Research Service, the excerpts from the *Mao Tse-tung Ssu-hsiang Wan-sui* documents contained in Stuart Schram's *Chairman Mao Talks to the People*, and other sources. Wherever possible, these allegations have been weighed against contemporaneous evidence, particularly the original texts of Mao's speeches and the reports of foreign observers in Yenan. Further research in this area depends upon release of new information by the Chinese themselves.

Finally, it should be noted that this study has not made use of the files of the Bureau of Investigation, Republic of China, except for those documents cited by other authors or included in the Yushodo Bookstore Microfilms.[7] These files should tell us more about the Chinese Communist movement during this period, especially the base areas outside Yenan, and I commend them to those scholars who wish to continue the search. Similarly, I have consulted only those Russian materials available in English. A more complete bibliography appears at the end of this book.

CHAPTER ONE

The Politics of War
(1935–1943)

Chinese Communist foreign policy at the close of World War II was shaped within the contours of the Communists' own political and military history. During the previous decade, Mao had asserted his dominance over rivals who favored a united front with the Chinese central government and its foreign supporters. After the searing Rectification Campaign of the early 1940s, few in the Party would risk a challenge to the Maoist tenet of rural "self-reliance." Meanwhile, Communist military commanders who favored, in opposition to Mao's notion of "people's war," a more ambitious conventional strategy, were forced to disperse their armies into smaller guerrilla units and abide by the teachings of Maoist orthodoxy. When the situation on the battlefield changed, the generals would be quick to resume the march along the "forward and offensive line." Both the decimation of those within the Party who favored the united front and the resurgence of the Red Army helped shape Yenan's choices in dealing with the great powers after 1944.

The Political Struggle: Mao versus the Returned Students

Mao Tse-tung rose to power by displacing incumbent Party leaders with whom he differed in background, experience, and basic policy preference. Mao was a man of the interior. He built his political base in the countryside, and he favored a strategy of relying on the peasants rather than trusting the good will of the Chinese bourgeoisie or its foreign supporters. His rivals were trained in the cities and abroad. They had seized control over the Party through the intervention of Stalin and they followed a policy, initiated by Moscow, of forming a united front with the Kuomintang. These differences and the way they were resolved influenced the Chinese Communist movement throughout the 1940s.

Mao's identification with the Chinese countryside long predates his rise to the apex of Party leadership. In an age when most of the radical intellectual youth of China flocked to the treaty ports or sought their fortunes abroad, Mao remained a man of the interior. He was twenty-four when he first left the inland province of Hunan to visit the great cities along the coast, and his recollections of that trip suggest little of the modern, nationalist, and anti-imperialist spirit that animated urban China in the wake of the May Fourth Movement.[1] Unlike many of his contemporaries, Mao never left China to study or travel abroad. He spoke no foreign language. Even after he began to rise in the Party hierarchy, he spent much of his time in Hunan rather than in the cosmopolitan cities along the coast.

Mao was not actively anti-urban or anti-foreign, however. He was a man of considerable education in both western and Chinese studies and preached a doctrine of European origin. His early writings stress the collective force of the Chinese people—undifferentiated between urban and rural, even between class and class—in the fulfillment of China's destiny.[2] This staunch nationalism helped make him an enthusiastic supporter of the Kuomintang during the 1920s and a serious student and practitioner of the strategy of the united front from that time on. But for Mao the turning point of the movement came in 1927, when Chiang Kai-shek's bloody purge of the Left ended the First United Front. The Central Committee of the CCP went underground in Shanghai; Mao and a band of followers took to the hills. From then until the Communist victory in 1949, Mao viewed China and the world from his mobile base in the countryside.

Indicative of Mao's rural orientation were the enemies he made, most notably the "Russian returned students" led by Wang Ming (Ch'en Shao-yü), Ch'in Pang-hsien (Po Ku), and Chang Wen-t'ien (Lo Fu). These men spent their early years in and around Shanghai, joined the Communist Party, and went to Moscow to study. Backed by Stalin and the Comintern, they returned to China in 1930 and took over the Central Committee, then operating underground in Shanghai. Shortly thereafter, Wang Ming was recalled to Moscow to take up the post of chief CCP representative to the Comintern, while Ch'in and Chang moved their operations to the security of Mao's rural base. Despite their youth (Wang was just 27 when he became general secretary of the Party; Ch'in was 24), and their dependence on Moscow, which earned them the epithet the "28 Bolsheviks," these students managed to displace Mao's "Real Power Faction" and dominate the Kiangsi Soviet during the last two years of its existence (1933–34).

Mao regained the upper hand in January 1935, at the midpoint of the Long March. Initially, his control over the movement was far from complete; the first challenge to him came from the returned students. The issue was whether a united front of all Chinese to combat the threat of Japanese aggression should be given more emphasis than the continuation of class struggle within China. At the Seventh Comintern Congress, held in Moscow in August 1935, Wang Ming obliquely criticized Mao for promoting class struggle and flatly asserted that the united front "determines everything."[3] Mao replied some months later that the Party must combine both programs: "to join together civil war in China with national war" against the common enemy.[4] For the next few years, the debate continued.[5] Neither Mao nor Wang ever embraced one goal to the exclusion of the other, but each argued for a different priority: Wang stood for the united front, Mao for class struggle.

The positions staked out in this debate revealed different conceptions of the course the revolution should take and, connectedly, the social base on which it should stand. For Mao, the previous attempt to cooperate with the urban bourgeoisie had proved catastrophic; it was the program of mass mobilization in the countryside, aimed against both the cities and the landlords, that enabled the revolution to survive and prosper. "Can the countryside defeat the cities?" he asked. "The answer is that it is difficult, but it

can be done."[6] As for how it was to be done, in "On the New Democracy," the keynote statement of Communist policy for the
period of the War of Resistance, Mao explained that the "Chinese
revolution is essentially a peasant revolution and . . . the resistance to Japan now going on is essentially peasant resistance. Essentially, the politics of New Democracy means giving the peasants
their rights. . . ."[7] Wang Ming's strategy called for broadening the
social base of the revolution to give a greater role to the cities. In
his view, the weakness of a purely rural base had been demonstrated by the near-destruction of the movement in 1934–35. Pressing the class struggle in the countryside weakened national unity
and alienated both landlords and the urban bourgeoisie. A moderate social policy coupled with support for the united front would
win their support.[8] In August 1940 Chang Wen-t'ien offered the following reply to Mao's New Democracy:

. . . the danger of the Left deviation manifests itself in the wavering of the
anti-Japanese united front policy. . . . In certain areas some comrades
have completely forgotten about united front work while carrying out the
anti-friction struggle with the die-hards. Some even carry on the struggle
so that the united front period will quickly pass away and the days of land
revolution will quickly arrive. In this, moreover, they feel elated. . . .[9]

Finally, the choice of strategy and social base was directly tied to
foreign policy. After the middle of the 1930s, all the non-Fascist
powers wanted the same thing in China: peace within the country
and national unity to oppose Japanese aggression on the mainland.
If the Communists were to win aid and comfort from the great
powers, they would have to come to terms with the Nationalist
government—in short, restore the united front. As we shall see,
this was the goal of American policy during the last year of the war.
But it was no less true of the Russians, and much earlier. To protect
the Soviet Union against threats from both east and west, in 1935
the Comintern instructed all foreign Communist parties to join
their respective bourgeois compatriots in the common cause of
resisting Fascism. Wang Ming, as CCP representative to the Comintern, articulated this policy with regard to China. Moscow, in turn,
backed Wang in his debate with Mao. And Soviet support for the
Nationalist government—in signing the Non-Aggression Pact of
1937 and providing military aid during the years that followed—left

Yenan with little choice but to join a Second United Front with the Kuomintang or alienate their most likely foreign ally.

Mao never openly criticized Moscow for its role in China, but there can be little doubt that he would have preferred less interference in Chinese Communist affairs. Soviet foreign policy was geared to Russian national interests, which did not necessarily coincide with those of China, the CCP, or its chairman, a lesson which Mao had first learned during the 1920s. Throughout the 1930s, Moscow secured its eastern flank by alternatively appeasing Japanese expansion and propping up the Nationalist government to serve as a buffer against it. In either case the Chinese Communists were ignored. To allow Moscow to dictate Party policy was, in Mao's eyes, to entrust the direction of the revolution to an uncertain ally which might at any moment compromise Yenan's interests to those of the Russian state. Relying on the foreigner was no less risky than passing the initiative to the Chinese landlords and urban bourgeoisie. As Wang Ming pressed for cooperation with Chungking and Moscow, Mao responded with the call for "self-reliance."

"Self-reliance" did not mean a renunciation of external assistance, for Mao recognized that Yenan's position was too precarious and the power of the foreigners too great to permit a policy of blind autarky. Nor did he assert the full implications of this slogan from his first day in office. Rather the idea crystallized gradually in response to events at home and abroad. An important turning point came in the fall of 1939, when Moscow concluded the Nazi-Soviet Pact and reached a cease-fire with Japan, revealing a willingness to pacify the Fascist powers. Finally, in the spring of 1941, the signing of the Soviet-Japanese Neutrality Pact and the accompanying Frontier Declaration in which Moscow pledged to respect the territorial integrity of the puppet state of Manchukuo confirmed the widom of "self-reliance" and elicited the following response from Yenan:

The return of the four Northeastern provinces of China [i.e., Manchukuo] is our affair. Under no circumstances can we entertain a hope, as certain speculators do, that the U.S.S.R. will start a war with Japan and that we shall be able to take advantage of this.

Following the U.S.S.R.'s statement that it will not attack Manchuria, these people began to maintain that the U.S.S.R. has acted incorrectly.

Such people are, to say the least, craven tricksters. We must return all the lost land of China. We must fight our way to the Yalu River and drive the Japanese imperialists out of China. This is the sacred task of the whole Chinese people.[10]

The intra-Party struggle of the late 1930s and early 1940s revolved around these two clusters: Wang Ming's adherence to the Comintern line of seeking a united front with the urban bourgeoisie versus Mao's "self-reliant" class struggle in the countryside. The policies adopted by Yenan reflect the degree to which Mao had to compromise. After the outbreak of war in 1937, the Communists and Nationalists agreed to form the Second United Front, and radical land reform gave way to the practice of "reducing rent and interest." The persistence of Wang's influence was due to many factors, but of particular relevance to the story that follows was the role of the professional commanders of the Red Army. Their preference for conventional military methods was more compatible with Wang Ming's efforts to forge together Communist and Nationalist armies than with Mao's strategy of waging "people's war" and a "struggle on two fronts."

The Strategic Debate: Mao versus the Generals

Since the early 1930s, Mao and the Chinese Communist high command had differed on the issue of basic military strategy.[11] After the outbreak of the war, Mao argued that Yenan should accept a long period of "strategic stalemate," during which the Communists would avoid meeting superior Japanese forces in head-on battles and instead rely on small, widely dispersed units to harass and wear down the larger, stronger enemy.[12] Only later, as the balance began to tilt in their favor, should the Communists move to the "strategic counter-offensive" and adopt the more aggressive "mobile and positional warfare" appropriate to that stage. The military commanders placed greater confidence in the strength of the Red Army and saw danger in Mao's caution. Guerrillas could make no dent in the Japanese war machine, they argued, and to expand their forces without using them in battle would invite lethargy and decay. The generals favored a strategy of "mobile warfare": the determination to hold some fixed lines, even at the risk of fighting set-piece battles, rather than "trading space for time"; and reliance on large regular armies rather than smaller guerrilla or self-defense units.[13]

Closely connected to the question of strategy was that of the nonmilitary role of the army. Counting heavily on regular forces, the generals wanted to concentrate their resources on training, equipping, and commanding the Red Army in battle. To divert their energy to the tasks of political mobilization and production was to weaken their fighting capacity and risk defeat. Mao insisted that divorced from its peasant base the army could not survive or expand. To wage a "people's war," he argued, the soldiers must be taught not just to fight, but to respect and help the peasants who supported them. The commitment of a substantial portion of military resources to training and arming village self-defense forces, carrying out mass mobilization, and engaging in production was a prerequisite to eventual victory.

In sum, Mao's military program envisioned gradual expansion from a peasant base against both Japanese and Nationalist fronts. In his view, war would provide the opportunity and the Red Army the means to wage a political and economic struggle in the countryside. The commanders wanted to free their troops from the distractions of mass mobilization and social change, to form large armies and march forward to meet the enemy. Favoring this conventional strategy, they saw the obvious advantage of cooperation with and assistance from the central government.[14] It is not surprising that Wang Ming found among these military men his strongest allies in the debate on the united front.[15]

The resolution of this debate and the turning point for the Communists in the War of Resistance came with the Hundred Regiments Offensive of August 1940. In all likelihood, this offensive was planned and executed by P'eng Teh-huai, the highest officer in the Red Army headquarters in Shansi, east of the Yellow River and beyond direct supervision of Yenan. Chu Teh, the Communist commander-in-chief, who remained in Yenan throughout the war, probably supported the undertaking. Mao almost certainly opposed it.[16] The Hundred Regiments Offensive was a massive effort aimed at destroying rail lines and disrupting Japanese com-

munications throughout north China. One of its goals was to restore confidence in the flagging United Front and keep the Nationalists in the war at a time when international events may have
tempted Chungking to accept a negotiated settlement. Despite
early Red successes, the Japanese soon mounted a counterattack.
By the end of the year, the casualty figures were: Japanese, 4000;
Communists, 22,000.[17] The Hundred Regiments was the only large-
scale offensive mounted by the Communists during the war, and it
ended in catastrophe.

The harvest of P'eng's ill-fated venture came the following year.
Deciding to get tough with Red units in north China, which up
until that time had been left largely alone, the Japanese launched
the "three-all" campaign: "kill all, burn all, destroy all." The purpose of scorching north China was to put an end to the close cooperation which had existed between the Communists and the populace, and the results were devastating for both. In the single year of
1941, the size of the Communist Eighth Route Army plunged from
400,000 to 300,000, the population under Communist control was
reduced from 44 to 25 million, and thousands of Party cadres were
killed or abandoned their posts.[18]

This backlash could not have come at a worse time, for the Communists were also facing serious problems at home. The Second
United Front had begun to unravel as early as the middle of 1939.
Finally, in January 1941, government forces wiped out the headquarters of the Communist New Fourth Army in a celebrated incident that ended cooperation between the two parties. Chungking's subsidies to Yenan were cut off, the economic blockade of
the Red areas was tightened, and a virtual cold war ensued.

Finally, international events turned against the Communists. In
1939 Moscow halted all aid to China, and in June 1941 the Germans
invaded Russia, eliminating the latter country as a force in East
Asia.[19] While it lasted, Soviet assistance had been a significant factor in the Chinese resistance to Japan. Although this aid went exclusively to Chungking, it had helped to keep the Nationalists in
the war and may have had some effect in damping down Chiang
Kai-shek's anti-Red campaigns. With the aid cut off and the very
survival of the Soviet Union in doubt, the target of the Kuomintang
war effort might easily swing toward Yenan. (Fortuitously, the

American entry into the war in December 1941 helped keep Chiang's anti-Communist impulses dormant and his resistance to Japan alive.)

These developments placed the Communist movement in peril and prompted a sweeping change in Yenan's practices. As a result of military defeat and economic strangulation, production in the Communist areas fell, taxes rose, and soaring inflation threatened to wipe out the popular support which Yenan had built up during the first three years of the war. Forced to retrench, large military units were broken up and dispersed, both to avoid head-on collisions with the Japanese and to reduce the drain on the public coffer. "Crack troops and simple administration" became the slogan of the day as military and Party cadres withdrew into the villages to aid in production and preserve a minimum of their hard-won gains. At the end of 1941, Yenan announced that "guerrilla" warfare had replaced the more aggressive "mobile-guerrilla" formula as the correct strategy for Communist forces.[20] In sum, the Communists were forced to hunker down, to think less about expansion and easy victory, and to contemplate the long, difficult struggle for survival in the countryside.

While hard on the movement as whole, these events served to justify Mao's warnings and press him farther along the path he had begun to map out. The collapse of the United Front and the removal of Soviet influence from the Far East silenced Wang Ming. Japanese devastation of north China made guerrilla warfare the only viable military option. Severe economic hardship demanded that greater attention be paid to the plight of the peasants. History had proven Mao right, and he seized the chance to shape the future after his own vision. His instrument was the first great political upheaval aimed at remaking the thoughts and reorganizing the personnel of the Chinese Communist Party, the Cheng Feng (Rectification) Campaign.

Cheng Feng: Mao Takes Command

The Rectification Campaign of 1942–44 was the most important single enterprise of the Yenan decade. Its central message—that the theory of Marxism must be made to square with the reality of rural China—has left an imprint on all aspects of Chinese Communism down to the present. Not the leàst was its influence on foreign relations. For the teachings of Cheng Feng decreed that the Communists would treat the world without on the basis of "self-reliance" and the creation of their own power from within.

The methods of Rectification have become the model for all subsequent political campaigns in China. Cheng Feng was in the first instance a great study session. The texts were prescribed by the leadership and discussed in small group meetings. The campaign was not a purge in the Stalinist sense, but it was most certainly a struggle in which many cadres were criticized; some were dismissed from the Party, tortured, or even put to death. It was a baptism in fire, an attempt to galvanize the movement behind an orthodoxy of Maoist thought in which the threat of physical and psychological violence made the lessons more meaningful.

The targets of Rectification included all those who had opposed Mao's program of rural revolution. Wang Ming and the returned students were branded as "dogmatists," rootless individuals whose experience was limited to their reading of foreign dogma, who knew and cared little about the real problems of the Chinese countryside.[21] The professional military commanders, most notably P'eng Teh-huai, were censured for "warlordism" and criticized for concentrating on conventional warfare while ignoring the broader needs of popular resistance.[22] Unnamed comrades were charged with favoring premature attacks on "strongholds and centrally located cities."[23] To combat such abuses, Yenan stripped local commanders of much of their authority, transferring it to the Party committees at the same level.[24]

Finally, Cheng Feng was aimed at the many middle- and lower-echelon cadres who had left the cities to join the Party after the outbreak of the war. These students and intellectuals of urban and petty bourgeois background had come to Yenan out of a nationalistic impulse and knew little of Marx, Lenin, or the Chinese countryside. They had formed a natural constituency for the policies advocated by Wang Ming. When the United Front broke down, they were disappointed; and when the Japanese extermination campaigns got underway, they were frightened and deeply disillusioned. Little in their urban bourgeois upbringing had prepared them to deal with uncouth peasants or to obey strict Party discipline. Yet, after 1941, if the Communist movement was to survive and prosper in the countryside, these young men and women would have to learn and accept the Maoist revolutionary vision. The deeper purpose of Cheng Feng was to effect this transformation.[25]

The message of the Cheng Feng documents was that urban-oriented cadres must adapt themselves to the tasks of rural China. As true revolutionaries, Mao warned, we must not "raise our heads and look at heaven," but must "look downward" at the problems and opportunities beneath our feet.[26] Book-learning was a bourgeois preoccupation of no intrinsic value. What mattered was the ability of Party members to apply their learning to the practical problems of the Chinese countryside. This dichotomy between urban bookishness and rural practicality ran throughout the Cheng Feng documents.[27]

Closely connected to this critique of the shortcomings of urban man was a circumspect view of foreign influence. Cheng Feng was not, at least in its ostensible manifestations, anti-foreign. Seven of the 27 documents assigned for study were written by Stalin or other Soviet authors, and none of the CCP's own works departed from the general line of support for the Soviet Union. The spirit of the movement, however, stressed independence, self-reliance, and a synthesis of the Marxist-Leninist tradition with the concrete problems of China to create a new and uniquely Chinese form of Marxism. In this sense the purpose of Cheng Feng was to sink wholly indigenous foundations under the CCP, to make it stronger within and less vulnerable to manipulation from without. The problem with the urbanites, as Mao told a gathering of cadres in early 1942, was precisely their uncritical adoption of foreign tutors:

China is a country with an extremely broad petty bourgeoisie; our Party is surrounded by this class and it produces a great many of our Party members. To a greater or lesser degree, they cannot help dragging the tail of this petty bourgeois class into the Party. If the radical and one-sided nature of the revolutionaries of petty bourgeois origin is not brought under control and reformed, subjectivism and sectarianism are very easily produced. The manifested form of these is foreign formalism and foreign dogmatism.[28]

During the years when Soviet fortunes on the European front were at their lowest, Mao sought to circumscribe Stalin's influence within the Chinese Communist movement and to put his own imprint on Party policies at home and abroad. The Comintern, which played such an important role in the early history of the CCP and posed, through such agents as Wang Ming, a continuing threat to Mao's authority, was an anathema to the principles of Cheng Feng. Commenting on its dissolution in May 1943, the chairman reaffirmed the value of "self-reliance," which, he implied, had been a hallmark of Party policy since his ascendancy in 1935:

The Chinese Communist Party has been through three revolutionary movements. These revolutionary movements have been continuous and uninterrupted and extraordinarily complex, even more complex than the Russian Revolution. In the course of these revolutionary movements, the Chinese Communist Party had already acquired its own excellent cadres endowed with rich personal experience. Since the Seventh World Congress of the Communist International in 1935, the Communist International has not intervened in the internal affairs of the Chinese Communist Party. And yet, the Chinese Communist Party has done its work very well, throughout the whole Anti-Japanese War of National Liberation.[29]

The men and ideas that emerged from Cheng Feng would leave their imprint on the story of Yenan. A single figure, Mao Tse-tung, dominated Chinese Communism as no one before him. Mao was the first man to assert his leadership over the movement without Soviet or Comintern support. He rode to power aboard a program of rural revolution and self-reliance which was in marked contrast to that of his predecessors. Mao's was the voice of Rectification, and he picked the men who dominated the Party from that time on.

What is most striking about the post–Cheng Feng leadership is the absence of people who would speak for the united front, for cooperation with the urban bourgeoisie and with the foreign powers that favored unity in China. The returned students, who had played this role since 1930, had not been purged, but they were removed to the outer fringes of power. In their place were a new set of figures with Soviet (K'ang Sheng and Ch'en Yun) and urban (Liu Shao-ch'i, Chou En-lai, P'eng Chen, An Tzu-wen, Po I-po) experience. What distinguishes this new group is the fact that its members had gained ascension in the Maoist leadership by signing on to the program of Cheng Feng.

Liu Shao-ch'i, who more than any other person was responsible for the migration of urban youth to Yenan during the war, wedded his Party from the "white" areas to that of Mao's in the "red" rural hinterland. Liu won his place at Mao's side by supporting the chairman in the debates with Wang Ming, by contributing heavily to the ideas and organization of Party Rectification, and by promoting the cult of personality which crowned Mao's triumph at the Seventh Party Congress in 1945.[30] In exchange, Liu emerged at the end of the war as second only to Mao in the Yenan hierarchy. Despite their efforts, Liu's Cultural Revolution critics were unable to find a substantial instance of conflict between these two men during the War of Resistance. Clearly, Liu did not continue the work of Wang Ming.

Unlike the returned students, the military professionals who opposed Mao throughout the war retained their posts atop the Communist high command. While Mao could argue with them, the generals were not expendable. Cheng Feng and the events that prompted it had driven them into the background. But when the situation on the battlefield changed—and it was to change dramatically in 1944—the commanders in Yenan and throughout the base areas would regroup their forces and prepare to take up the march along the "forward and offensive line."

Rapid military expansion would have a significant impact on all parts of Yenan's program, especially its relations with the central government and the foreign powers. Early in the war, when the Japanese threat was dominant, the preference of the commanders for conventional military techniques served to bolster the United Front. Later, as resistance to Japan gave way to conflict within China, their enthusiasm for large-scale offensive operations would bring the Communists into conflict with Chungking and the Allies. The momentum of the Red Army would then dominate decision making in Yenan, for few members of the new Party leadership would argue to slow the armed advance in deference to the united front and its foreign supporters.

Those who passed through the fires of Cheng Feng had learned to face inward, away from the cities and the world outside, to the problems and potentials of the Chinese countryside. They would be loath to speak for reviving the united front, and cautious in their view of the foreigners. In 1936 Edgar Snow was surprised to find that socialist internationalism was more than mere rhetoric to the Chinese Communists: "But I saw it, and heard it, and felt it. This idea of having behind them such a great ally—even though it has been less and less validated by any demonstrations of positive support from the Soviet Union—is of primary importance to the morale of the Chinese Reds."[31]

A decade later, Jack Belden, another American journalist who visited the Communist areas, was told that the Russians had made "many mistakes, which we don't have to repeat" and that "their basic program may not be suited to China."[32] Po I-po, a leading figure in the new Party leadership, explained: "Cheng Feng taught us that the Chinese Communist party must have its own principles. It was not necessary that we travel the same road as the Soviet Union."[33]

In 1944 rapid and profound changes on the battlefield would beckon the Red Army out of the villages of north and east China and invite the resumption of an armed offensive. The commanders would be there to signal the advance. But who in Yenan would speak for a pause, a probing of the united front and of the foreign powers beyond? What would the Chungking government and the foreigners do to merit such a compromise? And how would Yenan choose between gradually augmenting its influence through peaceful negotiation and outright military expansion?

CHAPTER TWO

Fight or Talk
(January–July 1944)

The Chinese Communists stepped onto the stage of world politics following the military collapse of their principal rival, the Kuomintang. A Japanese offensive, launched in the spring of 1944, chewed up Nationalist defenders in east China and crippled the government in Chungking, creating new opportunities for Yenan to enhance its power and attract foreign support. Chaos throughout the country invited the Communists to expand their holdings by force of arms. Turmoil in Chungking gave them a chance to broaden their appeal by joining a move toward governmental reform. These events brought Yenan to the attention of the Americans, one of the parties most interested in the military and political changes then underway in China. But a policy of armed expansion was, in several respects, incompatible with attempts to expand the united front and win new friends at home and abroad. Thus a strategic choice—to fight or to talk—came to occupy Communist policymakers, a choice which would remain at the center of their attention for the next two years.

The Ichigo Offensive

Yenan's opportunities came when a Japanese offensive, codenamed Ichigo, destroyed the status quo on the mainland which had persisted throughout most of the war. By the end of 1938 the lines of control in wartime China had been firmly drawn (see Map 2). The Japanese occupied all the major cities and lines of communication in the north and east, including the Yangtze River as far as Hankow, and the port cities of Amoy, Swatow, and Canton in the south. Chinese puppets helped them keep order in these areas. The Communists, directing events from their capital in Yenan west of the Yellow River, generated "base areas" between and around the lines of enemy control. There were nineteen bases in all, forming a chain of huge stepping stones across the breadth of north China from Kansu to the coast. The Nationalists, while moving their capital to the security of Chungking in the remote southwest, claimed jurisdiction over all the Japanese left untouched, in the central, southern, and western portions of the country. The vast landscape of the south, beyond the reach of the Japanese army, provided a haven for Allied bombers. And this is what led to the scramble for China that broke out in 1944, ending six years of military and political stalemate.

In the debate over Allied strategy on the mainland of Asia, General Claire Chennault, founder of the famed Flying Tigers and an early proponent of air war, prevailed over General Joseph Stilwell, commander of all U.S. forces in the China-Burma-India Theater, whose priorities lay with the creation of an effective Chinese land army.[1] Backed first by Chiang Kai-shek and then by President Roosevelt, Chennault won access to the bulk of the tonnage flown over the Hump from India, and he used these supplies to build a string of airfields across south China, the most important of which lay along the line running diagonally through Hengyang, Lingling, Kweilin, and Liuchow.[2] Bases at Kweiyang and Kunming formed the reserve area. By the winter of 1943–44, Chennault's bombers had begun to take their toll on Japanese supply lines up the Yangtze and along the coast.[3] If the Americans moved their B-29 Super-Fortresses up to these fields in China, they could threaten the whole Japanese position on the mainland, as well as the home islands themselves.

Tokyo's response to this situation was the massive Ichigo Offensive, an attempt to establish a line of overland communications from Peiping in the north, down through Hankow, thence to Canton in the south and to Hanoi and the Japanese strongholds of

Map 2. Occupied China, 1938–44.

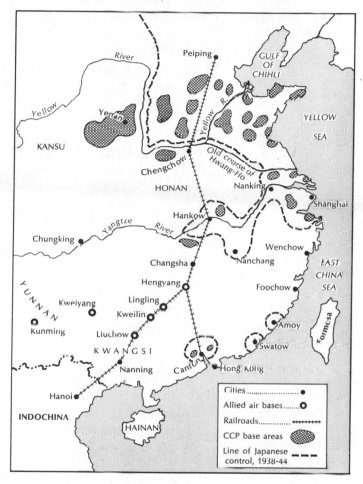

Southeast Asia.[4] The goals of the offensive were, first, to drive the American air force out of east China; and second, to cut off Allied forces on the mainland from the sea and preclude their linking up with an American landing on the coast. Aimed at offsetting the steady erosion of Japanese might in the Pacific, this was Tokyo's bid to make sure that the axis of control in East Asia continued to run along a north-south rather than an east-west line.

During 1944 Ichigo was a rapid and total success. The first phase of the offensive began in April, when the Japanese struck the key rail juncture of Chengchow and sent government forces in Honan scurrying in all directions.[5] Having secured a supply line to the north, the Japanese immediately pushed south from Hankow. By the end of the year, they achieved all their principal objectives. They secured the line from Peiping to Canton and Hanoi, albeit with some fragility in Kwangsi Province. They destroyed the American airfields in east China and forced Chennault's bombers back to the mountain retreats of Kweiyang and Kunming. Finally, they strengthened their defense against an American landing by capturing Wenchow and Foochow, two major ports on the coast opposite Formosa. In contrast to the setbacks suffered in Burma and the Pacific, 1944 was a banner year for the Japanese in China.

The East China Crisis shook Chungking and the whole Nationalist enterprise. Chinese forces mustered little resistance to the enemy onslaught, and in some cases, such as the brief battle for Honan, they simply dropped their weapons and fled. By December, when Ichigo reached its high-water mark, Chungking had lost a half-million soldiers and effective control over the large part of eight provinces—Honan and all those south of the Yangtze except Yunnan.[6] Enemy forces were advancing into the mountains toward Kweiyang, from which point they could threaten Chungking itself.[7] The Nationalist military position was collapsing, and given the political impotence that war and the Kuomintang had conspired to produce, the fate of that regime appeared in doubt.

Option One: Military Expansion

The widespread disorder wrought by the East China Crisis invited the Communists to expand their holdings by force of arms. The

Japanese move south depleted the ranks of the enemy adjacent to Red bases in north China. The collapse of the Nationalist position below the Yellow River opened up a whole new frontier for Communist expansion in that direction. Finally, the approach of the U.S. Navy from the Pacific argued for a move east to link up with Allied forces on the coast. On all these fronts, military commanders in Yenan and the outlying base areas saw the chance to reconcentrate dispersed guerrilla forces into larger units and go on the offensive.

From the Communist point of view, the most immediate and compelling consequence of the Ichigo Offensive was the opening of a vacuum of power across the breadth of north China. As early as 1942, the Japanese "three-all" campaign, which had forced Yenan to disperse its regular units and to resort to guerrilla warfare, had begun to subside. In the summer of that year, American advances in the Pacific triggered the redeployment of Japanese troops to the east. By the spring of 1944 this process had drained eight divisions, a full quarter of the best Japanese forces in China, from the mainland. Then Ichigo took its toll: initially seven and finally fifteen divisions moved south to take part in the offensive.[8] By the middle of the year Japanese strength above the Yellow River was a mere shadow of its once-proud self.[9]

Communist forces which had gone underground just a few years earlier were quick to reassert their claims. In 1943 they began to retake blockhouses and fortresses abandoned by the Japanese. By the end of the year they still held only one *hsien* (county) seat outside their home base in Shensi,[10] but the pace of Communist expansion accelerated in the wake of Ichigo. The first opportunity came in Honan.

Centrally located between the Yellow and Yangtze rivers, site of the juncture of the north-south and east-west trunk rail lines, Honan was valuable real estate, which explains why the Nationalists held onto the province following the outbreak of the war. It was also an area of chronic grain deficits, and in 1944 a serious famine rocked the province, taxes were not remitted to reduce starvation, and popular dissatisfaction with the government ran high.[11] When the Japanese attacked along the Peiping–Hankow Railroad in April, angry peasants turned on their own troops. Poorly fed, ill-equipped, and confused, many Nationalist soldiers simply dropped their guns and fled. The Japanese took the railroad; but the peasants seized the abandoned weapons, and banditry and disorder spread.[12]

The Communists, driven out of Honan three years earlier, rushed back in from all sides. During the latter half of 1944, they seized all or part of 29 counties and established new base areas on both sides of the Peiping–Hankow Railroad.[13] By year's end, Red holdings in north China had grown by 80,000 square kilometers, 12 million people, and sixteen county seats—twelve north of the Yellow River and four to the south, in Honan.[14] Communist authority was reaching rapidly toward the Yangtze, and their success in this area pointed to still greater opportunities farther south.

The Japanese thrust into south China drove the Nationalists out of major cities and lines of communication and reduced their ability to control the surrounding countryside. Cut off from Kunming, government armies to the east of the Hankow–Canton Railroad could not be resupplied. After the middle of 1944, the entire southeast began to slip from Chungking's grasp. While still nominally part of Nationalist China, the cities captured by the Japanese lay along an axis of traditional Communist strength.

After fleeing the embattled base areas in Hunan and Kiangsi in 1934, many Communist units had not joined the Long March but stayed behind to continue guerrilla operations. Most of these drifted into Anhwei and Kiangsu and coalesced around the New Fourth Army, which numbered more than 100,000 by 1944.[15] Several important units remained closer to the line traversed by Ichigo. The largest of these, 22,000 men under the command of Li Hsien-nien, operated along the border joining Honan, Hupeh, and Anhwei. After April, Li's forces moved north into Honan, where they helped capture four county seats, and south across the Yangtze into Hunan. At the opposite end of the axis, in Kwangtung, was Tseng Sheng and the East River Column, a force estimated variously from 2000 to 10,000. To the east, 4000 regulars under T'an Ch'i-lung made their base in Chekiang Province.[16] Smaller guerrilla units scattered throughout Hupeh, Hunan, and Kiangsi could be drawn together if and when Yenan decided to move south.

Finally as a corollary to new moves north or south, Yenan had to weigh the prospects for an American landing on the coast. In fact, by early 1944 the importance of China had already begun to diminish in the eyes of American military planners. The Chinese had proven themselves incapable of mounting a counteroffensive, and Ichigo drove the point home. Meanwhile, at the Teheran Conference (December 1943), Stalin assured Roosevelt that the Soviet Union would enter the war in the Far East after the defeat of Germany, offering an alternative source of ground forces for use against the Japanese army on the mainland. Despite these developments, however, throughout 1944 and into the spring of 1945, officials in the State Department and even the President continued to discuss a landing in China.[17] Admiral Chester Nimitz, commander-in-chief of naval forces in the Pacific, repeatedly told the press that the Americans were aiming at the China coast.[18] These statements were backed up by promising actions: air raids on the Philippines in August and on Formosa in October; and the landing on Leyte in the Philippines on October 19. It was in part the threat of an American landing that had prompted the Japanese to undertake Ichigo. The Chinese, both in Chungking and in Yenan, had good reasons to share these expectations.

Different members of the Chinese Communist leadership had different views on how to respond to these opportunities. Commanders in the outlying base areas, battered by the "three-all" campaign and reined in by Cheng Feng, were anxious to rally their forces and go on the offensive. The high command in Yenan was similarly optimistic about the prospects for military expansion and ready for action. But Mao, the author of "people's war" and responsible, as the man in the middle, for a wider range of political and economic concerns, urged restraint. His debate with the generals, which had gone on for some time, was evident in the spring of 1944 and would continue throughout the following year.

Speaking to a meeting of senior cadres on April 12, Mao noted that the Nationalist defense of Honan had collapsed without a battle and concluded that it would be the "fighting capacity" of the two Chinese factions that "will decide China's destiny." The test would come, Mao continued, in the battle for the cities. Therefore, the Party must "raise the work in the cities to a position of equal importance with that in the base areas," while in the base areas cadres must "learn how to administer the industry, commerce and communications of big cities." And the coming Seventh Party Congress must "discuss the problems of strengthening our work in the cities and winning nationwide victory." While promising an eventual move on the cities, however, Mao was careful to point out that the time was not yet ripe:

Our Party is not yet sufficiently strong, not yet sufficiently united or consolidated, and so cannot yet take on greater responsibility than we now carry. From now on the problem is further to expand and consolidate our party, our Army and base areas in the continued prosecution of the War of Resistance; this is the first indispensable item in our ideological and material preparation for the gigantic work of the future. Without this preparation, we shall not be able to drive out the Japanese invaders and liberate the whole of China.[19]

Mao's caution reflected in part the danger he saw in the actions of aggressive and independent commanders in the bases east of the Yellow River. "The old factions are gone," he told listeners, referring to the "dogmatists" and "empiricists" who had been the target of attack in the Rectification Campaign. "But what still exists in our Party to a serious extent, and almost everywhere, is a more or less blind 'mountain-stronghold' mentality."[20] The mentality of the "mountain-stronghold" (also called "mountain-top-ism") was a deviation of local or regional groups which had become ensconced in their independent duchies, cut off from the world outside and defiant of the central authority in Yenan. This tendency toward regional autonomy was the hallmark of warlordism, which had dominated the history of modern China. It had been attacked by that name in the course of Cheng Feng and remained a central concern to Yenan throughout the rest of the decade.

Another source of concern was the high command in Yenan. It was the chiefs of the Red Army—Chu Teh, P'eng Teh-huai, Ch'en I, and Liu Po-ch'eng—who had argued against Mao's cautious guerrilla tactics and for a more aggressive "forward and offensive line."[21] After the catastrophe of the Hundred Regiments Offensive, they had been forced to accept the go-slow strategy of "people's war" and mind the lessons of Cheng Feng. Now, in 1944, they wanted to resume the initiative.

In Yenan, Chu Teh spoke optimistically to American listeners about the prospects for Communist success in the old base areas south of the Yangtze. Knowing that such a move would lead to conflict with Chungking, Chu noted that the Communists would move south only with the government's permission.[22] Chu's chief of staff, Yeh Chien-ying, was much less diplomatic, telling American observer John Service flatly: "Chungking will not like it. But the Communists listen to the people, not to Chungking."[23] Finally, Service sought out Ch'en I, commander of the New Fourth Army, which would play a dominant role in any move south, and asked him about the possibility that the Kuomintang might be losing control of the areas along the Hankow–Canton Railroad. "General Ch'en gave me a sharp and seemingly surprised look," reported Service, "and said with some excitement: 'That is just what we are considering.' "[24] According to Ch'en, Yenan had thus far refrained from moving south because of its desire to avoid friction with the government. But with the Japanese threat against the Hankow–Canton line, there was a serious possibility that all of southeast China would be lost, and with it the chance to link up with an American landing on the coast. Ch'en made no prediction as to what Yenan would do, but he agreed that the situation was changing and concluded: "The possible near collapse of the Kuomintang in these areas, and the importance of the areas to the United Nations war effort must be considered."[25]

In sum, after the middle of 1944, new military frontiers—against the cities of north China, to the south, and along the coast—beckoned the Communists forward. The high command in Yenan and Red commanders in the base areas were looking to the future, taking the initiative where possible and urging the Party leadership to authorize bigger operations. Mao was listening to these voices, but he had reason for caution. And he was hesitant to move on the military front until he had explored the political opportunities, also produced by Ichigo, also below the Yangtze River, in the shrinking bastion of Nationalist China.

Option Two: The United Front

In the wake of the Ichigo Offensive, Yenan also had a chance to broaden its appeal by promoting the cause of peaceful political reform. Besides greatly reducing the sphere of Chungking's authority, the East China Crisis dealt a shattering blow to the stability and morale of the Kuomintang regime. While the government had always been viewed with some misgivings both in China and among the Allies, the collapse of the Nationalist army in 1944 drove its critics to seek for other alternatives. The most obvious alternative was some new political arrangement which would give a greater role to the Communists. Yenan could win new friends at home and abroad by offering to expand and strengthen the united front.

Chiang's critics were everywhere. At one extreme was Li Chi-shen of Kwangsi, around whom had coalesced the warlords of the southeast, those whose lands were traversed by Ichigo.[26] These regional military commanders had received little of the foreign aid which filtered through Chiang's hands, and when the government faltered they were the first to consider forming a separate regime and appealing to the Americans directly. Second, there were the minor parties that made up the "third force," wedged between the Communists and the Kuomintang, and sharing a commitment to civil rights and the rule of law, democratization of the government, and national unity in resistance to Japan.[27] In May 1944 representatives of these warlords and minor parties approached the Americans with a plan to unite dissident groups in China in case the government collapsed. Finally, within the Kuomintang itself, the liberal Political Study Clique pressed for an understanding with Yenan. The Communists were aware of all these developments, and while Yenan voiced no public approval, Communist agents in Nationalist China offered their cooperation.[28]

The foreign powers represented in Chungking, most notably the Americans, also began to address the problem of reforming the Chinese government to make it more effective in the resistance to Japan. During the first two years after Pearl Harbor, the United States had done its best to aid China's cause, and by implication to bolster the position of the Kuomintang and Chiang Kai-shek. Given the limits on American resources, much of this support was symbolic. Washington led the way in abrogating the humiliating unequal treaties and secured for China a place among the "Big Four," which would presumably police the postwar world. More concretely, President Roosevelt sought to expand the material assistance reaching Chungking by insisting—over the opposition of Churchill and the British chiefs of staff—on the campaign to re-open the Burma Road. And he made certain that the aid sent to China was the type Chiang wanted, primarily for air rather than ground forces.[29] Washington, like Moscow before it, channeled all its assistance through the Nationalist government; none reached Yenan.

Americans in China, both official and unofficial, were never much impressed by the image of "democratic China" portrayed in the western press and saw clearly the corruption and ineptitude which Kuomintang censorship tried to conceal.[30] By the latter half of 1943, these views began to find their way into foreign publications and to gain a hearing at the highest levels of the American government.[31] As a result, Roosevelt's commitment to Chiang peaked at the Cairo Conference at the end of the year. In early 1944 the two leaders clashed over the question of whether or not American-trained and -equipped Chinese forces would fight in northern Burma, and much of the confidence that remained between Chungking and Washington was broken.[32]

The East China Crisis was the last straw. In the spring of 1944 Roosevelt appointed Vice-President Wallace to go to Chungking to boost the Chinese war effort. Wallace arrived on June 21, just three days after the fall of Changsha, the first major city below the Yangtze captured by the Japanese. He told Chiang that Washington was unhappy with events in China and that the time had come for the Communists and Nationalists to "call in a friend" (Roosevelt) to help settle their dispute. Chiang parried this attempt to interfere in what he considered a domestic matter, but Wallace secured one important concession: permission for an American military observer section to visit Yenan.[33]

Viewed from Yenan, these events formed a clear and promising pattern. A number of Chiang's supporters at home and abroad had found that his government, at least in its present form, could no longer claim a monopoly on the cause of national resistance and that China needed some new political arrangement which, among other things, would give a greater role to the Communists. Some dissident elements, such as the more conservative warlords, would not make reliable partners. But the Americans, the left wing of the

Kuomintang, the minor parties of the "third force," and a wide range of liberally oriented students, intellectuals, and publicists shared with Yenan the immediate goal of restructuring the government on a broadly representative basis. Taken together, they offered a large and attractive audience which would respond favorably to a Communist call to restore the united front.

Yenan stood to gain substantial benefits from such an appeal. An agreement with Chungking would bring relaxation of the blockade against the Communist areas, at least some material assistance to strengthen the war effort in the north, and public recognition of Yenan's role in the resistance to Japan.[34] If Chiang refused to cooperate (and this was possible, if not probable), the offer to restore the united front would score important points among his critics. One target was the urban bourgeoisie. They could help restrain the government's more aggressive anti-Communist impulses, and their support would be increasingly valuable at the close of the war, as the Communists moved toward the cities and sought recognition as a legitimate claimant to power at the national level. Similarly, the United States would continue to play a pivotal, and Yenan could hope flexible, role in China. At a minimum, the Americans could try to persuade Chiang to accept reforms and withhold their support if he refused. At a maximum, they might send a portion of their military aid to the Communist armies, with or without Chungking's approval. The Allies had already armed Tito's partisans in Yugoslavia; perhaps they would follow the same course in China.[35]

Insofar as he chose to work with these urban and foreign interests, Mao would rely heavily on Chou En-lai. Following the formation of the Second United Front in 1937, Chou had taken his liaison group to meet with Nationalist representatives in Hankow and, after the fall of that city in 1938, in Chungking. Chou's ostensible task was to coordinate with the government the common effort against Japan, but he also established a wide range of contacts through whom he advertised the Communist cause, with considerable success. Besides handling all political and diplomatic affairs in the Nationalist capital, the Communist liaison office was permitted, under the terms of the United Front agreement, to publish a daily paper, *Hsin Hua Jih Pao* (New China Daily), which was second only to Yenan's *Chieh Fang Jih Pao* (Liberation Daily) as the authoritative voice of the Party, and a periodical, *Ch'ün Chung* (The Masses). In addition to Chou, the major figures in the group included Tung Pi-wu, Teng Ying-ch'ao, Wang Ping-nan, Ch'en Chia-k'ang, and Chang Han-fu. The Chungking office served as a nerve center for two satellite missions, one in Kweilin under Li K'o-nung and a second in Hong Kong under Liao Ch'eng-chih and Ch'iao Kuan-hua (Ch'iao Mu). Both branch offices were closed in 1941, but their operations continued underground.[36]

Reared in an upper-class family in Kiangsu, a traditional cradle of the Chinese scholar-gentry, well educated, urbane, and articulate, Chou En-lai was by both birth and training a diplomat.[37] While in his teens, he studied in Japan and later spent four years in France, where he joined the Paris branch of the Chinese Communist Party and met many of its future leaders. He traveled in England, Germany, and Belgium and visited Moscow in 1928, 1930, and 1939. After returning to China, Chou was elected to the Central Committee and the Politburo in 1927. Chou's resilience, the hallmark of a successful diplomat both within the Communist movement and outside it, is demonstrated by the fact that he is the only member of the 1927 Politburo who kept his post until 1949, and also until his death in 1976.

Chou's relationship with Mao was complicated. In the early 1930s Chou and the returned students combined to remove Mao from control over the Red Army and substitute their own military strategy of the "forward and offensive line" for Mao's guerrilla warfare. After the outbreak of war against Japan, Chou sided with the military professionals in opposing Mao's sectarian attitude toward the United Front. As Mao's power within the movement grew, however, Chou adapted to the changing circumstances. In 1943, at the height of the Rectification Campaign, Chou warmly applauded Mao's leadership and (echoing the message of Cheng Feng) stressed the independence of the Chinese Communist movement (implicitly from Soviet influence) and the creation of a new ideology which "is indigenous and has grown roots in the soil of China."[38]

We can only speculate on Mao's reasons for welcoming Chou into the fold of his own leadership. Perhaps Chou's charm helped the chairman forget past differences and anticipate future confidence between the two men. Perhaps Mao felt he needed a strong figure to displace Wang Ming in the area of united front and diplomatic work. Perhaps Mao genuinely respected Chou as one colleague who was as masterful in his area of political activity as Mao was in his own. Whatever the reasons, Mao and Chou formed a classic partnership: the strategist and the practitioner; "one making plans inside," as Chang Kuo-t'ao observed, "and the other negotiating outside."[39] Throughout the war and beyond, Chou remained Mao's right arm in united front and foreign affairs.

These were the opportunities opened up by the Ichigo Offensive: the united front and the armed advance. In some ways, the two fit together. Expansion of Communist power, by whatever means, would give Yenan greater leverage in the negotiations to reform the Chinese government. Moves against the cities or the coast of north China, which were held by Japanese and puppet forces, could not be criticized by anyone who favored an Allied victory. If the Communists were beating the enemy, naturally their claim to rule China would be enhanced.

In other ways, however, Communist military expansion was incompatible with efforts to achieve peaceful reform. Any attempt to move south, either through the central corridor opened up by the Japanese advance or against the coast of Nationalist-held Chekiang and Fukien provinces, would lead to conflict with the government and expose Yenan to the charge of inciting civil war. Conversely, if the Communists delayed the move south in hopes of winning concessions in Chungking, they might lose a chance to seize power throughout the country. Chinese moderates and foreign powers represented in Chungking favored national unity to fight Japan and forestall a civil war. But the questions of whether, when, and how much this constituency would reward Yenan for its efforts at peaceful reform remained to be answered. In the meantime, a yawning vacuum of power beckoned the Communists south.

Within the Party each policy option had its adherents. A broadening of the Communist appeal at home and abroad would depend heavily on the work of Chou En-lai and his diplomatic apparatus in Chungking. The process of Rectification, however, had quenched much of the enthusiasm for this line among the leadership in Yenan. Thus a serious move in this direction could come only at the initiative of Mao, whose role in Cheng Feng protected him from charges of being soft on the foreigners and the Chinese bourgeoisie. At the same time, it remained to be seen how long Red Army commanders in Yenan and the outlying base areas would restrain their forces in deference to the united front. The generals were ready to move, and when they did, a major thrust of their operations would be into areas where conflict with the government was certain. Like all effective politicians, Mao could try to play both sides of the street while keeping his options open. But in the end, he would have to choose.

CHAPTER THREE

The American Connection
(August–October 1944)

In the summer of 1944, Yenan first opted for a peaceful expansion of the united front. The arrival of the U.S. Army Observer Section gave Mao a chance to appeal for American diplomatic and material assistance. Circumstantial evidence suggests that the Communist high command agreed to delay the expansion of Red forces into Kuomintang territory while efforts to forge the American connection hung in the balance. At first, this strategy seemed to work, for Washington tried to include the Communists in a unified Chinese army under General Stilwell's command. In the end, however, Stilwell was recalled, signaling the retreat from a more flexible American policy toward China and triggering the dispatch of Communist forces south.

The Dixie Mission

Yenan had every reason to welcome the U.S. Army Observer Section, nicknamed the Dixie Mission because it was sent to rebel territory to answer the question, "Is it true what they say about Dixie?"[1] The arrival of the Dixie Mission demonstrated for the first time publicly that Washington could and would impose its will on the Nationalist government, which had tried to prevent contact with the Communist areas. It constituted a quasi-official recognition of Yenan by the United States government. It gave the Communists a chance to make their case for foreign assistance directly and with the evidence of their military and political successes at hand. Finally, it opened a direct line to Washington and offered hope that this connection would pay dividends in the months to come.

We shall never know for sure what the Communists thought of their American visitors, but we can guess. At one level, CCP propaganda presented a dry, formalistic, and unflattering picture of the United States. In this view, the structure of America's capitalist economy dictated the "imperialist" behavior of the United States government. Before the war, the United States, Great Britain, Japan, and the other "imperialist" powers were pictured as colluding with the Nationalist regime to exploit and oppress the Chinese people. Following the Japanese invasion of China, the Communist press continued to trace the twists and turns of international events: ever alert to the possibility of drawing the capitalist countries to China's side; but no less willing to condemn backsliding in the direction of a "Far Eastern Munich."[2] Finally, after Pearl Harbor, the structure of world politics congealed into its wartime mold. From then until the eve of the victory over Japan, the term "imperialist" was discarded and readers of the Yenan press were told of a global struggle between "Fascism" on one side and "Democracy," including all Allied countries and people, on the other.

At another level, Communist propaganda had always distinguished between bad governments and good people, and direct contact with American citizens confirmed the view that Yenan had friends on the other side of the Pacific. During the late 1930s, before the imposition of the Kuomintang blockade, several foreign journalists had visited the Communist areas and reported favorably on what they found.[3] The most celebrated of their number, Edgar Snow, told the world in *Red Star over China* about the achievements and the vision of the Communist revolution. This experience taught Yenan that there were fair-minded and influential foreigners who could be convinced by what they saw and whose message would redound to the Communists' favor. In Chungking, Chou En-lai cultivated these people and invited them to Yenan. His efforts bore fruit in the spring of 1944, when a foreign Press Party was allowed to tour the Communist areas, ending the five-year drought on news from the north brought on by the blockade.[4] More important, in the summer came the Dixie Mission.

The eighteen men who made up the first contingent of the Dixie Mission arrived in Yenan on two flights, in July and August.[5] They represented all the major U.S. agencies in China: Army, Air Corps, Navy, State Department, and Office of Strategic Services (OSS). The head of the mission was Colonel David Barrett, a plump, vigorous professional soldier who had spent two decades in China, spoke the language fluently, and had great empathy for things and people Chinese. The chief political reporter was John Service: the son of a missionary family who had grown up in China, a Foreign Service officer, and contact man in Chungking between Chou En-lai and the top American officials. The Dixie Mission had orders to gather intelligence on the location and movement of Japanese forces in north China and on the political, military, and economic status of the Communists themselves.

From the outset, the Communists gave their visitors the fullest cooperation. They paid for feeding and housing the Americans and waited on their personal needs. Several members of the high command—Chief of Staff Yeh Chien-ying, P'eng Teh-huai, Ch'en I, and Nieh Jung-chen—gave extensive briefings on the military situation and tailored their research to suit American needs. Mao, Chou, and Chu Teh met the Americans for frequent and long conversations. At lower levels, cadres were assigned to each member of the mission to provide information and assistance in a variety of areas: enemy and Communist order of battle, weather, targets, rescue of downed airmen, communications, coastal defense, propaganda, and interrogation of Japanese prisoners. Special units guided the Americans on long excursions to Communist bases behind enemy lines.[6] Finally, the Communist press celebrated this new partnership with an enthusiasm evident in its Fourth of July editorial:

Democratic America has already found a companion, and the cause of Sun Yat-sen a successor, in the Chinese Communist Party and the other democratic forces. . . . The work which we Communists are carrying on today is the very same work which was carried on earlier in America by Washington, Jefferson, and Lincoln; it will certainly obtain, and indeed has already obtained, the sympathy of democratic America.[7]

American journalists and government officials who visited Yenan in 1944 liked what they saw. The winnowings of historical debate in this country have identified a handful of Foreign Service officers with a special sympathy for the Communists and for a policy of giving them aid. But it was Colonel Barrett who, after less than a month in Yenan, first recommended sending arms to the Communists. "I have been in China too long to be easily deceived," wrote Barrett in his report of August 18, calling for immediate military assistance, "and since the Section came to Yenan, we have certainly been subject to no high pressure salesmanship except a burning desire to convince us that they want to fight the Japanese and help the people."[8] At least until spring of the following year, this judgment was shared by virtually all members of the Dixie Mission and the press party.

Policymakers in Yenan knew they were scoring points. They could read the favorable news stories which appeared in the American press and were reprinted in *Chieh Fang Jih Pao*.[9] Or they could listen to one journalist (Harrison Forman) who made numerous speeches to audiences in the Communist areas promising large-scale American aid. And as John Davies found when he first joined the mission in November, "the forthrightness, energy and efficiency of the Americans who compose the Observer Section has made an excellent impression on Yenan leaders."[10]

Americans and Chinese developed a close rapport in wartime Yenan. During the day they worked together in the common crusade against Fascism. At night, they mixed easily at dances in the Pear Orchard, where Mao revealed his earthy rhythmic skills, and at dinners, remembered for the good food and bad wine.[11] What some of the Americans saw and the way they reported it rang with an excitement and optimism which has made their accounts despised, honored, and always engaging. At the same time, these Americans communicated some of their own spirit, which must have given promise to those in Yenan who hoped for American aid.

Mao's Diplomatic Initiative

No sooner had the Dixie Mission arrived in Yenan, than enemy advances revived the search for political realignments which had been going on throughout China. On August 8 the Japanese overran Hengyang, site of the first American air base south of the Yangtze, signaling the start of the action. In Kweilin, the warlord Li Chi-shen sought American aid for a separate government in south China. In Chungking the American embassy sounded out sympathetic members of the Kuomintang on a plan to bring the Communists into a joint "war council" which would exercise command over all Chinese armies. Minor party spokesmen discussed plans to form a federation, which would concentrate their efforts and magnify their influence. In Yenan, Communist propaganda organs stepped up the pressure on Chiang, accusing the Nationalist governor of Shansi of making a secret deal with the Japanese, and for the first time calling the Communist areas the "center of democratic China."[12]

What lay behind Yenan's verbal flourishes? Were the Communists prepared to expand "democratic China" southward and risk conflict with Chungking? Or were they simply trying to isolate Chiang Kai-shek and win support among the growing legion of his critics? The answer is both: but first diplomacy, then war.

As policymakers in Yenan discussed plans for an opening to the Americans, preparations for the move south began in Nanniwan, a village just outside the Communist capital. In 1941, at the height of the Japanese "three-all" campaign, Wang Chen led his 10,000-man brigade to Nanniwan. During the most difficult years of the war, Wang built this village into a showpiece of "self-reliance," and the "spirit of Nanniwan" took its place in the lexicon of the Communist movement. Wang, like Mao, was a native of Hunan, the province south of the Yangtze most deeply affected by the Japanese advance, and he had risen in the Party as a labor organizer in this region. In August, training and equipping of Wang's forces got underway.[13] When Yenan decided to move south, Wang Chen and the Nanniwan Brigade would lead the way.

Before launching an offensive which might strain relations with Chungking, however, Yenan would test its chances on the diplomatic front. Perhaps because he saw potential opposition from within his own ranks, Mao had put off an early meeting with John Service.[14] A hasty move toward the Americans would expose Mao to charges that he had compromised the staunch nationalism which was one foundation stone of Communist success. To protect himself against such criticism, the chairman called a meeting which on August 18 issued the Central Committee directive "On Diplomatic Work."[15] This document, which by its own assertion marks the beginning of Chinese Communist foreign policy, set forth the central theme of Yenan's diplomacy for the next two years: to secure foreign assistance, without compromising the gains of the movement to date or its commitment to self-reliance.

The Central Committee saw the arrival of the Dixie Mission as an important turning point, separating the previous history of expansion from within and the "beginning of our participation in the unified international anti-Fascist front as the start of our diplomatic work." While acknowledging the gains of the past, the Party center predicted that cooperation with the United States and Great Britain (the directive made little mention of the Soviet Union) would enable the liberated areas to attain "even greater growth" in the future and foresaw the "possibility" of continuing this cooperation after the war. To secure these objectives, the directive instructed cadres to welcome foreign military, diplomatic, cultural, and religious missions; foreign economic aid, capital investment, and technical cooperation; and military assistance in the form of "ammunition, drugs and equipment."

While opening the door to the outside world, "On Diplomatic Work" warned against the danger, recurrent in the past century of Chinese history, of fear of, passivity toward, and reliance on the foreigners. It told cadres not to ask for assistance of any kind, but to demonstrate their energy and determination and to "arrange it so that the foreigners would offer us help themselves." This quest for foreign aid, Yenan explained, must not erode the commitment to self-reliance:

We must intensify the feeling of national self-respect and faith in ourselves, but without boycotting foreigners; we must study the positive experience of others while improving cooperation with them, but without worshipping and flattering the foreigners. This is what constitutes the correct national platform, this is what constitutes the essence of the prototype of the new man in new democratic China.[16]

Perhaps this directive was part of a broader agreement, which would give Mao time to talk with the Americans while preparations for the move south went forward. In any case, securing support from within the Party solved only a fraction of the chairman's problem. Before him lay the more difficult task of weaning the Americans away from their policy of recognizing and aiding only Chungking. Time was running out, for the opportunity to win American assistance was subject to fast-breaking events along the narrow line separating Communist and Nationalist forces. Finally, on August 23, Mao summoned Service for an unusual six-hour conversation which the latter described as "the clearest indication we have yet received of Communist thinking and planning in regard to the part they hope to have in China's national affairs in the near future."[17]

Service was well acquainted with the public version of Yenan's wartime policy: a united front of all parties and classes for the liberation of China from Japanese domination.[18] The New Democracy, as Mao called it, prescribed cooperation with the Nationalists as the legitimate government of China. In the liberated areas, local governments were chosen by democratic election and CCP members were limited to one-third of the total seats to assure the representation of all parties. Under a mixed economy, Yenan promoted cooperative enterprises while guaranteeing the rights of private property, production, and commerce. An agrarian policy of "reducing rent and interest" rather than redistributing land was designed to secure the support of rich peasants and landlords. Finally, all these practices were to continue for some time to come. "The fundamental policy of democracy," Mao told one foreign journalist, "has been unchanged. It will remain unchanged under any conditions, because concrete conditions in China dictate continuation of democratic policies for a long time to come. What China needs most is democracy—not socialism. We are still very far from socialism."[19]

With regard to foreign policy, in his talk with Service Mao emphasized the same theme of unity against Fascism, minimizing the role of the Soviet Union in China and maximizing that of the Americans. Moscow would decide its own policy in the Far East, but given Russian losses during the war and the needs of postwar reconstruction, Mao considered Soviet assistance to any party in China unlikely. "And for us to seek it would only make the situation in China worse," the chairman insisted. "China is dis-unified enough already!"[20] He denied the necessity for Soviet-American conflict over China: "Russia only wants a friendly and democratic China. Cooperation between America and the Chinese Communist Party will be beneficial and satisfactory to all concerned."[21] Finally, if such cooperation could be secured, Mao saw a bright future for CCP–American relations:

Even the most conservative American business man can find nothing in our program to take exception to.

China *must* industralize. This can be done—in China—only by free enterprise and with the aid of foreign capital. Chinese and American interests are corelated and similar. They *fit* together, economically and politically. We can and must work together.

The United States would find us *more cooperative* than the Kuomintang. We will not be afraid of democratic American influence—we will welcome it. We have no silly ideas of taking *only* Western mechanical techniques. Also we will not be interested in monopolistic, bureaucratic capitalism that stifles the economic development of the country and only enriches the officials. *We will be interested* in the most rapid possible development of the country on constructive and productive lines. First will be the raising of the living standard of the people (see what we have done here with our limited resources). After that can come the "national defense industry" that Chiang talks of in his "China's Destiny." We will be interested in the welfare of the Chinese people.

America does not need to fear that we will not be cooperative. We must cooperate and we must have American help. This is why it is so important to us Communists to know what you Americans are thinking and planning. We cannot risk crossing you—cannot risk any conflict with you.[22]

This offer to open China's doors to foreign trade and investment is surprising, especially when compared with Chiang's program of high tariffs and state monopolies.[23] Mao's vision extended far into the future, however, and it could be realized only if the United States first agreed to change its policy toward China. The threat of civil war, Mao warned, was growing. Allowed to go unchecked, reactionary elements in Chungking would eventually attack the Communists and *"China will become a major international problem."*[24] Only Washington could prevent this catastrophe. If the Americans agreed to act, Mao had a plan for averting civil war.

The chairman's program unfolded in two stages. Initially, he wanted American support for the creation of a coalition government, which would draft a constitution, hold free elections, and establish a truly democratic regime. If the Kuomintang refused these reforms, the next step would be for the United States to begin sending arms to Yenan. Mao never requested aid directly— this would have put him at a disadvantage, and the Central Committee directive told him not to. Instead, he appealed to American self-interest. To aid only Chungking divided the Chinese people and invited civil war; to aid all those forces fighting the Japanese would bring victory that much closer.[25]

Mao's proposals raised the stakes in Yenan's ongoing negotiations with Chungking. In the talks held sporadically during the previous year and a half, the Communists had sought recognition for their liberated areas and some control over a unified Chinese army, while the Nationalists insisted that Red forces be turned over *prior to* reform of the government command structure.[26] By calling for a coalition, Mao was demanding not just autonomy but a share of the national government itself. His suggestion that the Americans bypass Chungking and send arms directly to Yenan introduced an element which would change the whole political balance in China.

It seems unlikely that Mao expected Chiang to accept the Communist proposal. Relations between the two parties in China had a long and bitter history. After the middle of August, Communist propaganda attacks on Chungking had grown more caustic. In his talk with Service, Mao called the generalissimo a "gangster" and charged that "even Hitler has a better claim to democratic power." Other high officials in Yenan voiced similar misgivings.[27] That the Communists would reveal these attitudes while trying to convince the Americans of their own good faith demonstrates the depth of their disdain for Chiang Kai-shek and their pessimism about chances for an agreement with him.

Mao's target was Washington. The Central Committee directive prohibited requests for arms and ammunition, and Mao presented the idea to Service only in an indirect fashion. Some of the Communist generals—Chu Teh, Yeh Chien-ying, and Lin Piao—were less reticent to talk about their need for weapons. In September a "qualified person in Yenan" (almost certainly Mao himself) issued an open call for aid on the front page of *Chieh Fang Jih Pao*. Finally, if the Americans would not agree to bypass Chungking, perhaps a de facto alliance could be created through a rendezvous of Communist and American forces on the coast. Knowing that whoever ushered the Allies ashore would get something in return, Mao stressed to Service that "the Americans must land in China" and promised Communist cooperation.[28] Throughout 1944 and well into the following spring, the Communist press and leading figures in Yenan remained strong advocates of an early, large-scale American invasion of the mainland.[29]

The Bid Is In

Mao's bid for American support (and also, although unknown to the Communists, Barrett's proposal that the United States send them arms) reached Chungking at an opportune time. On September 5 the People's Political Council (PPC), a public forum for airing the views of all political parties, convened in the Nationalist capital to discuss the gathering crisis. On the seventh, Lingling, the next American air base south of Hengyang, and Wenchow, a major port on the east coast, fell to the Japanese. Under considerable pressure, Chiang lifted the ban on criticism of the government. *Ta Kung Pao*, a major daily paper representing liberal-to-moderate independent opinion, sharply attacked the government for mismanaging the national defense and blamed the losses on the minister of war.[30] Meanwhile, within the halls of the PPC, as one American journalist reported, the fat was in the fire: "Never before have delegates to the People's Political Council spoken so sharply to Government Ministers about corruption, inefficiency, repression, the shocking treatment of Chinese soldiers and other evils of the moribund regime."[31]

Yenan made the most of the generalissimo's troubles. Communist representative Lin Tsu-han told the PPC that the Kuomintang should relinquish one-party rule and organize a coalition government which included all anti-Japanese parties. The Council refused to deal with this issue, but on October 10 leaders of the minor parties announced the formation of the Chinese Democratic League, which joined in support of Yenan's proposal.[32] From this point on, as Lyman Van Slyke has observed, the Communists "had the KMT in a corner. If the KMT made concessions to the League, the CCP would be the principal beneficiary. If the KMT refused to do so, the League's criticism would help isolate the KMT and destroy public confidence in it."[33]

Meanwhile, outside this wholly Chinese gathering but parallel to it, the Americans pressed Chiang to adopt reforms which would give a larger role to the Communists. In the summer of 1944 Chennault's promise that his bombers could provide their own defense against a Japanese ground attack was discredited, and the Chinese army was in retreat. The solution, at least from Washington's point of view, was to hand the ball to Stilwell. On July 6 Roosevelt advised Chiang to place Stilwell in command of all Chinese forces—including the Communists. Chiang parried this request by asking the President to send a representative to China to discuss the terms of Stilwell's investiture. Roosevelt agreed, and on September 6 Patrick J. Hurley arrived in Chungking to take up the task.[34]

Stilwell had first seen the Communists in 1936, while on a trip through north China in his capacity as American military attaché. "They have good intelligence work," he wrote at the time, "good organization, good tactics. They do not want the cities. Content to rough it in the country. Poorly armed and equipped, yet scare the Government to death."[35] Thereafter, Stilwell's respect for the Communists never slackened, and on one occasion, in 1943, he proposed to the generalissimo that they be armed and used in operations in north China. At the same time, Stilwell kept his distance from Yenan. His focus was on Burma and on rebuilding the Nationalist army. Getting mixed up with the Communists would only damage these efforts, so Stilwell ordered his military staff to stay away from them. When asked about commanding the Chinese army, however, Stilwell agreed only on the condition that the Communists be included and that he retain the power to arm them through his control over lend-lease.[36] In retrospect, it is hard to imagine that Chiang ever intended to grant the American this much authority, but for the better part of two months the talks dragged on.

Although the content of these negotiations was not made public, the Communists either learned or guessed what they were about.[37] The last presidential envoy to China was Vice-President Wallace, whose visit had led to the dispatch of the Dixie Mission. The arrival of Hurley less than three months later amidst the rapidly declining military situation obviously had an important purpose. Publicly, Yenan suggested that the talks with Hurley should deal with allocation of Allied materiel. Privately, Mao and several other top Communist officials discussed with foreign visitors the appointment of an American Allied supreme commander in China.[38] Communist agents in Chungking assured Stilwell that they would fight under his command and invited him to visit Yenan. Stilwell agreed, and they went away, reportedly much pleased.[39]

Yenan was willing to place its forces under an American commander, but not without exacting a price. Chou En-lai told Service that such an arrangement was possible only after "American supplies and men are coming into China in significant magnitude and the counter-offensive is actually in sight."[40] Yeh Chien-ying agreed. "The supreme Allied Command should consider that we can take charge of *our front* if we have the equipment," he told Service. "Without equipment we can only continue guerrilla tactics." Mao too refused to promise immediate cooperation with an Allied commander.[41] Remembering the lesson of the Hundred Regiments Offensive, Yenan would not turn its poorly armed guerrillas over to an American general to cast them lavishly onto the Japanese barricades. The Communists would fight for Stilwell, but only after their forces had been properly armed and trained for conventional warfare.

For the time being, policymakers in Yenan could do nothing but wait. They had filed their appeal for a coalition government and for American aid if this should fail. The Japanese advance and the talks on Stilwell's command were proceeding at a pace over which Yenan had no control. Meanwhile, in Washington, the Roosevelt administration was preoccupied with the upcoming election. Coverage of the campaign in the Chinese Communist press strongly favored the familiar and friendly Roosevelt over the "isolationist" Republican, Thomas Dewey. Both Mao and Chou told Service that they expected no change in American policy until after the election.[42]

The Recall of Stilwell and the Move South

If there was an understanding among Communist leaders to delay the move south pending an American response to Mao's proposals, it was dissolved by news that General Stilwell had been relieved of his command and recalled to the United States. Stilwell left China on October 21. The story of his dismissal broke immediately: Stilwell and the Communists wanted to fight the Japanese; Chiang did not; when push came to shove Chiang demanded Stilwell's ouster, and Roosevelt complied. Many observers in China could agree with one American reporter's view of what this meant: "Inside China it represents the triumph of a moribund antidemocratic regime that is more concerned with maintaining its political supremacy than in driving the Japanese out of China. America is now committed at least passively to supporting a regime that has become unpopular and distrusted in China."[43]

Yenan's reaction to these events was restrained. The Communist press made no comment at all until after the American election. Then, a laudatory editorial entitled "Roosevelt Reelected" assured readers that whatever his past mistakes, in the future the President would "certainly continue to aid the Chinese War of Resistance, promote the internal reunification of China, promote the reform of the Chinese Government and enable the Chinese people to develop their proper role in the anti-Fascist war in Asia."[44]

While Communist propaganda remained unchanged, the recall of Stilwell had a dramatic impact on Yenan's military and by implication foreign policies. It was the departure of the American general that triggered the decision to move Communist forces south. Based on information he received in Yenan the following spring, Service reported that "the decision to start expansion into Southeast China was made immediately after General Stilwell's recall, which [the Communists] interpreted as an American decision to support Chiang and the Central Government only."[45] The order to Wang Chen was issued on October 25, four days after Stilwell's departure. On November 1, 5000 men of the Nanniwan Brigade left Yenan for the south.[46]

The recall of Stilwell was a serious blow to Mao's diplomacy and probably served to erode what little support remained within the Party for a policy of cooperation with Chungking and the foreign powers. Clearly, Chou En-lai backed Mao's efforts in this direction. But the lessons of Cheng Feng must have been well learned, for among the many attacks leveled against Mao's opponents in the intervening years, no one has been accused of tilting toward compromise with the Kuomintang or the foreigners during this period.

Criticism did come from other directions. According to Michael Lindsay, an Englishman who worked for the Communists in Yenan during the war, Mao and Chou "seriously risked their positions and influence" by agreeing to work with the Americans. Lindsay, and later Mao, suggested that some of this opposition came from hard-line anti-imperialists, apparently identified with the pro-Soviet returned students.[47] Some of it may also have come from the military. P'eng Teh-huai was suspected of being aloof from or even hostile to the Americans, and according to Colonel Barrett, "with a few shots of *pai-kan* ('white dry') under his belt, [Ch'en I] talked in a manner which sounded anti-foreign in general and sometimes anti-American in particular."[48] On balance, however, the commanders of the Red Army cooperated fully with the Dixie Mission and made no secret of their interest in obtaining American arms. If there was any circumspection on the part of the generals, it was not because they were anti-foreign but because they favored the vigorous expansion of Communist forces which had been delayed by pursuit of the American connection.

Throughout the summer and fall of 1944, Mao worried about the pace and direction of the military advance. On one hand, the Communists had to expand into newly exposed areas and eventually into the cities, if they were to emerge from the war as a force at the national level. But Mao was concerned that in making this transition headstrong commanders would sacrifice popular support for the promise of quick victory, that Communist soldiers would forget the lessons of fighting a "people's war," and that the spread of a "mountain stronghold" mentality would throw the movement out of Yenan's control.[49] These dangers were evident in the present situation, for a failure of military discipline could upset the chance to win American assistance. Conversely, Mao must have seen that American arms, channeled through Yenan and distributed under his watchful eye, would give him the same leverage over potential "warlords" in the base areas beyond the Yellow River that Chiang exercised over his own minions in the south.

After the middle of 1944, the potential power of the Communists was greater than either the scope of their military control or their status in the national political order—and they knew it. With the

rapid changes on the battlefield, the movement was heaving up-
ward and outward. Mao tried to convince the Americans of this
fact and win their support for Yenan's emergence, but he failed. In
the wake of the Rectification Campaign, few people in the Party
would speak for the united front, and now, after the recall of Stilwell, the generals were in the ascendant. It was the surprise visit of
Patrick Hurley, rather than any further initiative by Yenan, that kept
alive hopes for the American connection.

CHAPTER FOUR

The American Initiatives
(November 1944–February 1945)

After the recall of Stilwell, policymakers in Yenan turned their attention to the battlefield. American initiatives, first by Hurley, later by the Army and the OSS, kept alive the prospects for winning American aid, and Mao and Chou made every effort to secure American cooperation. The expansion of Yenan's forces to the south, however, promised more substantial and certain rewards. The Communists would hear the Americans out, but they would not compromise this chance for armed advance to satisfy Chungking or its foreign supporters.

The Hurley Initiative

Patrick Hurley, the first top U.S. official to visit Yenan, offered the Communists what appeared to be real hope for winning American support. Their initial round of talks seemed promising. But once back in Chungking, Hurley reversed his position, the negotiations broke down, and prospects for cooperation with the Americans were bleaker than ever.

On the afternoon of November 7, Hurley arrived, unannounced, on the runway in Yenan. Although the Communists had no idea why he had come, they greeted his appearance as an unexpected windfall. Within a week of Hurley's arrival in Chungking, Chu Teh had invited him to Yenan, and Communist representatives sought him out to discuss their proposal for a coalition government. The Communist press praised his efforts in the talks held in Chungking. Reports of Stilwell's recall credited Hurley with trying to reorganize the Nationalist cabinet and unify all Chinese forces under an American command.[1] After the departure of Stilwell and the resignation of U.S. Ambassador Clarence Gauss (on November 1), Hurley emerged as the most important American in China. Unblemished by the Stilwell affair and for the moment in command of his country's policy, Hurley was the most powerful foreigner ever to visit Yenan and obviously the man Mao would have to deal with if the Communists were to win American arms.

Hurley's decision to visit Yenan reflected the continuing deterioration of the Allied position below the Yangtze. After the capture of Lingling in September, the Japanese pressed on against American air bases at Kweilin and Liuchow.[2] If these two cities fell, U.S. bombers would have to retreat to Kweiyang, high in the mountains to the west and far from their prime targets in central and eastern China. Meanwhile, stunning blows against the Japanese navy in the western Pacific, MacArthur's landing in the Philippines, and the beginning of air raids against Formosa brought the Americans provocatively close to the China coast. But while Chungking was preoccupied with its own defense, the Japanese had little trouble seizing Foochow, a major port opposite Formosa which would be pivotal in any battle for control of the southern shoreline. The American advance, offset by the Nationalist retreat, raised the obvious question of what Chinese forces, if any, would meet an American landing party on the coast.

With leaders in Yenan still ignorant of the purpose of Hurley's visit, the talks opened on the morning of November 8.[3] Hurley and Barrett attended for the American side; Mao, Chou, and Chu Teh represented the Communists, with interpreters and secretaries also present. Since Hurley had initiated the meeting, he dominated the first session. His message was simple and to the point. The United States did not want to interfere in the internal politics of China. Acting as a friend, his mission was to "bring about a unification of the Chinese military forces for the defeat of Japan in cooperation with the United States." To that end, he produced a five-point plan for resolving the impasse between Yenan and Chungking. Hurley assured his listeners that this document was to serve only as a basis for discussion, but anyone who had followed the negotiations could see that these five points were simply a restatement of the familiar—and to the Communists unacceptable—Kuomintang position, requiring all Chinese armies to submit to the government's command. Mao asked whose idea the five points were. Hurley replied that "it was his idea, the basis was his idea, but it had been worked on by all of us." After a brief exchange the meeting adjourned to give the Communists time to study the proposal. The two sides agreed that the content of the talks would remain confidential so that publicity would not undermine their chances for success.

When the meeting reconvened in the afternoon, Mao took the floor. The chairman ignored the proposal Hurley had put forward and tried to force the Americans onto the defensive with a vigorous attack on the Kuomintang regime:

The policy of the Chinese Government has been a hindrance of the unity of the whole Chinese people. . . . They tried all means to attack [the liberated areas] and to send spies into our territories . . . The greater portion of the Kuomintang Army has lost its fighting power . . . the source of this crisis lies in the policy of the Kuomintang authority and the corrupt government apparatus which just collapses at the mere encounter of the Japanese attack.[4]

Hurley defended the generalissimo, charging that Mao's allegations were "what the enemies of China have been saying." The chairman retorted that he was merely repeating the views of President Roosevelt and Prime Minister Churchill.[5] After this exchange Hurley retreated a step and the atmosphere cooled, but Mao had won the debate.

From this point on, Hurley took an active part in composing Yenan's response.[6] The Communist Five Point Proposal reflected its joint authorship. On the Communist side, the proposal called for the creation of a coalition government. On the American side, Hurley contributed a string of clauses which would commit the new government to every guarantee of liberty and democracy from

the Bill of Rights to the Four Freedoms.[7] Finally, at his own initiative, Hurley signed the document to indicate that he considered its
terms "fair and just."[8]

There is no way of knowing what Mao and company thought of
this surprising and bizarre visit. Hurley had arrived in Yenan bearing the shopworn demands of the Nationalist government, now in
a new wrapping for which he himself claimed credit. Then, after a
single lecture by Mao, he joined in drafting and ratifying a document which everyone in Yenan (save, perhaps, Hurley) must have
known the generalissimo would never accept. Was this a victory?
Or would Hurley, who had turned 180 degrees during his three
days in Yenan, be spinning in circles after a week back in Chungking?

Whatever his thoughts, the chairman moved quickly to maximize
the value of Hurley's signature and strengthen the tenuous link between Washington and Yenan. On the day of Hurley's departure,
Mao wired the President, thanking him for sending a representative and informing him of the proposed agreement that had been
arrived at through these "good offices." Four days later, Roosevelt
replied, tersely but auspiciously: "I look forward to vigorous cooperation with all the Chinese forces against our common enemy, the
Japanese invaders of China."[9] Whatever doubts the Communists
may have had about Hurley, their hopes rode with him as he carried their proposal to Chungking.

Once back in the capital, Hurley's support for the Communist
Five Points proved short-lived. Initially, he pressed the reluctant
Chiang to accept Yenan's offer and told one associate that "if there
is a breakdown in the parleys it will be the fault of the Government
and not the Communists."[10] Similarly, he declined to help draft
Chungking's reply, a three-point proposal which rejected the formation of a coalition government and insisted on government control over Communist forces. Barrett dates the shift of Hurley's sym-
pathies toward the Kuomintang from his appointment as
ambassador on November 17, and he may be right.[11] Soon thereafter the new ambassador began to press Chou En-lai, who had returned with Hurley to represent Yenan in the talks, to accept the
government's three points. Chou insisted that such an important
decision would have to be referred to the Communist leadership,

and on December 7 he returned to Yenan.[12] On the plane with him was Colonel Barrett, whom Hurley charged with the task of persuading Mao to accept the proposal and send Chou back to Chungking to continue the negotiations.

In Yenan, Mao and Chou received Barrett the following day. They had already decided to reject the government's offer, for even before the meeting began they informed Barrett that Chou would not return to Chungking. The Communist Five Points were not an "asking price," Mao told Barrett, they were Yenan's "final terms." In any case, the chairman had never been sanguine about the chances for an agreement with Chiang; what bothered him more was Hurley's apparent reversal. After reviewing Hurley's role in drafting the Communist Five Points, Mao found it "difficult . . . to understand" how the American could ask Yenan to accept the government's reply.[13]

If Chungking and Washington refused to support a coalition, Mao threatened, the Communists would have no choice but to move toward the creation of a separate government. This was the first suggestion of what would become the ultimate weapon in Yenan's diplomatic arsenal. The formation of a separate government in north China, long achieved in fact but denied in convenient fiction, would formalize the division of China and dash American hopes for wartime and postwar unity. If the United States would not aid Yenan, the chairman warned, "there is still England and the Soviet Union."[14] No one could take seriously the reference to England, but the possibility of a Chinese Communist–Soviet alliance, coupled with the civil war which would result if a basis for unity could not be found, was one scenario the Americans wanted to avoid. Knowing this, Mao regularly sweetened the prospects for CCP-U.S. cooperation with assurances that the Soviet Union would not play a large role in China. But the converse argument also had its utility, and Mao made sure that Barrett did not miss the point.

Still interested in the possibility of American assistance, Mao coupled these threats with an offer of continued cooperation. During Chou's stay in Chungking, high officers in the U.S. military headquarters, now headed by Stilwell's successor General Albert Wedemeyer, had begun to discuss plans for aid to Yenan. Chou may have learned of these developments and passed the information on to Mao. Whatever his source, the chairman told Barrett: "General Wedemeyer says that if we can come to an agreement with the Generalissimo, he can give us arms and can send United States Army officers to train us and work with us."[15] The Communists were not willing to pay the price Chiang was asking, the chairman continued, but they were prepared to cooperate with the Americans:

If the United States abandons us, we shall be very, very sorry, but it will make no difference in our good feeling toward you. We will accept your help with gratitude any time, now or in the future. We would serve with all our hearts under an American General, with no strings or conditions attached. That is how we feel toward you. If you land on the shores of China, we will be there to meet you, and to place ourselves under your command.[16]

Whether spontaneously or by design, the mood of the meeting was stormy. In contrast to the diplomatic calm that had prevailed in the earlier talks with Hurley, Mao unleashed on the lowly Barrett a wide slice of human emotion. Several times he flew into a violent rage and shouted over and over again: "We will not yield any further!" "That turtle's egg, Chiang!" "If Chiang were here I would curse him to his face!" Throughout this performance Chou never lost his temper, but backed the chairman up with cold logic. "I left the interview," Barrett recalled, "feeling that I had talked in vain to two clever, ruthless and determined leaders who felt absolutely sure of the strength of their position."[17] Finally, Mao had (again Barrett's phrase) "one more shot in his locker." As the meeting drew to a close, he told the American that Yenan might find it necessary to publish the Communist Five Points which bore Hurley's signature.[18]

In the aftermath of this nasty exchange, Mao and Chou held firmly to their position: since Chiang had refused to discuss the formation of a coalition, it was up to the Americans to proceed to the question of military aid. "We completely desire," Chou wrote the ambassador, "to continue to discuss with you and General Wedemeyer the concrete problems of our future military cooperation and continue to keep the closest contact with the U.S. Army Observers Section in Yenan under the command of Colonel David D. Barrett." In the meantime, however, Chou would not return to

Chungking, and he confirmed to Hurley the decision to publish the Communist Five Points.[19]

Yenan could expect few concessions from the American embassy, for Mao's statements had put Hurley in a very ugly temper and pressed him further toward his eventual destination of all-out support for Chiang Kai-shek. In his reply to Chou, the ambassador repeated his position in favor of continuing talks in Chungking and against publication of what he considered a confidential document.[20] Between Hurley's quest for a political settlement and Yenan's demand that they move on to the question of aid, there was little room for compromise.

Six weeks after the recall of Stilwell, a month from Hurley's visit to Yenan, Mao and Chou had come down hard on their terms for dealing with the Americans. They would talk about arms, or they would not talk at all. The mood in Yenan, according to one American observer, was confident and tough:

> The Communists, on their part, have no interest in reaching an agreement with the Generalissimo short of a genuine coalition government. They recognize that Chiang's position is crumbling, that they may before long receive substantial Russian support and that if they have patience they will succeed to authority in at least North China. They are now so confident and so little concerned with Chungking that if the current negotiations break down, they intend to bring together the heretofore decentralized areas which they control under a centralized administrative federation. This would be a blow to Chiang which he could not effectively counter.[21]

Military Expansion: "Our Task in 1945"

Yenan's confidence, and by extension its diplomatic pluck, was a direct reflection of the situation on the battlefield. At the end of 1944, Nationalist fortunes continued to decline, while the Communists made gains throughout south China. Red military commanders in the outlying base areas wanted to rally their forces and take the offensive. Under the pressure of these events and his own generals, Mao began to prepare for the transition from guerrilla to conventional war.

During the final months of 1944, the Nationalists were unable to blunt the Ichigo Offensive. In November the Japanese captured

Kweilin, Liuchow, and Nanning, removing the last vestige of American air power from east China and threatening its refuge in Kweiyang. If Kweiyang fell, the enemy would have a clear shot at the Nationalist capital. In early December American and British civilians were evacuated from Chungking and there was discussion of moving the government to a more secure location farther west. According to one American journalist in Chungking, "the next sixty days might determine whether China would be knocked out of the war."[22]

The view from Yenan, by contrast, yielded an expanding military horizon to the south. Almost half of Honan, including 90 percent of the territory once held by the Nationalists, was about to fall under Communist control. An American observer confirmed that the province was in a state "bordering on chaos," while Communist guerrillas (including Wang Chen's brigade) were "slowly filtering in from the north of the Yellow River, subduing robber bands and organizing the peasantry."[23] Meanwhile, Yenan claimed its first victories below the Yangtze: in Hunan, southern Kiangsu, and Chekiang, the latter two involving sharp clashes with government forces.[24]

Commanders of Communist units outside Yenan drew courage from these events and pushed for a more aggressive policy than that authorized by the Party center. From October 1944 to January 1945, Raymond Ludden, one of the Foreign Service officers attached to the Dixie Mission, traveled behind Japanese lines in Shansi, Hopeh, Suiyuan, and Chahar provinces. Ludden described the mood in these north China bases:

The further one proceeds east in Communist controlled areas of north China the more outspoken and bitter becomes criticism of the Kuomintang Government. This is especially true among field commanders of the Eighth Route Army and their political commissars.

At the headquarters of the Shansi-Suiyuan and Shansi-Chahar-Hopei Communist Base Areas I heard much more frank discussion of the Communist plans for expansion than I heard at Yenan. This was especially true after the fall of Kweilin [on November 10] and the rapid Japanese advance into Kweichow province. Communist leaders pointed out on numerous occasions that Communist planning envisages the organization of Communist guerrilla units in all areas of eastern China evacuated by Kuomintang forces and that it was hoped eventually to have a connected series of Base

Areas extending from present bases in the north to the small Communist Base Area on the East River in Kwangtung Province. If, say the Communists, the Japanese establish a line from north to south through China, that line must be harassed throughout its length by active guerrilla operations and the people must be organized to support and to participate in such operations.[25]

The officials Ludden talked to were not optimistic about the prospects for Communist expansion into the Japanese enclaves of Manchuria and Inner Mongolia, but they pointed to a much different situation in Honan, where recent victories rested on the "large quantities of arms and equipment abandoned by retreating Kuomintang forces during the spring and summer of 1944 and collected by Honan peasants."[26] They were confident they could repeat this process farther south and were anxious to push in that direction.

Responding to news from the front, and perhaps also to these pressures from within the Red Army itself, Mao stepped up preparations for a wider war. On December 15 he instructed the Shensi-Kansu-Ninghsia Border Region Congress on "Our Task in 1945." Ostensibly, the main task of the Party was to promote the formation of a coalition government. But the hard core of Mao's message was a call to arms. The chairman appealed to followers in the Communist-controlled areas to expand their guerrilla operations into both Japanese and Nationalist territories. And he called on those in Japanese occupied (largely urban) areas to prepare to drive out the invaders: "At present this task must be raised to a position of equal importance with the work of the liberated areas. This is extremely urgent work and, no matter how difficult, it should be done."[27] Mao had not foreclosed on the American connection, for he urged continued cooperation with the Allies, who had "already reached Leyte Island in the Philippines and may land in China."[28] But the thrust of his speech and the program of military expansion outlined in it ran directly against the grain of the united front. One member of the Dixie Mission called it "the strongest statement that had yet come out of Yenan" and a signal that the Communists had begun active expansion into central and southern China.[29]

While signaling a military advance, Mao remained deeply concerned about the dangers inherent in this move. Most of the "tasks" he pointed to were aimed at avoiding the abuses which might accompany the resumption of large-scale warfare. Only an emphasis on production and frugality would offset the costs of expanding the army. Only the practice of reducing rent and interest, rather than the more radical redistribution of land, would assure the support of rich peasants, landlords, and other centrist elements. Only attention to the policy of "support-the-government and love-the-people" would prevent the "bad habits of old-time armies" such as "adopting an overbearing attitude, violating the people's interests, bad disciplinary conduct and not paying due respect to the government."[30]

Finally, to strenthen his grip on the army during this transition from guerrilla to conventional warfare, Mao turned to the one general who had supported his military-political program throughout the war: Lin Piao. Lin Piao had commanded the Communist forces at P'inghsingkuan, the first major engagement with the Japanese at the beginning of the war. Unlike P'eng Teh-huai, Lin had learned from this experience that "mobile war" was too costly for the ill-equipped Red Army. In 1938 he returned to Yenan, where he became a major proponent of the guerilla strategy avocated by Mao. With the exception of years spent in Moscow for medical treatment (1939–42), Lin served throughout the war as president and head of the Rectification committee of K'ang Ta (Resistance University), the school where future cadres trained for the task of waging people's war in north China.[31]

At the end of 1944, as the process of military expansion toward the south, the coast, and the cities began to unfold, Lin Piao turned his attention to the problems of conducting large-scale conventional operations across a broader geographic area. In November he called for a stepped-up military training program which would "raise the political awareness and the tactical and technical level of our troops, strengthen our ability to cooperate in making war and establish the courage and determination to dare to fight in distant regions, to fight large-scale battles and to [seek] thorough victory."[32] At the beginning of December Yenan established an artillery school to prepare the military technicians who would guide "the transition from the present, dispersed guerrilla warfare to concentrated, conventional warfare."[33] Lin took charge of the training of artillery, engineering, and mechanized units, which would be indispensable in "carrying out the great counter-offensive, fighting mobile and positional warfare and attacking the enemy's strongest fortifications." After months of schooling under Lin's watchful eye, these units would join him in the massive Communist invasion of Manchuria launched in the fall of 1945.[34]

The Wedemeyer Initiative

Against the background of these events, policymakers in Yenan had no inclination to grasp at foundering American support. Communist forces were on the move; if Hurley wanted to talk, he would have to talk about arms. On his side, Hurley insisted the Communists consider a political settlement on terms which fell far short of their own plan for a coalition government. This deadlock in relations between Yenan and the American embassy was not broken. It was bypassed by a surprise offer from the U.S. Army and the OSS to supply Communist forces.

American officials first approached Yenan on the subject of military cooperation at the end of October, when Mao and company helped draft plans for a hypothetical landing of American forces on the China coast.[35] Following reports from the Dixie Mission and the decline in Kuomintang fortunes, the U.S. Army Headquarters in Chungking began to consider ways of strengthening the Communists—news of which, as noted above, had already reached Yenan.[36] In early December, Wedemeyer ordered his chief of staff, General Robert McClure, to devise a tentative plan and submit it to the government for approval.

The McClure plan envisaged an American airborne unit of 4000 to 5000 technicians that would lead joint Communist-American sabotage teams behind Japanese lines. The Communists would supply manpower, intelligence, and logistical support. U.S. Army officers would command the teams and retain control over all weapons, munitions, and military equipment.[37] McClure submitted this plan to Hurley and to the Nationalist minister of war. Before receiving a response from the government, however, he also showed it to Barrett and asked him to find out what assistance the Communists might provide if the plan received official approval. By coincidence, Barret was joined on the flight to Yenan by Lieutenant Colonel Willis Bird, the number-two figure in the OSS in China, who also had a plan for joint U.S.–CCP military operations.

Mao, Chou, Chu Teh, and Yeh Chien-ying received the two colonels on December 15, and listened as they presented their projects. The OSS, like the Army, wanted to place technicians with Communist units to carry out sabotage, but Bird was more specific about the aid he could offer in return. Under the terms worked out in Yenan, the OSS would provide "complete equipment for up to twenty-five thousand guerrillas" and "at least one hundred thousand Woolworth one-shot pistols for [the] People's Militia." The Communists understood that both plans required ratification by the American and Chinese governments, but the two emissaries were clearly behind the schemes, and their enthusiasm showed. Bird assured General Yeh that among the Americans in Chungking, "there were many people that recommended such a plan as it was felt we should assist in killing the Japs in North China." And he may have implied, as he later reported, that the theater command had "already agreed on [the] principle of support to [the] fullest extent for [the] Communists and feel it is an OSS type project." [38]

The Communist response to these offers was to renew contact with Hurley, who, it appeared, must have had a change of heart. On December 16 Chou wrote the ambassador that Yenan agreed not to publish the Communist Five Points. Negotiations with the government could not resume until Chiang agreed to form a coalition. But Chou's real purpose in writing was "to avail myself of this opportunity to extend to you, General Wedemeyer and General McClure our very best wishes." On the same day, Mao also wrote the ambassador, citing Roosevelt's pledge to cooperate with "all anti-Japanese forces in China," and thanking Hurley for "the kindness of Colonel Barrett whom we hope will soon return to Yenan." [39] Their point was implicit but unmistakable: To fulfill the dictum of the American President and implement the plans just presented in Yenan, what was needed was not Chou's return to Chungking (to discuss political unification), but Barrett's return to Yenan (to finalize plans for military aid).

Hurley refused to budge. Again he demanded that Chou return to Chungking. Again Mao replied that Barrett must come to Yenan.[40] And again the stalemate was punctuated by an unannounced visit of Colonel Barrett with yet another plan for military cooperation and aid.

The proposal Barrett presented to the Communist leadership on December 27 called for a much larger American operation in north China.[41] U.S. Army Headquarters in Chungking had learned that a paratroop division might come to China to take part in the final stage of the war against Japan. This division, 28,000 strong, would be dropped into Shantung to establish a beachhead for the eventual American landing. Barrett asked the Communists if they could support the division until the U.S. Army took over. He emphasized, as he had previously, that the plan was tentative and required prior approval from Washington.

Yenan's leaders welcomed the prospect of having such a large American force in their territory and assured Barrett that they would take care of the division until regular American supply agencies could assume the task.[42] They undoubtedly saw this second visit as further evidence that the Americans were planning to land in north China and that arms and ammunition would go to those forces willing and able to help the Allies ashore. More important, they thought they saw a fissure between American diplomatic and military officials in China which they could manipulate to their own advantage.

The evidence now fit together and called for a change of tack. Hurley had turned aside Mao's request to send Barrett to Yenan and refused to discuss the question of military assistance. Yet Barret had twice come to Yenan, and military cooperation rather than political unification had been the subject of his mission. This indicated that the American embassy and the army headquarters were running on separate tracks: Hurley, in short, did not know what Wedemeyer was up to. Given the time limit imposed by the Communist move south, this discovery offered Yenan a new and daring option. Rather than continue the laborious exercise of reeducating Hurley—a task which would be increasingly difficult as the civil conflict spread—the solution was simply to bypass the recalcitrant ambassador and deal directly with U.S. Army Headquarters in Chungking.

Yenan's initiative came in two telegrams to Wedemeyer on January 9 and 10. The first message set forth the top-secret offer for Mao and Chou to visit the White House, "as leaders of a primary Chinese political party." The second message told of documented information on "negotiations between our allies [the central government] and our enemies for [the] sellout of American interest in China," and invited Wedemeyer to Yenan to examine the evidence in person. Chou told the American official who transmitted the telegrams that Wedemeyer alone should receive them and decide on their "disposition stateside," adding that "General Hurley must not get this information as I don't trust his discretion."[43]

Mao and Chou knew that their gambit might backfire, but they were racing against events that put their diplomatic program on a tight schedule. Communist officials told members of the Dixie Mission that compromise with the government was no longer possible, that army leaders were leaving Yenan for the south, and that all of south and southeast China behind Japanese lines "will be completely in Red hands within 6 to 12 months." George Hatem, an American who had lived in Yenan for several years and enjoyed the confidence of Communist policymakers, described the pressures under which they were working: "Time for decision between Chiang and [the] Communists is now. We will have either ballots or bullets now. If America bolsters Chiang with arms and economic help and not us, America will suffer the responsibility for results within China and our future relations with her."[44]

Given the limited information available to Communist policymakers and the rush of events surrounding them, perhaps Mao and Chou had no choice but to try this end run around Hurley's diplomatic blockade. From the outset, however, their efforts were doomed. The ambassador learned of the plot before it could hatch and demanded a full investigation, which convinced him that U.S. Army officers had caused the breakdown of negotiations and that Yenan had tried to deceive the American government. He dismissed Barrett from the Dixie Mission, and thereafter his antagonism toward the Communists mounted.[45]

The Last Wartime Talks

When Mao learned of Barrett's dismissal, he understood that the scheme to bypass the ambassador had failed and agreed to Hurley's long-standing request that Chou return to Chungking to resume talks.[46] Embarrassed by these events, the chairman would try to repair relations with the Americans, but Yenan had no reason to compromise nor to expect concessions from Chungking. By the beginning of 1945 both Communist and Kuomintang armies were moving forward, and neither party had the least inclination to yield at the negotiating table what it might soon win on the battlefield.

The new year brought an upturn in Nationalist fortunes. December 1944 marked the end of the long slide down the East China Crisis and the first signs of recovery which would restore government domination over the Yangtze by the end of the war. At the beginning of the month, the Japanese withdrew from Kweichow Province. This was no general retreat, but it relieved the threat to Chungking, a mood of elation spread through the Nationalist capital, and from this point on, confidence in the government continued to rise.[47]

News of Allied successes elsewhere also served to buoy the spirits of those in Chungking. During the last three months of 1944, the Americans took command of the western Pacific: Nimitz's forces mauled the Japanese navy in the Second Battle of the Philippine Sea; B-29s based in Saipan began to strike Tokyo; MacArthur liberated Leyte and prepared for the invasion of Luzon. In early January, Nimitz repeated his pledge to land in China, and for the first time American planes from the Pacific struck the coast of the mainland.[48] In February, a line of trucks and jeeps traveling overland from India on the newly christened "Stilwell Road" entered Kunming. With the capture of northern Burma, supplies reaching the front in China more than doubled between January and July.[49] The American-trained and -equipped Chinese forces that fought, effectively, in Burma would soon be available for service at home. As long as the east China front held, the Allied pincers movement from Burma and the Pacific promised relief for beleaguered Chungking. Barring a turn for the worse, Chiang had no incentive to cede to the Communists what he had denied them during the crisis of 1944.

Yenan also had reason to be confident. At the end of 1944, the Communist press first reported guerrilla activities south of the Yangtze. After the beginning of the new year, Li Hsien-nien's 5th Division scored victories in Hunan and Kiangsi, while Wang Chen's brigade ignited guerrilla operations in Hupeh before moving on to the old base areas farther south. To the east, Red forces established the Kiangsu-Chekiang Military Region, then proceeded south, finally linking up with guerrilla units below Hangchow.[50]

Predictably, the talks which opened in Chungking at the end of January produced no results. In the Communist view, Hurley's support for the government made compromise impossible. Chou refused to sign the final comminiqué, which he claimed was in part the work of Hurley and "was entirely favorable to the Kuomintang and did not present the true facts." The talks ended on a bitter note; the government charged Yenan with bad faith and Chou told the press that the Communists were prepared to accept Chiang, but "want him to be a Roosevelt, not a Hitler."[51]

Chou also failed to repair relations with Wedemeyer's headquarters. According to one American observer in Yenan, Chou's mission to Chungking was to explore "the possibilities of direct contact with high ranking American military men." On the day of his departure (January 22), Yenan sent the Americans the documentary evidence of alleged Japanese-Nationalist collusion along with a request for $20 million in aid. After the Bird-Barrett affair, however, Wedemeyer became wary of contact with the Communists and issued orders prohibiting discussion of cooperation or aid with members of any political party in China.[52]

Chou returned to Yenan empty-handed. On February 19 Hurley and Wedemeyer left Chungking for Washington. Both the American embassy and U.S. Army Headquarters were closed to the Communists, and neither could be reopened until the return of the chief executives. Their flirtation with diplomacy ended, policymakers in Yenan now looked to the battlefield.

After the recall of Stilwell, it was American initiatives—from Hurley, Wedemeyer, and the OSS—that kept U.S.–CCP relations alive.

Policymakers in Yenan, including the high command of the Red Army, were willing to entertain these offers. But Communist forces were on the move, and there was no inclination to slow this expansion in deference to anyone, Chinese or foreign, down below in Chungking. When the ambassador pulled back his own offer, then those of the Army and the OSS, the Communists were disappointed. But this had little impact on the main thrust of their military advance.

These events must have further eroded support within Yenan for the strategy of working through the united front. Mao and Chou had taken the lead in talks with the Americans and the Nationalist government. Their efforts had produced nothing. Meanwhile, the military offensive, which had already touched off clashes with government forces on the lower Yangtze, was paying substantial dividends and promising more. The wind was blowing in the direction of those who argued for armed struggle, and Mao and Chou had to lean with the wind.

CHAPTER FIVE

From the Countryside to the Cities
(February–April 1945)

At the beginning of 1945, in the wake of his disappointing experience with the Americans, Mao turned inward, away from the cities and the foreigners, back to the roots of Cheng Feng. Speaking to a gathering of labor heroes in Yenan, the chairman reminded his listeners that they were living in the countryside and criticized the "many cadres" who "approach rural affairs from an urban viewpoint."[1] Echoing a prominent theme of Party Rectification, he noted the link between this rural orientation and a foreign policy of self-reliance:

> We want to hit the Japanese aggressors hard and make preparations for seizing the cities and recovering our lost territories. But how can we attain this aim, situated as we are in a countryside founded on individual economy, cut up by the enemy and involved in guerrilla warfare? We cannot imitate the Kuomintang, which does not lift a finger itself but depends entirely on foreigners even for such necessities as cotton cloth. We stand for self-reliance. We hope for foreign aid but cannot be dependent on it; we depend on our own efforts, on the creative power of the whole army and the entire people.[2]

This spirit of self-reliance was to dominate the Chinese Communist movement until the end of the war. The Americans, to be sure, remained a potent force in Chinese politics. Meanwhile, Allied victories in Europe relieved the pressure on Moscow's western front and brought the Russians back into the China tangle. Both great powers supported China's unity and urged all factions in that country to reach a peaceful settlement. In the final analysis, however, neither the Soviet Union nor the United States proved decisive in the formation of Yenan's policies. Rather, it was events on the battlefield and the internal dynamics of the Chinese Communist Party itself that set the course toward civil war.

The Russians Are Coming

After the middle of 1944, with the opening of the second front in Europe, Moscow began to turn its attention back to the Far East. Since the outbreak of war with Germany in 1941, the Russians had been preoccupied with their western front and had had little time for China. On their return, they found their most powerful ally deeply involved in that country and supporting a program of national unification to strengthen the resistance against the common enemy. Moscow joined this effort, urging all factions in China to resolve their differences and concentrate on driving the Japanese from the mainland of Asia.

Soviet retrenchment in the Far East actually began before the German invasion (June 1941), with the signing in April 1941 of the Soviet-Japanese Neutrality Pact.[3] This agreement guaranteed neutrality between the signatories in case of war with a third party and would last for five years, with an automatic extension unless denounced one year before its expiration, in other words, no later than April 13, 1945. By the end of 1941, both parties were at war and neither showed any interest in undermining their agreement while preoccupied elsewhere.

Given these priorities, the Soviet press paid little attention to China during the next two years. When it did look east, Moscow's picture of China remained essentially unchanged: the War of Resistance against Japan was just; the United Front of all Chinese was the best means of waging that war; and the leadership of the Nationalist government in the war was unquestioned. Moscow mentioned the Communists only in connection with the larger problem of China's resistance, and one Soviet publication asserted that Yenan and Chungking "share the same point of view on all important questions relating to home and foreign policy."[4]

In Yenan, these years (1942–43) marked the high tide of the Rectification Campaign, when foreign influence and the position of the Russian returned students came under scrutiny and attack. The Communist press never wavered in its support for Moscow, but some statements—on the dissolution of the Comintern, for example—reveal an underlying mood of independence. According to Pyotr Vladimirov, head of a three-man Soviet delegation to Yenan from 1942 to 1945, during the period of Cheng Feng Mao spoke disparagingly of Stalin and treated Comintern representative Wang Ming with a heavy hand.[5] In contrast to his later offers of cooperation, the chairman reportedly ordered the Chinese Red Army to avoid diversionary moves against Japanese troops which would have relieved pressure on the Soviet border.[6]

After the lifting of the siege of Stalingrad in early 1943, the event which marked the turning point of the war on the Western Front, Moscow was able to devote greater attention to the Far East, and the Soviet press joined that of other Allied countries in pointing up the shortcomings of the Nationalist regime.[7] In the spring of 1944 relations between Moscow and Chungking were rent by armed conflict on the border between Sinkiang and Outer Mongolia and by Chiang's growing conviction that the Russians were encouraging Yenan to expand its forces and defy the government's control.[8] Meanwhile, Chungking's failure to give effective leadership to the cause of Chinese national resistance undermined Soviet interests in that quarter. In early December, the high-point of the East China Crisis, V. Avarin, a leading Soviet commentator on the Far East, described the situation as follows:

Judging from all the evidence coming from China and from the events occurring in that country, the influence of reactionary land-owners, speculators, and war profiteers has noticeably increased in recent years within the leadership of the Kuomintang. The final word in the determination of military strategy is often left to generals who hide their pro-Japanese sentiments under a mask of patriotism just as the "father of treason," Wang Ching-wei, did in his time.[9]

Despite such attacks, the aim of Moscow's press campaign was to rectify rather than undermine the Nationalist regime. The Russians viewed Chiang, warts and all, as the man best able to protect their interests in the Far East. To side with the Communists would justify Chiang's suspicions, divide China along ideological lines, weaken the resistance to Japan, and drive Chungking into the arms of the Americans. Thus, while pointing a finger at Kuomintang weaknesses, criticism in the Soviet press was actually less severe than that which appeared in many liberal journals in Britain and the United States at this time. Moscow never attacked Chiang Kai-shek by name, paid relatively little attention to the Communists, and refrained from drawing overt contrasts between Yenan and Chungking.[10] The Russians praised Chinese Communist military efforts; however, as Avarin made clear, what Moscow wanted in China was not revolution but an effective united front:

All impartial observers notice unanimously the true patriotism motivating the democratic forces which have become grouped around the 8th Route Army. . . . It would seem . . . that from the point of view of the national interests of China, the struggle of the 8th Route Army and the Partisans should be supported and encouraged. . . .
   . . . There is no doubt that some elements among the ruling circles of the Kuomintang strive by all possible means to hinder a real unification of all living forces of the people which would be so necessary for a true regeneration of China.[11]

Privately, Stalin and Foreign Minister V. M. Molotov communicated a similar view to American representatives in Moscow. Stalin told Ambassador Averell Harriman that despite his shortcomings Chiang was "the best man under the circumstances" and must be supported. The Chinese Communists, he continued, "are not real Communists, they are 'margarine' Communists. Nevertheless they are real patriots and want to fight the Japs."[12] On this occasion (June 1944), as throughout the war, Stalin affirmed his support for American efforts to improve Chinese resistance and unify the country under Chiang's leadership.

According to Vladimirov, Mao grew more responsive to the Russians as their power and interest in the Far East increased. In January 1944, for example, the chairman answered a probing and skeptical telegram from Georgi Dimitrov, former chairman of the defunct Comintern, assuring him that Yenan's intra-Party struggle was over, that former Comintern representative Wang Ming was being treated well, and that the Communists supported the United Front with the Kuomintang.[13] In the fall, Vladimirov noted a sharp decline in the influence of K'ang Sheng, the man Dimitrov held responsible for the excesses of Cheng Feng.[14] In view of Russian losses in the war, Mao reportedly offered to send 10,000 officers to Siberia for training and to join the eventual Soviet invasion of Manchuria.[15]

During the same period, the Chinese Communist press backed Moscow to the hilt. In the fall of 1944—at the height of Mao's campaign to forge the American connection—tensions began to appear between Washington and Moscow on a number of issues: the structure and operation of the proposed postwar international security organization; the progress of the Western Front in Europe; and the make-up of the future government of Poland. Rather than duck these issues in deference to the Americans, *Chieh Fang Jih Pao* reprinted the regular Soviet press attacks on their Allies.[16] In the lead editorial of November 7 commemorating the Bolshevik Revolution, Yenan flatly stated its preference for Moscow:

The Soviet Union is the first and up to the present the only country in the world to eradicate classes. Therefore, their democratic system is more thorough than that of any other country. The broad people are truly masters of the country.[17]

As the year 1944 drew to a close, the news from Moscow confirmed the promise of a new Soviet role in the Far East. On November 7 Stalin publicly denounced Japan as an aggressor.[18] On December 2 *Izvestia*, the official organ of the Soviet government, echoed Avarin's themes criticizing Chungking and calling for unity in China.

According to Vladimirov, the *Izvestia* article, which was reprinted in *Chieh Fang Jih Pao*, raised expectations in Yenan about the possibility of Moscow's support and encouraged a harder line in talks with the Americans. If true, this may have influenced Mao's treatment of Barrett in their stormy meeting on December 8; and the outcome of this meeting, in turn, may have led the Communists to look more hopefully to a possible Soviet connection. In any case, Yenan continued to reprint articles from the Soviet press which hinted at the entry of the Russians into the war with Japan. Mao asked Vladimirov about Moscow's intentions toward the Soviet-Japanese Neutrality Pact, whose denunciation prior to the April 13 deadline would be a clear sign of Russian plans in the Far East. In contrast to his earlier treatment of the Soviet mission, Mao became openly solicitous. After the middle of December, Vladimirov concluded, "The new reorientation towards Moscow becomes a fact."[19]

The Foreign Policy of "Self-Reliance"

Vladimirov was wrong. During the spring of 1945, Yenan did keep an eye on the great powers, but neither Moscow nor Washington could persuade the Communists to halt the slide toward civil war. Mao and his colleagues read with interest the news of the Big Three Conference held at Yalta in the Crimea on February 4–10. The agreements reached at Yalta restored, for a time, the spirit of unity among the Allies and confirmed their commitment to a program of unifying China around the leadership of Chiang Kai-shek. While only part of this was known to observers in China, after Yalta Vladimirov and Service each assumed that his respective country could have a decisive influence on the course of Chinese Communist policy. In fact, Yenan was going its own way—away from both great powers and toward civil war.

China was a minor issue at Yalta, discussed between Stalin and Roosevelt only and excluded from the agreements made public at the conclusion of the conference. It was, however, a subject of the secret protocol, also adhered to by Churchill, in which the Russians pledged to enter the war against Japan within three months after the defeat of Germany. In exchange, Moscow received American and British backing for a number of important concessions in the Far East, most notably in Manchuria. Stalin offered to cement the deal by signing a treaty with Chungking—a promise that the Soviet Union would support the Nationalist government after the war. Chiang learned of this protocol in May.[20] There is no evidence that Yenan knew of it before the treaty was announced in August.[21]

Those agreements which were made public at Yalta dealt not with China, but with relations among the Big Three and with the postwar settlement in Europe. Nevertheless, the Yalta Declaration—optimistically dubbed by the editors of *Hsin Hua Jih Pao*

"The Magna Charta of World Democracy"—had a particular appeal for Yenan. This document contained a pledge to enable the liberated peoples of Europe "to restore their sovereignty and to establish their own democratic governments" along lines which were identical to the CCP's own proposal for a coalition regime. The conferees also agreed to convene the United Nations Conference in San Francisco on April 25. Yenan saw in these accords a chance to lay the onus for continued disunity on Chiang Kai-shek. For as the Communist press pointed out, only a Chinese government which met the standards of the Yalta Declaration (that is to say, a new coalition government) should enjoy the right to attend the United Nations Conference in San Francisco.[22]

By offering the Russians attractive concessions in Manchuria and tying these concessions to a new Sino-Soviet treaty, the agreements reached at Yalta strengthened Moscow's commitment to the government in Chungking. During the weeks that followed, the Soviet press continued to criticize the Nationalists for their shortcomings, but also called for greater Chinese unity under the leadership of Chiang Kai-shek.[23] Finally, in the middle of April, V. Avarin issued what one expert has called "the sharpest attack on the Kuomintang that had appeared in the Soviet press during the entire war."[24] The problem, said Avarin, lay with Nationalist failures. But the solution lay in national unification:

It is difficult to say at present whether or not this hope will be realized. One thing, however, is clear: without the adoption of urgent measures to democratize the political life of the country and to achieve national unity, China cannot occupy the place in the general family of democratic nations to which it aspires.[25]

Even without knowledge of the secret protocol, observers in China could see that the developments at Yalta increased the likelihood that the Soviet Union would enter the war against Japan. Vladimirov reported that Soviet entry into the war would be decisive in shaping Yenan's policy. With the Russians out, the Communists had to avoid alienating Chungking and, connectedly, Washington. With the Russians in, on the other hand, they could risk a civil war. And until the middle of April, when Moscow's decision on the future of the Soviet-Japanese Neutrality Pact became clear, Yenan would wait.[26]

Vladimirov was wrong, however, about the weight of the Russian factor in Yenan. This was demonstrated on February 21, when the CCP Central Committee decided to establish an all-China federation of trade unions.[27] All observers in China considered such a move the first step toward formation of a separate Communist state, which would terminate the United Front and lead to civil war. Mao knew that this act would be unpopular in both Washington and Moscow, but he reportedly told the Central Committee that they could expect little from either capital and that Yenan must proceed with the separatist program whatever the attitude of the Allied powers. Finally, while plans for the labor federation went forward, announcement of the new government itself was delayed, not in deference to Moscow, but to await the results of the upcoming Kuomintang Congress, which would probably adopt a hard line against the Communists and provide Yenan the excuse for an open break.[28]

In assessing Yenan's attitude toward the Russians, John Service was closer to the mark than Vladimirov. Service, like all foreigners who visited Yenan, found the Communists hesitatnt to discuss their relations with Moscow, but by the spring of 1945 he had assembled a report which remains the best insight we have into this subject.[29] The Chinese Communists, like almost everyone else at this time, saw a prolonged war in Asia. They expected the Russians to enter the war and welcomed their entry, but realized that they would have to wait until a considerable time after the defeat of Germany—perhaps until the spring of 1946. They had no doubts about where Moscow would strike: it would be a "direct attack by the Red Army against the Japanese army in Northern Manchuria." When the Soviet attack came, "Simultaneously the Communists will commence active infiltration into southern Manchuria." In fact, Service observed, they had already begun operations in eastern Hopeh, Jehol, and southern Liaoning, while "political organizers" were infiltrating Manchuria. The success of these efforts was demonstrated by the rescue of several American airmen downed in these areas and by the response of the Japanese, who had stepped up pressure against Communist activities in Manchuria. As the offensive developed, Service reported, there would be a link-up of Soviet and Chinese Communist forces: "There is obviously no doubt in the minds of the Communists that the Russians will recognize and cooperate with whatever Chinese forces they meet in Manchuria, i.e., the Communists. This is so taken for granted that it is not worthy of mention." Since the Soviets would demand no concessions in Manchuria ("the days of Russian imperialism are over," Service was told), "such a course of development will leave the Chinese Communists in control of Manchuria."

There was reason to doubt, however, that Chinese Communist leaders were so confident of Soviet support. In the past, Soviet aid in China had gone exclusively to the Nationalists, and Moscow could renew this practice in the future. Yenan, along with the rest of the world, had watched during the fall of 1944, as an indigenous uprising was crushed by Nazi forces in Warsaw while the Russian army sat supinely outside the city, and Stalin dickered with the Polish government-in-exile which would take power after the war. Similarly, Moscow made little protest against the destruction of the Greek Communist Party by the British in 1944–45. The lesson—that Russian interests rather than the needs of local liberation forces would dictate Soviet policies—could not have been lost on observers in China.

It was a sign of their caution that leaders in Yenan told Service that Russian aid would go to "whatever Chinese forces they meet in Manchuria." The Russians would need the cooperation of local forces for intelligence, supplies, and the maintenance of public order. Yenan's determination to take charge of the Manchurian countryside (first signaled by Service and confirmed by other American observers)[30] rested on the assumption that Soviet policy would be governed, at least in part, by events on the battlefield. The best means of winning Russian cooperation and aid was to secure a firm base of Communist power. Self-reliance, Service concluded, was the cardinal theme of Yenan's revolutionary strategy and no less of its approach to the Soviet Union.[31]

While his analysis of Chinese Communist–Soviet relations was remarkably perceptive, Service, like Vladimirov, overestimated the importance of his own country in Yenan's calculations. Chinese Communist leaders perceived—correctly—that following the Yalta Conference, Washington would hold high-level meetings to discuss the situation in China (among other things). Hurley and

Wedemeyer returned to the States to represent the established line. The Communists did not know that professional diplomats in the State Department would challenge Hurley with a proposal to send arms to Yenan.[32] But they did know, especially after the Barrett-Bird affair, of the sharp divisions among American officials in China and of elements in the diplomatic corps, the Army, and the OSS who favored a change in policy. Admiral Nimitz had arrived in the American capital and told reporters that the "final assault on the Japanese Empire will probably be launched from positions in China." "All these reports deserve our close attention," concluded the editors of Hsin Hua Jih Pao. "Washington is discussing Pacific strategy and is eyeing the China problem anxiously. The outcome of these conferences may have far-reaching effects on us."[33]

To reach the President, Yenan submitted a bid for support on the latest issue in the see-saw battle with Chungking. In keeping with the propaganda line that emerged following the Yalta Conference, the Communists wanted a share of the Chinese delegation to the United Nations Conference to be held in San Francisco on April 25. While in Chungking, Chou had approached Hurley on this issue, but he had been rebuffed. On March 9 a second message to the ambassador, then back in Washington, asked him to inform the President of the U.N. matter and named Chou En-lai, Tung Pi-wu, and Ch'in Pang-hsien as Yenan's prospective delegates. On the following day Mao received a note from Roosevelt mentioning that he would soon meet with Hurley to discuss the situation in China. At Yalta the President had supported the formation of coalition governments, which included Communists, in the countries of liberated Europe. Yenan had reason to hope that he might apply the same principle to China. Service reported that the decision whether or not to move toward formation of a separate government would depend on whether or not Washington delivered on the issue of Communist representation at the U.N. Conference: "The convening of the Communist Party Congress is being delayed to await clarification of this issue."[34]

The test of Service's prediction came at the end of March, when Chungking invited Tung Pi-wu to join the Chinese delegation to San Francisco. Although the Communists had asked for three places and preferred to send Chou rather than Tung, they agreed to the arrangement. Service thought that while the Communists were engaged in the Conference they would not proceed with the creation of a separate regime.[35] But he was wrong. On April 1, after agreeing to send a representative to San Francisco and before learning of the outcome of the talks in Washington, Mao told Service (who was preparing to leave Yenan for a possible return to the States) that the Communists had decided to convene the "Chinese People's Liberation Union," a step toward separate statehood.[36] Whatever line the Americans adopted, they would have to learn to live with two Chinas.

Throughout the first half of 1945, both the Soviet Union and the United States urged Yenan to seek an accommodation with Chiang Kai-shek, but neither was willing to insist that Chungking accept a real sharing of power such as that envisaged in the CCP plan for a coalition government. The Communists were in no mood for this kind of advice. Privately, Yenan's leaders assured foreign visitors of their commitment to the Allied cause, and the Party press made no criticism of either great power. Perhaps the official proclamation of a separate government was postponed to await further developments on the foreign policy front or to delay what would have been a conspicuous slight to the cause of Allied unity. But the Communists made no attempt to conceal the fact that they were moving toward civil war.

The Slide toward Civil War

Two factors dictated Yenan's move toward civil war. First, in the spring of 1945, events on the battlefield favored Communist expansion against both Japanese and Nationalist lines. Red forces were doing well, and with more effort they might do better. Second, among the leaders gathered in Yenan for the Seventh Party Congress, the balance tilted sharply toward those who favored military expansion against the resistance of the Nationalists at home and the disapprobation of the great powers abroad. Proponents of the united front, weakened by Cheng Feng and discredited by the conflict with Chungking, were conspicuous by their absence.

The confident mood in Yenan reflected the continuing expansion of Communist horizons. According to Peking's own account, during the first half of 1945, Communist forces recovered 29 *hsien* seats (almost twice the number captured by all Red units in 1944) in the Shansi-Hopeh-Shantung-Honan region. After crossing the Yangtze River, Wang Chen's southbound army reportedly liberated all or part of nine *hsien* in the vicinity of Changsha, capital of Hunan. Farther east, an American observer in Anhwei Province reported that in February, a force of 8000 Communists crossed the Yangtze into Chekiang, where fighting broke out with Nationalist troops. A lengthy study by the U.S. Army found that during the first half of 1945 the Communists extended their control into areas previously held by the government in Honan, Hupeh, Anhwei, Chekiang, and Kwangtung, as well as in north China. The report concluded that the Reds were holding back on the Japanese front but pressing the attack against the Nationalists "whenever they feel that they are strong enough to drive out the Chungking forces." Finally, at the end of March, after a lull of more than three months, the Japanese resumed their east China offensive with successful advances in Hupeh and Hunan. With Chungking on the ropes, Yenan's military prospects brightened.[37]

Against this background of deepening conflict, relations between Yenan and Chungking worsened. On March 1 Chiang announced that the National Assembly would convene on November 12, the eightieth anniversary of Sun Yat-sen's birth. The Communist press blasted this speech, which explicitly ruled out the formation of a coalition government and demanded that Communist forces submit to government control.[38] According to Service, leaders in Yenan viewed the March 1 statement as a virtual "declaration of war":

The door to compromise has not quite been closed—but has almost been. There is no expectation that the Central Government will make any compromise in the present situation. American policy and the attitude of the Ambassador are partially blamed for this. Chiang is spoken of in the most derogatory terms and there no longer seems to be a willingness to consider him as the necessary head of the State.[39]

These events must have strengthened the hand of hard-line elements in the debate which preceded the Seventh Party Congress. The course of this debate is revealed by the "Resolution on Some

Questions in the History of Our Party," an important Central Committee document issued on April 20. Later attributed to Mao, the "Resolution on History" marked the conclusion of the Rectification Campaign and the chairman's final statement both on the power struggle at the top of the Party and on the correct line to be pursued by those below.

Ostensibly, the focus of the Central Committee's attack was on Mao's chief rivals, the Russian returned students, and specifically Wang Ming and Ch'in Pang-hsien. The charges leveled against these men, however, suggest that they were not the only or perhaps even the most important targets of the intra-Party struggle. Wang Ming's most recent crime was in fact of a "rightist" variety—offering to sacrifice the leadership of the revolution to Chiang Kai-shek under the slogan "all through the united front." But the charge made in the "Resolution on History" harked back to an earlier period when both Wang and Ch'in allegedly directed the last of the "three 'Left' lines." The significance of this reversal can be explained by examining the specific errors attributed to the Left line and the groups within the Party who may have shared in them.

The crux of the leftist deviation lay in pressing for " 'big actions' [armed insurrections] throughout the country." More specifically this meant: an effort to win quick victories, rather than adherence to a strategy of protracted warfare; an attempt to capture cities, rather than the cultivation of rural areas and a strategy of surrounding the cities from the countryside; reliance on positional, rather than guerrilla or mobile warfare; and, finally, a sectarian class policy, a refusal to seek support of intermediate elements including the rich peasants, rather than promoting cooperation with a wide range of classes.[40] The irony of this indictment was that Yenan itself had adopted a policy of "big actions." Thus the purpose of the swing against the Left was to head off such deviations as the battle for China unfolded:

This enlarged plenary session of the Central Committee emphatically points out that we are now approaching the change in the situation, the very change to be brought about by our rural work and waited for by our city work. . . . Only at the present moment, at the final stage of the Anti-Japanese War, when the army under our Party's leadership has grown powerful and will become even more so, is it correct to give the same weight to the work in the enemy-occupied cities as the work in the liberated areas and to work hard for all the conditions necessary for annihilating the Japanese aggressors in the major cities from both within and without, and then shift the focus of our work to the cities. This will be a fresh change full of historical significance . . . and comrades of the whole Party must prepare for this change with full consciousness and must not repeat the mistake of the exponents of the "Left" line in regard to the shift from the city to the countryside during the Agrarian Revolutionary War.[41]

The threat of leftist behavior came primarily from elements within the Red Army which tended toward being overly aggressive, professionally specialized, separated from the masses and from broader political concerns. Mao had attacked excesses of this type throughout the Rectification Campaign and more recently in his address on "Our Task in 1945." At the beginning of the year, the chairman assailed unnamed people, who opposed diverting military units to the task of production, and insisted that the Communists must avoid the illusion of quick victory and prepare for protracted war. Similarly, the "Resolution on History" called upon the army to "oppose the purely military approach . . . shoulder the threefold task of fighting, carrying on mass work and raising funds . . . [and] wage a people's war in which the main forces are linked up with the local forces, the regular army with guerrilla units and the militia and the armed sections with the unarmed sections of the masses."[42]

There is some evidence to tie this general attack to specific figures within the military leadership. In the spring of 1945 members of the high command in Yenan talked freely about the expansion southward. "Give us a year," they boasted to Service, "and we will have all East China from the borders of Manchuria to Hainan [Island]." According to Vladimirov, Chu Teh, over the opposition of Mao, demanded the transfer of large Red Army contingents to the south and, again unlike Mao, expected a revolutionary explosion throughout China rather than gradual expansion of the base areas. Despite the criticism leveled against him during the Rectification Campaign, P'eng Teh-huai continued to defend the abortive Hundred Regiments Offensive. According to later charges, this conflict between P'eng and Mao continued through the summer of 1945.[43] Alone among the high command, Lin Piao reportedly argued that the Communists' knowledge of modern warfare was deficient and that they faced the danger of insufficient links with the people. It is perhaps indicative of these differences that after the war P'eng was demoted to command of the Northwest Field Army, the weakest of the Red armies located in a remote area, while Lin went on to lead the largest, best trained, best equipped troops into the vital Northeast.[44]

The most serious threat to Mao's military strategy probably came from outside Yenan. Almost half (21 out of 44) of the full members of the new Central Committee elected at the Seventh Party Congress in June were military men who had remained in the border areas during most of the war. Raymond Ludden had found these commanders to be more outspoken and aggressive than their counterparts in Yenan. Similarly, William Whitson has observed that they "must have provided persuasive professional military arguments for quickly preparing for postwar hostilities with the Nationalists."[45] At the Congress, Liu Shao-ch'i attacked those guilty of "warlordism" and "mountain-top-ism." According to one delegate, Mao circulated among the small discussion groups arguing that "the very deviation we ought to oppose and wipe out is mountain-top-ism."[46]

Despite the indictment leveled against them in the "Resolution on History," Wang Ming and Ch'in Pang-hsien escaped relatively unharmed. In part, this was due to the already low status of the returned students. Ironically, it was also because Mao emerged as the principal defender of his former rivals and intervened to secure for them seats on the new Seventh Central Committee. The chairman's objective may have been to reassure Moscow that elements experienced in the work of the Comintern and friendly to the Russians would remain in the Maoist leadership.[47] These men would be less of a threat to Mao under his own roof than as outsiders who could be invested as a rival center of power under protection of the invading Soviet army.

More to the point, however, is that Mao had to defend them at all. There was apparently little sympathy within the post–Cheng Feng leadership for Wang Ming and the other figures who had favored close cooperation with the Kuomintang and its foreign allies. There is no evidence that Liu Shao-ch'i, the chief spokesman for those students and intellectuals who had come to the base areas from the cities, ever promoted these policies during the war. It is ironic that Chou En-lai, who more than anyone else had a "bureaucratic interest" in the success of the united front, was the one Communist official on record as strongly supporting the divisive step toward formation of a separate government.[48] Following the Rectification Campaign, no important figure in Yenan—save Mao himself—would speak up for a policy of compromise with Chungking and the great powers. By contrast, enthusiasts for armed expansion were legion.

In the spring of 1945 Chinese Communist armies were on the move. The problem facing policymakers in Yenan was how to assure a rapid yet orderly and effective expansion. Elements in the military and in the outlying base areas pressed for "big actions," a resumption of the armed advance, with little or no concern for its political implications. Both Moscow and Washington urged restraint, a sentiment which was undoubtedly shared by the majority of Chinese not wedded to either of the rival parties. But the evidence on the debates which preceded the Seventh Party Congress suggests that no one in Yenan argued for a pause in deference to the government, to centrist elements in China, or to the foreigners. With the great powers seeming to favor Chungking and the opportunities on the battlefield beckoning, Mao sounded the call for self-reliance. The Chinese Communist movement was welling up from within and finding its own way toward civil war.

CHAPTER SIX

The Seventh Party Congress and
The Civil War
(April–July 1945)

At the Seventh Congress of the Chinese Communist Party in the summer of 1945, Yenan, against the advice of both great powers, decided to cut its ties to Chungking and set out to seize power by force of arms. Initially the Communists tried to shield this decision behind rhetoric which would convince Washington, Moscow, and other interested parties that their commitment to national unity was still intact. But events on the battlefield soon persuaded Yenan's leaders that the time had come for open civil war, which they hoped would divide the great powers in China and bring the Russians in on the Communist side.

"On Coalition Government"

The Seventh Party Congress was the most important gathering of the Chinese Communist leadership during the war. Seventeen years had passed since the previous Congress was convened by the then outlawed CCP in Moscow. Delegates to the Seventh Congress began to arrive in Yenan as early as 1940, but the pressures of war, conflict with Chungking, and the Party's own internal divisions led to repeated delays. Finally, at the beginning of 1945, top Party and army leaders gathered for a series of meetings to prepare for the main event.[1]

The Congress opened on April 23. In attendance were 752 delegates (544 regulars, 208 alternates) representing an estimated Party membership of over 1.2 million. The Congress heard three major speeches (Mao Tse-tung's political report [April 24], Chu Teh's military report [April 25], and Liu Shao-ch'i's report on the revision of the Party Constitution [May 14–15]), elected a new Central Committee (June 9–10), and approved a new constitution (June 11). A number of lesser figures, including Chou En-lai, Lin Po-ch'ü, Jen Pi-shih, and Okano Susumu, leader of the Japanese Communist Party living in Yenan, also addressed the full assembly, which adjourned on June 11.[2]

The most important speech delivered at the Congress, indeed the most important document to emerge from Yenan during the last year of the war, was Mao Tse-tung's political report, entitled "On Coalition Government." Chairman Mao spoke from a new summit of power. The movement he led had grown from the few thousand refugees who had reached north China at the end of 1935 to an enterprise of national scope, claiming a population of 95 million and for the first time a serious rival to the central government itself.[3] Mao was the chief architect of the political-military strategy which catapulted the Party to these heights, and this had helped him consolidate his power. The Congress confirmed Mao's leadership, and the new Party constitution installed the thought of Mao Tse-tung as the "guiding principle of all its work."

As the title suggests, "On Coalition Government" was an appeal to the domestic and foreign constituents of the united front by promoting the Communist program for peaceful unification. Mao refrained from criticizing Chiang Kai-shek, while calling for a moderate reduction of rent and interest, rather than land redistribution, and for a broad united front from above (with the KMT) and below (within the liberated areas).[4] Beneath this veneer of propaganda, however, "On Coalition Government" showed that Yenan had reached a consensus on a set of policies which pointed toward civil war. Mao called on the people in both occupied and liberated China to fight to expand the area under their control. He urged underground forces to prepare for the liberation of Japanese-held cities. And he announced, for the first time publicly, that Yenan would convene a People's Assembly of the Liberated Areas—a first step toward formalizing the existence of two Chinas. "Comrades!" the chairman said in closing, "As soon as this Congress is over we will go to the battlefield to defeat the Japanese aggressors and build up a new China. . . ."[5]

The news from Washington undoubtedly contributed to Yenan's decision to advance on the battlefield and risk a split with Chungking. Although details of the debate on China policy were not made pubiic, it was clear that Hurley had emerged victorious and that no American aid would reach Yenan. Confirmed in his position and instructed to return to China, the ambassador told reporters (on April 2) that Chinese and Americans in Chungking "are all now one team" and, in an indirect slight to the Communists, announced that "there can be no political unification in China as long as there are armed political parties and warlords who are still strong enough to defy the national government."[6]

Despite this setback and under pressure to avoid an open rift, Yenan accepted the news with public equanimity. The Communist press denied Hurley's charge that "armed political parties" had caused China's disunity and lamented the decision to refuse aid to Yenan, but in the same breath promised continued cooperation:

Even under such circumstances, we can assure the nation and our Allies that we are still able to prosecute the war of resistance. And although our Allies will not give us help in arms, we are quite willing to give them any possible help if they desire it, and provided that they fight against the Japanese.[7]

In a similar vein, the Communist press treated Roosevelt's death on April 12 with a great display of sympathy, and a week later offered a vote of confidence in his successor: "We expect much from President Truman. In him we have faith."[8]

This rhetoric persisted in Mao's address to the Party Congress, whose theme of "coalition" itself was in part a sop to the foreigners. On one hand, Mao warned that Yenan was carefully weighing the actions of Washington and London: "Any foreign Government that helps the Chinese reactionaries to stop the Chinese people's pursuit of democracy will be committing a grave

error."[9] But he balanced this warning with an expression of gratitude for past Allied contributions to China's cause. Pending judgment that they had committed some "grave error," the Communist
press remained friendly to, or at least remarkably tolerant of, the
Americans.[10]

The tensions inherent in Mao's position—between conflict with
the Nationalists and cooperation with the Americans—mounted as
the split between Yenan and Chungking widened. By the middle of
May, Nationalist forces finally repulsed the Japanese advance in
east China and were in hot pursuit of enemy units retreating to
their strongholds on the Yangtze.[11] Buoyed by these signs of success, the Kuomintang Congress confirmed the decision to convene
the National Assembly, an act which was certain to meet with sharp
criticism in Yenan. Reports followed of serious clashes in Honan,
Hunan, and Kwangtung, where Communist and Kuomintang forces
fought for control of those areas vacated by the Japanese.[12] By the
early summer of 1945, both parties in China were moving toward a
resumption of civil war.

Yenan Breaks with the Americans

The renewal of fighting among Chinese did not alarm the Communists, for they had been pointing in this direction for some
time. Nor did it necessarily mean a break with the Americans, for
Yenan hoped to thrust the onus for conflict onto Chungking and
persuade both great powers to play an even-handed role in the
coming civil war. During most of May, Yenan remained satisfied
with American behavior and the diplomatic charade continued. At
the end of the month, however, events took a turn for the worse:
the Communists lost the race to the sea, conceding to Chungking
the fruits of union with American forces on the coast; reports of a
possible settlement between Tokyo and Washington suggested
that the Americans might be handed control of enemy-occupied
China; and evidence of an OSS-KMT plot indicated that the Americans might use their position to help restore Nationalist power
throughout China. Signs that Washington had begun to slide from

the station of wartime ally to that of opponent in a civil war prompted Yenan to attack American "imperialism" and seek Soviet support in the coming battle for China.

Both the persistence of Yenan's open door to the Americans during April and May and its closing at the end of this period reflected the course of the battle for control of the coast. Hurley's press conference on April 2 ended all hopes that Washington would willingly send arms to Yenan. But the possibility of linking up with an American landing party and creating a de facto alliance with U.S. forces along the coast remained a viable option, at least in Communist eyes. In the spring of 1945 the Communist press promised that, once armed, its three million regulars and militiamen could hold a portion of the coast for an American landing: "The combination of the Allied nations' rich resources and our inexhaustible manpower spells victory."[13]

In large part, this propaganda was self-serving. Most Communist military expansion was inland rather than on the coast and against Kuomintang rather than Japanese forces. The biggest battles against the Japanese occurred not along the sea, but in Hopeh, Chahar, Jehol, and southern Liaoning.[14] Granting all this, there is still substantial evidence that the Communists challenged the enemy for control of the coastline of northern and central China and that the struggle continued well into May (see Map 3).

Shantung. According to Communist and Japanese sources, during the last two years of the war more fighting occurred between their forces in Shantung than on any other front. While the heaviest fighting was in the central mountainous regions, in late 1944 and early 1945 there were also significant battles along the coast near the Hopeh and Kiangsu borders. Commenting on the military situation for April 1945, *Chieh Fang Jih Pao* reported that the Japanese had recently begun a full-scale "mop-up" in Shantung aimed "especially [at] the coastal regions, where the enemy can strengthen his control to deal with the Allied landings." Despite this resistance, during May the Communists claimed victories on the coast between the cities of Jihchao and Kanyu.[15]

Kiangsu. By the end of 1944 Communist forces began to move toward the key port of Lienyunkang in northern Kiangsu. It is indicative of Japanese priorities that they brought in troops from the

Map 3. North China Coast.

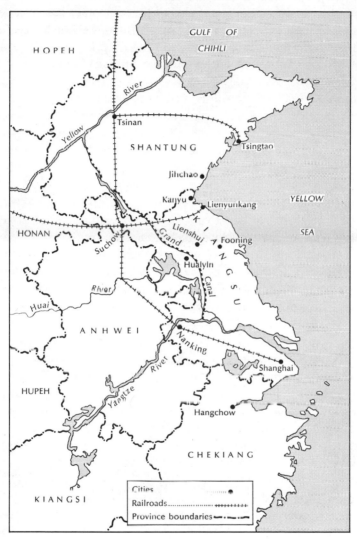

HOPEH

GULF OF CHIHLI

Yellow River

Tsinan

SHANTUNG

Tsingtao

Jihchao

Kanyu

Lienyunkang

YELLOW

SEA

HONAN

Suchow

Lienshui

Grand

K I A N G S U

Fooning

Hualyln

Canal

Huai

River

ANHWEI

Nanking

Yangtze River

Shanghai

HUPEH

Hangchow

CHEKIANG

KIANGSI

Cities .... ●
Railroads .... ╫╫╫╫╫
Province boundaries ━ ∙ ━ ∙ ━

Hopeh-Honan-Shantung region, where the Communists were also claiming victories, to attack Red forces at Huaiyin and Lienshui "in order to destroy the threat of [CCP] forces against the seacoast." Despite this resistance, by the end of March Yenan claimed control of the shoreline below Lienyunkang and reported victories farther south between the Grand Canal and the coast. On May 5 Yenan announced the capture of Fooning, a county seat near the edge of the Pacific.[16]

Shanghai. Finally, Communist forces moved across the Yangtze to join the newly created Kiangsu-Chekiang Military Region surrounding Shanghai. In January two to three thousand Red troops reportedly crossed into Chekiang to link up with local guerrillas and "prepare to 'greet' an American landing party." Eight thousand more waited north of the river in Anhwei. In April Yenan claimed the capture of two county seats northwest of Hangchow. Reports followed of Communist advances toward Shanghai, and by the middle of May Yenan described the coming struggle for the Yangtze Delta, an obvious target for Allied landing parties, as one of particular "strategic importance."[17] Even Tokyo admitted that the Communist offensive threatened "to strike the Japanese in the back in conjunction with the heralded American landing on the China coast."[18]

These reports kept alive hopes for a rendezvous with the Americans, for in the middle of May Vladimirov could still write of expected landings along the coast. By the end of the month, however, Yenan learned that reinforced Japanese defenses had succeeded in blunting the Communist attack. For the first time, the Communist press admitted that its troops had been forced onto the defensive.[19] The problem was not only with the Japanese, moreover, as one member of the Dixie Mission explained:

The Chungking armies in the South are making what seems to be good headway against some sort of Japanese resistance—the Communists never figured that even American equipment and personnel could beef up Chungking so that it could fight offensively. As a result of Chungking's advances—particularly toward the Hankow–Canton railroad line—the Communists who as little as two or three months ago were speaking of their capabilities for linking up between Canton and Hankow, grabbing the South China coastline, and sealing off the whole region in expectation of an American landing, are now commonly speaking of the possibility that their Canton guerrillas will be overrun and will have to go underground.[20]

After the first of June, Yenan could boast no more victories on or near the coast. The race to the sea was lost.

News that Communist forces had failed to capture the coast removed an important incentive for courting the Americans. But a more serious blow to Yenan's policy came from signs, also reaching the Communist capital at the end of May, that the Americans had taken a sharp and dangerous turn to the right. The first of these involved rumors of an early peace settlement between Washington and Tokyo.

The attention paid by the Chinese Communist press to the eradication of Fascism and the punishment of Fascist war criminals is indicative of the importance Yenan attached, not simply to victory, but to the way in which that victory was consummated.[21] A protracted war would give the Communists ample opportunity to expand the area of their control and prove to skeptics both at home and abroad that they, rather than the Kuomintang, were the rightful rulers of China. This interest in defeating the Japanese *in China* helps explain Yenan's willingness to see an American army invade the mainland and its unswerving support for the goal of "unconditional surrender." Conversely, a settlement which left the Japanese and puppet forces in China intact, due either to a compromise with Tokyo or to a direct assualt on the home islands which bypassed the mainland, would be less welcome in Yenan. Naturally, the decision on the final disposition of Japan rested with the great powers, so delegates to the Seventh Party Congress followed with interest the course adopted by Moscow and Washington in the summer of 1945.

Again, through the first half of May, news reaching Yenan favored the continuation of a tolerant attitude toward the United States. Moscow's renunciation of the Soviet-Japanese Neutrality Pact (April 5) raised hopes that the Russians might enter the struggle in the Far East, but even after the defeat of Germany (May 8) no declaration of war was forthcoming. While the United States remained the backbone of the war effort, there were few arguments for attacking Washington, despite its unfriendly policy in China.

The importance of American firmness was underlined by reports, which appeared in the respected *Ta Kung Pao* on May 10, that Tokyo was "casting an insinuating glance at Soviet Russia, as a gesture of peace feelers."[22] The Communist press responded by noting that both Great Britain and the United States supported the goal of unconditional surrender, but that to crush Japan promptly and at the lowest cost, "the Asiatic war must be transformed into a common struggle participated in by all important anti-Fascist nations."[23]

Rumors of Japanese "peace feelers" abounded during the remainder of May. Increasingly, however, the alleged target shifted from Moscow to Washington and London. Finally, on May 29, *Ta Kung Pao* printed an apparently credible report that Great Britain and the United States had received another offer.[24]

While the threat of a Soviet-Japanese understanding disturbed Yenan, the hint that the United States might agree to a compromise settlement was even more alarming. Prior to Pearl Harbor, Chinese Communist propaganda had stressed the danger that the "imperialist" powers, both Fascist and non-Fascist, might resolve their differences and turn against the forces of revolution in China and around the world.[25] The precedent of the Siberian Intervention of 1918 suggested that the temptation to adopt this course would be greatest as the war neared its end. After Pearl Harbor, Yenan emphasized the solidarity of all "democratic" forces—both socialist and capitalist—in the common struggle against Fascism. At the end of May 1945, however, with the war against Japan nearing its conclusion and signs of a possible deal between Washington and Tokyo beginning to surface, the Communists retreated to their earlier view. On June 1 *Hsin Hua Jih Pao* pointed out that "the target of Japanese 'peace overtures' today has been shifted to the United States of America and Great Britain," and charged that "pro-Fascist elements" in these two countries had "heavily overshadowed the meaning of the Asiatic war of emancipation with their calculations of a war for colonies." "The nauseous attitude of certain Allied people," *Hsin Hua Jih Pao* editors noted, recalled the "tragic history of 1918."[26]

A second indication that American policy had taken an unfavorable turn came nearer to home. Also at the end of May, Yenan learned of an attempt by the OSS to assist the Kuomintang in expanding its operations north of the Yellow River into what the Communists considered their own liberated areas.

The Communists knew of the OSS presence in Yenan as well as

the fact that this agency maintained close relations with Tai Li, head of the KMT secret police, who was known for his persecution of Communists south of the Yellow River. Through the first half of 1945, there was no indication that OSS activities in the liberated areas bore any connection to Tai Li or other government agents, and Communist leaders showed no reluctance to cooperate with the OSS. They welcomed Colonel Bird when he visited Yenan in December, and reports from the Dixie Mission in the spring of 1945 show that neither the course of American policy nor the activities of the OSS had caused the Communists to reassess their attitude.[27] The incident that occurred at the end of May changed all that.

On May 29 Communist forces captured four American OSS agents and one Chinese, a member of the KMT (Tai Li) Secret Service Police, shortly after they parachuted into the T'ai Hang region of southeast Shansi. Neither the Communists nor the Americans in Yenan had been forewarned of this expedition, which was run out of the OSS office in Sian. The Communists soon discovered that the purpose of the mission was to establish liaison with two Chinese puppet generals and eventually to supply them with arms through the cooperation of the OSS and the Nationalist army south of the Yellow River. While the Americans argued that these puppets would be used against the Japanese, Yenan claimed that they were already fighting against Communist forces in the T'ai Hang base. The Communists' suspicions of American motives mounted when they learned that the Chinese "interpreter" in the group could not speak English.[28]

When news of this incident reached Yenan, the Communists were already looking for signs of Kuomintang-American collusion. In his address to the CCP Congress, Mao had warned that Chungking would try to induce the Americans to play the role of British General Ronald Scobie, the commander of Allied forces in Greece who attacked the leftist Greek resistance army in an effort to install a rightist government and ignited the Greek civil war.[29] Vladimirov observed that the menace of American "Scobieism" was driving Mao closer to Moscow. Service explained the reference to Scobie as evidence that the Communists were preparing to move on Japanese-occupied cities and expected the Kuomintang "to try to involve American forces in its own attempt to gain control of the same cities."[30] With the danger of "Scobieism" in the air, the May 29 incident had a chilling effect on the delegates to the Seventh Party Congress, as a report from the Dixie Mission explained:

> The Communist attitude towards OSS is not basically unfriendly. They have known of our relations with Tai Li and naturally they don't like them. But they have all along given every indication that [they] were quite willing to deal with OSS, despite these relations, as the organization of the U.S. Army which appeared best adapted to cooperation along the general lines of guerrilla warfare. The development of OSS operations down below [the Yellow River], however, and particularly those based at Sian, has brought it about that even before there has been any discussion of the general Army or OSS plans for utilizing the Communists, the Communists are already beginning to feel the impact of OSS operations. And the point of impact is at the very heart of Communist strength—China north of the Lung-hai [Railroad].`
>
> To understand Communist reaction to our operations from Sian one must realize the prime bogey which the Communists believe will develop from U.S. Army support of Chungking. The Communist analysis is that American armies will land, and will eventually knife into areas of their control. The KMT armies will walk in behind. The KMT will bring in local magistrates. The Communists will refuse to accept them. At the initiative of one side or the other fighting will start. The U.S. Army, if only to keep its supply lines clear, will give active military support against the Communists.
>
> The Communists take our operations in areas of their control as being spearheads for the KMT.[31]

Finally, the arrest, on June 6, of John Service and two editors of the leftist magazine *Amerasia* on charges of illegal dissemination of secret government documents contributed to the appearance of a swing toward anti-Communism in the United States. The Chinese Communists rejected what they considered a legalistic explanation of Service's crimes and insisted that these arrests were an attempt by reactionary elements in control of the State Department to silence those who favored support of Yenan.[32] Reports in the American press which described the arrests in the same terms helped confirm Yenan's view.[33]

The failure of Communist forces to link up with an American landing party on the coast, coupled with signs that Washington was tilting decisively toward the Nationalists, convinced Mao and the other delegates to the Seventh Party Congress to drop the united front and go it alone. The chairman announced the decision at the closing session of the Congress on June 11. Evoking the parable of "The Foolish Old Man Who Removed the Mountains," he directed the Party faithful to help raise the twin burdens of feudalism and imperialism from the backs of their countrymen, to go out and "fire the whole people with the conviction that China belongs not to the reactionaries but to the Chinese people."[34]

To remove the mountain of feudalism at home, Yenan decided to end its parley with Chiang Kai-shek, launch an all-out offensive to expand the area of Communist control, and match Chungking step for step by creating a separate government in north China to rival the National Assembly. The *Chieh Fang Jih Pao* editorial of June 14, which announced the results of the Congress, told its readers to "launch a counter-attack" on the "reactionaries," "destroy the Japanese invaders," and move on the cities:

If we want to [become] powerful, then we need the cities, we need the workers. In the future there will be a shift from the rural workers to the urban workers, a shift from guerrilla warfare to conventional warfare. This change must rely on the support of workers and other broad urban people. Only if we develop a true workers movement and an urban peoples' democratic movement can the Chinese people have a firm base to struggle for the realization of the New Democracy throughout China.[35]

As their armies advanced, Communist policymakers set in motion steps to establish a separate government. Shortly after the close of the Congress, Yenan announced that it would not send delegates to the People's Political Conference in Chungking, which was expected to ratify plans for the National Assembly.[36] Instead, concurrent with this session of the PPC, a Preparatory Conference of the Chinese Liberated Areas People's Representative Congress convened in Yenan. An official telegram set November 12 as the date for the opening of the Congress itself, underlining Yenan's determination to offer an alternative to the National Assembly.[37]

To remove the mountain of imperialism, the Seventh Party Congress agreed to a similarly hard line on foreign policy. "The U.S. government's policy of supporting Chiang Kai-shek against the Communists shows the brazenness of the U.S. reactionaries,"

Mao told the assembly. "But all the scheming of the reactionaries, whether Chinese or foreign, to prevent the Chinese people from achieving victory is doomed to failure."[38]

Communist propaganda organs picked up on Mao's themes, striking out at the "imperialists like Hurley" and warning that they would be taught a "lesson" if they continued to oppose the Chinese people. For the first time since the United States joined the war in Asia, the editors of *Chieh Fang Jih Pao* bypassed the American government and addressed their appeal directly to its citizens.[39] Mao, in two unsigned articles of July 10 and 12, branded Hurley an "imperialist" and charged him with "creating a civil war crisis in China."[40] Even the Potsdam Declaration (July 26), which reaffirmed the long-standing Communist demand for the unconditional surrender of Japan, met with an icy reception in Yenan.[41]

"Since I have been able to fight Japan with these few rusty rifles," Mao told a visitor on the Fourth of July, "I can fight the Americans too. The first step is to get rid of Hurley, then we'll see."[42]

Wooing and Warning Stalin

Yenan's break with Chungking and Washington came as a direct challenge to Moscow as well. During the spring and summer of 1945, the message emanating from the Soviet capital remained loud and clear: unification of China was a key to defeating Japan and restoring security in the region after the war; and while the responsibility for China's problems might lie with Chiang Kai-shek, the Chinese Communists must nonetheless make their peace with him. The Seventh Party Congress, as we have seen, rejected this advice. After the decision was made, Yenan sought to turn the Russians around, to secure Soviet support in the struggle against "reactionary" forces in China and in the West.

Those attending the Congress in Yenan found no encouragement for their independent line in the Soviet press.[43] Moscow published no news of the CCP Congress, in contrast to the extensive coverage given to a meeting of the French Communist Party two months later. The exchange of telegrams between Stalin and

Chiang at the conclusion of the war in Europe, on the other hand, suggested that the Russians favored Chungking. In early June, as the CCP opted for armed expansion, *Izvestia* demanded the formation of a coalition government in China.[11]

News of Soviet diplomatic moves reinforced this message. Following the resolution of the debate in Washington, Ambassador Hurley visited London and Moscow to seek support for the American program to unify China under Chiang's leadership. Stalin and Molotov assured the ambassador that they would back the Americans in this endeavor, and Stalin expressed approval of Chiang, whom he called "selfless," "a patriot." Back in Chungking at the end of April, Hurley told a press conference that Churchill and Stalin had agreed to Washington's policy. He amplified his views in private, whence the information circulated freely in Chungking and eventually to Yenan. Meanwhile, signs of a rapprochement between Moscow and Chungking served to corroborate this report. In April Molotov agreed for the first time to meet with Nationalist Foreign Minister T. V. Soong as a representative of the Big Four. In the middle of May Chungking announced that Soong would visit Moscow "in an attempt to strengthen Sino-Soviet relations and learn Soviet Russia's intentions in the Far East."[45]

Finally, the overall improvement in Soviet-American relations promised continued cooperation between the great powers in China. In late May, as signs of tension between Moscow and Washington began to surface, President Truman dispatched Harry Hopkins, symbol of the friendly relations which had reigned during Roosevelt's lifetime, to the Soviet capital for talks with Stalin. Privately, Stalin repeated his promise to promote the leadership of Chiang Kai-shek and to negotiate a treaty with Soong which would confirm the terms of the Yalta protocol and formalize Russian support for the Nationalist government. Publicly, the news from Moscow was sparse but uniform in its assurances of improved Soviet-American understanding. Although they did not mention China, beginning on June 7 the two sides announced a series of agreements resolving the various issues in question.[46]

Those following events in the Soviet capital could see that the Grand Alliance was alive and well. There was every indication that Stalin would support the American program to unify China around the leadership of Chiang Kai-shek. This news made a big impression on delegates to the CCP Congress, as one American observer in Yenan reported:

Hurley's statement, privately made in Chungking, but fairly openly discussed in Yenan, that he has Russia's OK for his policy touches the Communists in a very tender spot. It is quite apparent that they are not fully informed of Russian intentions, and have no formal guarantee of Russian support. They expect it in the long run, but anything which suggests that they may not get it in the short run, is bound to cause them a severe case of the nerves.[47]

Following the close of the Party Congress, Yenan launched a campaign aimed at exposing Soviet mistakes and persuading Moscow to join the Chinese Communists in the coming struggle. On June 19 *Chieh Fang Jih Pao* (*CFJP*) reprinted an expose, taken from the American press, of the April talks between Hurley and Stalin.[48] This report credited Stalin's support for American policy in China as the cause for Chiang's refusal to compromise with Yenan, by implication a reproof of the whole Soviet policy. Two days later the editors of *CFJP* abandoned their established line of praise for the political and economic compatibility of the Allies and attacked the "monopoly capitalism" which had sprung up in the United States and Great Britain, as well as in the Fascist camp, during the war.[49] In a reversal of policy which had been to advertise and celebrate the cause of Allied unity, the paper also began the practice of reporting points of conflict between Moscow and Washington.[50]

These efforts met with no apparent success, for at the end of June the talks between Soong and Stalin opened, and the news from Moscow indicated progress toward a Sino-Soviet rapprochement. Yenan responded with a more direct attack. On July 10 the April article by Soviet analyst V. Avarin covered half the front page of *CFJP*. An unprecedentedly sharp attack on the Kuomintang leadership, this article had been in Chinese Communist hands for almost three months. The other half of the page contained a diatribe, later attributed to Mao, against "His Worship Patrick J. Hurley."[51] The Avarin article, published after so long a delay, with such prominence and alongside Yenan's first public attack on the chief American "imperialist," served to underline the gap between the earlier promises of Soviet propaganda and the dalliance then underway in Moscow.

Despite these warnings, the Soong-Stalin talks recessed on an auspicious note. According to a report by Radio Moscow, the negotiations "took place in a friendly atmosphere and revealed broad mutual understanding." A brief pause freed Stalin and Molotov for their duties in Potsdam, but the talks would resume "in the nearest future."[52] The focus of Yenan's attention now shifted to the Big Three Conference, but the problem remained the same. Although the substance of the Potsdam meetings was not made public, the friendly atmosphere surrounding them pointed toward a common solution for China and the Far East.[53] Again Yenan reminded Moscow of the dangers of following the American lead:

The political situation in China during the past half year has been thrown to the brink of civil war by the policies of Hurley and Chiang Kai-shek . . . This dangerous situation raises a serious responsibility for the people of China's liberated areas, the democratic parties and various people's circles in areas under KMT control and the three Allied countries, Great Britain, the United States and the Soviet Union. *This responsibility is to correct the policy of Hurley and Chiang Kai-shek and end the threat of civil war.*[54]

The End of the War

The end of the war in the Far East came with unexpected speed. On August 6 the first atomic bomb fell on Hiroshima. On the eighth the Soviet Union entered the war. News that the Japanese had begun to sue for peace reached China on the tenth. On the fourteenth Tokyo announced its surrender. As the real estate of occupied China was thrown suddenly onto the market, all parties rushed forward to corner as much as they could, as quickly as possible.

Abandoning its concern about Leftist excesses, Yenan sounded the charge. "If there is any opportunism during this period," Mao told cadres about to leave for the front, "it will lie in failing to struggle hard." On the eve of Japanese surrender, the editors of *CFJP* announced "The Urgent Task before Us": "From the country to the cities, from guerrilla warfare to mobile warfare—because of the sudden change in the current situation, the changes foreseen by our Seventh Party Congress must now be quickly realized."[55]

The Japanese army posed the immediate obstacle to Communist expansion, and CCP propaganda stressed that the war was against the foreign intruders. But the real question at this time was, which Chinese would take over from the defeated enemy? On August 10 Chu Teh ordered his armies forward to disarm and accept the surrender of Japanese and puppet forces. Chiang Kai-shek countermanded Yenan, telling the Communists to "remain in place and await orders."[56] Mao rejected Chiang's orders, publicly branded him "China's Fascist Chieftain," and reaffirmed the Communists' right to disarm the enemy. Finally, in a statement later attributed to Mao, Yenan admitted the truth of some time standing, that the real target of the Communist offensive was the Chiang regime itself: "If an autocrat and traitor to the people dares to attack them, the people must act in self-defense and resolutely strike back to frustrate the designs of the instigator of civil war. That is the way, the only way."[57]

The defeat of Japan also served to sharpen the conflict between Yenan and Washington. In early August General Wedemeyer outlined for the press American policy in China during the coming transition from Japanese to Kuomintang rule. The Americans would recognize Generalissimo Chiang as the Supreme Allied Commander in the China Theater; they would invite Nationalist authorities to take control of territory occupied by U.S. forces; and they would assist in the transportation of Nationalist troops to take over areas held by the Japanese.[58] The prospect of the Americans helping to restore Kuomintang control in occupied China confirmed Communist suspicions and hostility. In Yenan, Mao told Party cadres who would soon occupy sensitive positions in north and east China to take a hard line in dealing with their erstwhile allies:

U.S. imperialism wants to help Chiang Kai-shek wage civil war and turn China into a U.S. dependency, and this policy, too, was set long ago. But U.S. imperialism while outwardly strong is inwardly weak. We must be clear-headed, that is, we must not believe the "nice words" of the imperialists nor be intimidated by their bluster. . . . In the past we have openly criticized and exposed the U.S. policy of aiding Chiang Kai-shek to fight the Communists; it is necessary and we shall continue to do so.[59]

Yenan's policymakers worried less about the Nationalists and the Americans, both of whom were beyond salvation at this point, than about the Russians, who alone held some promise of assisting the expansion of Communist power in China. Yet success on this front was far from certain. Despite Yenan's earlier efforts to woo Stalin, the Potsdam Conference closed on August 1 with no indication that he had been moved. On the contrary, news that Soong had returned to the Soviet capital suggested that an agreement between Moscow and Chungking might soon follow. In his remarks to the press, Wedemeyer asserted that Stalin too acknowledged Chiang as the Supreme Allied Commander in China.[60]

Yenan tried to put the best face on a bad situation. On learning that the Russians had entered the war, Mao wired Stalin offering cooperation, the CCP press pledged to fight "shoulder to shoulder" with the incoming Soviet units, and Chinese Communist forces moved to meet the Russians north of the Great Wall. To buoy the spirits of those soon to join the battle, Mao assured cadres in Yenan that they could count on the aid of the Russians. But in a more candid moment he admitted that Communist strategy was to rely on its own resources and hope for the best. "On what should our policy rest?" Mao asked. "It should rest on our own strength, and that means regeneration through one's own efforts."[61]

As China's War of Resistance drew to a close, Yenan set out to fulfill the plans of the Seventh Party Congress: to seize the cities and railroads long held by the Japanese, even, or especially, against Nationalist and American opposition. The Communists had tried to persuade the Russians to join them, for Soviet cooperation—active at best, passive at least—would be needed if the enterprise were to succeed. With the great powers divided in China, the Communists might prevail in a test of strength; with the same powers united against an armed struggle, Yenan would have to find another road to power. While awaiting Moscow's response, Communist forces advanced and Yenan hoped for the best. These hopes were soon dashed, however, by news from the Soviet capital that slowed, for a time, the rush toward civil war.

CHAPTER SEVEN

The Reoccupation of China
(*August–October 1945*)

The end of China's War of Resistance also marked the end of Yenan's campaign of armed expansion and a return to the tactics of the united front. Russian entry into the war forced the Communists, for the first time, to heed Moscow's advice. The Sino-Soviet Treaty, signed on the last day of the war, signaled that the Russians would support the restoration of Nationalist authority and American efforts to unify China under the leadership of Chiang Kai-shek. Moscow flatly rejected Yenan's bid to drive a wedge between the great powers in China and secure Soviet backing in the civil war. Their previous diplomatic strategy in shambles, the Communists agreed to enter peace talks with Chungking, hoping by this show of conciliation to win the cooperation of both great powers as the struggle to retake occupied China unfolded.

The Sino-Soviet Treaty and the Chungking Talks

News of the Sino-Soviet Treaty reached Yenan on August 15. Publication of the texts of the treaty and accompanying agreements awaited ratification by both parties, but the Chinese Communists had followed the talks in Moscow over the preceding weeks and the significance of the act was unmistakable. Publicly Yenan responded (as it had to the Soviet-Japanese Neutrality Pact of 1941) by putting the best possible face on the unwelcome news. To observers in Yenan, however, the Communists appeared hurt and bewildered. The CCP liaison office in Chungking reacted to the treaty with open bitterness. Even one Soviet historian has agreed that the Chinese Communists were resentful and suspicious of Moscow's policy at this juncture.[1] The explanation offered to CCP followers behind closed doors was equivocal at best:

In order to maintain and to stabilize the peace in the Far East the Soviet Union has signed the Sino-Soviet Friendship Treaty. This [treaty] is beneficial to the people of China and the world, but not to Japan and all other warmongers. At the same time, however, in order to carry out its responsibilities under this treaty, the Soviet Union will not be able to aid us directly and will be under certain limitations.

In sum, this spokesman concluded, "The concrete policy of the Soviet Union cannot be understood. ([We must] proceed from hope.)"[2]

The Russians may have followed up the treaty by urging Yenan to seek a peaceful settlement with the Nationalists. Stalin later admitted this mistake.[3] And Mao explained it as follows:

They [the Russians] did not permit China to make revolution: that was in 1945. Stalin wanted to prevent China from making revolution, saying that we should not have a civil war and should cooperate with Chiang Kai-shek, otherwise the Chinese nation would perish.[4]

After Mao joined the Chungking talks, the Soviet press approved, saying that the "further development of China and the maintenance of internal peace depend upon the collaboration of [the CCP and the KMT]."[5]

However the message reached Yenan, its meaning was clear, and the Communists lost little time in responding. On August 15 the CCP Central Committee banned all criticism of the Kuomintang and the Americans and ordered cooperation with American forces in the field. The next day Yenan addressed its first statement to the American government (as opposed to the American people) since the close of the Seventh Party Congress. Finally, at the end of August, after repeated appeals from both Ambassador Hurley and Chiang Kai-shek, Mao flew to Chungking for talks aimed at ending civil strife and finding a basis for national unity.[6] The Communist position at the talks was moderate: criticism of both Chiang and the Americans ceased, and Yenan dropped the demand for a coalition in favor of a modus vivendi under which the Nationalist government would recognize the local authority of the Communist "liberated areas."[7]

Before leaving Yenan, Mao explained that he had agreed to the talks because "at present, the Soviet Union, the United States and Britain all disapprove of civil war in China."[8] The purpose of his mission was to shift the great powers away from Chungking and toward Yenan. Its success would be measured by the cooperation Communist forces received in the field: from the Russians in Manchuria and from the Americans in north China.

Meeting the Russians in Manchuria

The most important testing ground for Yenan's postwar strategy was Manchuria. Previous attempts by the Communists to penetrate this region had proven ineffective. The collapse of the Japanese and the inability of the Nationalists to take the surrender above the Great Wall left the Russians in control of the cities and railroads; all else was up for grabs. Mao had followed Moscow's advice in joining the Chungking talks. Now the Russians could repay him by helping Communist forces take control of Manchuria.

The Soviets entered the War in the Far East on August 8, advancing along two lines. The main force under Marshal Malinovsky followed the Chinese Eastern Railway across northern Manchuria toward Harbin, while Soviet and Mongolian units penetrated from the west into Jehol and Chahar provinces. They met a feeble and dispirited Japanese resistance. Within two weeks the Russians occupied all of Manchuria from Tsitsihar and Harbin in the north to Port Arthur and Dairen at the tip of the Liaotung Peninsula, as well as the major urban centers of adjoining Inner Mongolia. By the end of August the Soviet army was the arbiter of all principal cities north of the Great Wall and of the railroads connecting them.

Under the terms of the August 14 agreements, Moscow recognized Chungking's sovereignty over Manchuria and pledged to support the Nationalist government in restoring its authority throughout China. On V-J Day, however, Nationalist forces were confined to the south; it was not until November that the first government units reached Manchuria. In the interim, there was no effective Chinese authority in the Northeast. The Communists hoped to fill the vacuum.

With the Russian entry into the war and the sudden collapse of Japanese power, Yenan shifted its attention to the north. During the 1930s, efforts to develop a resistance movement in the Japanese puppet state of Manchukuo had been a dismal failure.[9] Beginning in 1944, the Communists below the Wall tried to fight their way into Jehol and southern Liaoning, but Japanese defenses proved impenetrable. Thereafter Yenan pursued more favorable opportunities in the south, and by the end of the war the largest CCP force near the Manchurian border numbered fewer than 10,000. With news of the Russian advance, however, Chu Teh ordered his forces northward and westward to meet the invading Allies.[10]

At the level of direct soldier-to-soldier relations, the first meeting between Russian and Chinese Communist armies was not very pleasant. The Russians viewed Chinese generally with disdain (they were "people of low culture" as one Soviet commander put it),[11] and the Red Army brooked no interference with its rapid and massive extraction of industrial "war booty" from the Northeast.[12] The few American observers on the scene reported that Russian officers treated the Chinese Communists in "summary fashion," while on their side the Communists were "bitter" about the treatment they received, "nettled" by the removal of Manchurian industry, and "plainly dubious about their well-muscled allies."[13]

Despite such friction, the pattern of Soviet behavior during the first three months of the postwar era decisively favored the expansion of Chinese Communist power north of the Great Wall. The first contact probably occurred at Kalgan, the capital of Chahar Province in Inner Mongolia and a strategic link on the railroad running west from Peiping (Map 4). Reports differ as to which forces reached Kalgan first, but there is general agreement that it was the advance of the Soviet army that made possible the Communist capture of the city and of the huge Japanese arsenal therein.[14] The Russians established their headquarters at Changpei, above the

Map 4. Manchuria and North China.

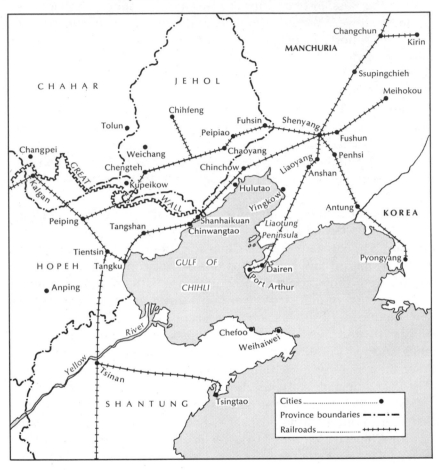

Great Wall, and maintained a liaison office in Communist-controlled Kalgan. Meanwhile, CCP representatives were allowed to visit Changpei "for the purpose of establishing a local Government."[15]

Farther east, "victorious rendezvous" were reported at Weichang and Tolun, also in Inner Mongolia. The Communists seized Chengteh, capital of Jehol Province, after the Russians had subdued the Japanese garrison and departed. To the south, at Kupeikow, the Soviets allegedly handed captured Japanese weapons directly to the Communists.[16] In one case, Shanhaikuan, a joint Soviet-Chinese Communist offensive liberated the city.[17] The Russians withdrew from Shanhaikuan shortly thereafter, leaving the Eighth Route Army in complete control, and during September they continued to deliver rifles to Communist forces in that area.[18]

By far the most extensive and significant contacts occurred in the pivotal Northeast. Movement of Chinese Communist forces into Manchuria proceeded along three lines: through Kalgan, across Chahar and Jehol; north along the Peiping–Shenyang Railroad from Shanhaikuan; and from Communist strongholds in Shantung across the Gulf of Chihli into the Liaotung Peninsula.[19] Following the last route, Communist representatives reached Port Arthur with a request to link up with Soviet forces in Manchuria. The Russians cooperated with this sealift as they did with the transport of Communist units by rail into Shenyang (Mukden).[20] According to Communist sources, as many as 100,000 troops and 50,000 political cadres were moved into the Northeast, primarily from Shantung and northern Kiangsu.[21] Aggressive recruitment from among the local inhabitants swelled their ranks. By the end of October, Lin Piao had begun to organize these forces into his Northeast Democratic Allied Army.[22]

In addition to providing logistical support, the Russians played a key role in transferring Japanese arms to the newly arrived Communist troops. Moscow has released figures on the number of weapons turned over to the Chinese Communists, which, if correct, were roughly equal to the materiel the Nationalists received from the Japanese army in China proper.[23] Communist officials in Chungking insisted that units of the Eighth Route Army entered the Northeast only as "civilians," without arms. At least one commander told his men to leave their guns in Shantung, assuring them that they would be re-equipped with Japanese weapons in Manchuria. He must have been right, for by early 1946 Yenan could claim an armed force of 300,000 in the Northeast.[24] It is clear that this army could not have been moved into Manchuria, recruited, supplied, or equipped without active Soviet cooperation.[25]

The Russians also assisted in the creation of new Communist political organs in the Northeast. As early as August, a variety of Party committees had been established at the district, *hsien,* and municipal levels, as well as in factories and other enterprises. When Communist forces reached Shenyang in late September, they found the city in Russian hands and a Chinese authority, such as it was, operating under the name of "The Shenyang City Kuomintang Party Headquarters." "After discussion between the Soviet Army and ourselves," the CCP commander reported, a new city government was organized, a garrison established, and local youth recruited into the Eighth Route Army. By the end of September, the Communists had spread out and set up new political organs in an area which extended to Changchun and Harbin in the north; Fushun and Kirin in the east; Penhsi, Liaoyang, Anshan, Yingkow, and Antung in the south; and Fuhsin, Peipiao, and Chaoyang in the west. Other elements of the CCP had gained a foothold in the administration and revived labor unions of the Russian-dominated cities of Port Arthur and Dairen.[26]

Finally, while providing aid and comfort to the Communists, the Russians obstructed the Kuomintang entry into the Northeast. No Chinese government representatives were allowed into Manchuria until October 12, when the Northeast Headquarters of the Nationalist army was set up in Changchun, the Soviet-occupied capital of Manchuria.[27] No Nationalist troops were permitted to enter the region until they began to fight their way in after the middle of November. On October 5 Moscow rejected Chungking's request to land troops at Dairen—in defiance of the August 14 agreement which made this city an open port and affirmed that "the administration in Dairen shall belong to China."[28] Later, Russian-Chinese Communist collusion prevented those troops from landing at the Manchurian ports of Yingkow and Hulutao. In sum, by the close of the Chungking talks on October 10, Mao could claim considerable success in the Northeast. Despite their promise to assist in the restoration of Nationalist control over the region, the Russians had kept government forces out, while providing timely and valuable aid to the Communists. One half of the postwar diplomatic strategy had paid off handsomely. Meanwhile, south of the Great Wall, Yenan sought similar cooperation from the Americans.

Meeting the Americans in North China

After the war, Yenan's interest in the Americans changed. Following the defeat of the common enemy, there was no longer any question of U.S. aid reaching the Communists; instead, with the reoccupation of Japanese controlled China, Yenan would try to reduce the American role in arming, training, and transporting Nationalist troops. It was in part to mollify Washington that Mao agreed to join the Chungking talks. Meanwhile, Yenan ordered its units in the field to avoid conflict with the American occupation. This was the other half of the diplomatic strategy which emerged in the wake of the Sino-Soviet Treaty: Its aim, to win American cooperation in north China.

During the first few weeks after the Japanese surrender, there was little cause for friction between Yenan and Washington. The Communists knew that the Americans would help Chungking retake control of occupied China, so it was no surprise when the airlift of Nationalist armies into Nanking and Shanghai began in early September. Yenan made no protest against these moves, in part because Mao was in Chungking talking peace and unity, and in part because the Communists were in no position to challenge the government in south China. Attempts to contest the Nationalists for control of the lower Yangtze had failed, while Communist units below the Yangtze had been cut off and threatened with destruction.[29] In Chungking, Mao offered to withdraw his forces from south China in exchange for right of passage through Nationalist lines.[30] As long as they remained on or below the Yangtze, the Americans posed no threat to Yenan.

The situation changed in October with the landing of the U.S. Marines on the coast of north China. North China, that broad expanse stretching from the plateau of Shensi Province in the west across the plain to the coast of Shantung, was the heartland of Communist power. Here the Communists had built their sprawling base areas during the war. Now, after the war, these base areas separated the huge Nationalist armies in the south from the coveted prize of Manchuria. While many crack Communist units flooded across the Great Wall, those that stayed behind sought to block the Nationalist advance northward. The Communists dominated the hinterland, where they could easily destroy railroads and disrupt the long government supply lines from the Yangtze overland to Peiping.[31] Yenan's blockade was threatened by American control of the coast and the transport of Nationalist forces through this narrow corridor by sea and air.

News of the American occupation of north China reached that country in late September. In line with the previously stated policy, it was reported that the Americans would disarm Japanese units in the area and assist in the transfer of authority to the Nationalists, whose troops would be flown in from the south.[32] On September 30 the first of an eventual 53,000 Marines, compromising two divisions, stepped ashore at Taku.

The First Marine Division occupied the Peiping-Tientsin-Chinwangtao triangle. It took over garrison duties in all the major cities of eastern Hopeh—Peiping, Tientsin, Taku, Tangku, Chinwangtao—as well as the Kailan coal mines near Tangshan, the most important source of fuel for all of east China. The First Division was also responsible for guarding the railroad between Peiping and Chinwangtao, though the Marines generally occupied only stations and bridges, using Japanese or puppet troops to patrol the more dangerous, exposed lines. In Shantung, the Sixth Division garrisoned Tsingtao but made no attempt to guard the railroad running inland to Tsinan. The First Marine Aircraft Wing, stationed at Peiping, Tientsin, and Tsingtao, provided transportation and reconnaissance for the entire area.[33]

At the time of the American arrival, all the major cities and railroads in both Hopeh and Shantung were controlled by the Japanese army with varying degrees of support from Chinese puppets. A token force of 1500 Nationalist soldiers took part in the American landing. There were no other government troops in either province. Communist guerrillas and regular units operated throughout the region, where they effectively controlled most of the countryside and some smaller cities and posed a constant threat to the major urban centers and lines of communication.[34]

The Communists were not happy about the American occupation, but neither were they ready to abandon the search for great-power cooperation. On the eve of the landings, Chou En-lai slipped into Tientsin to warn the American advance party that the Communists would resist with force any attempt to move the Marines to Peiping. Meanwhile, the Yenan press charged that American intervention would constitute "interference in the internal politics of China and aid to the Kuomintang."[35] When these warnings were ignored and the landing began, however, the Communists avoided conflict and promised to cooperate with the forces of occupation—a wise show of discretion at this point.[36] Hardened by fighting in the Pacific, backed by the enormous power of the Seventh Fleet, the Marines promised trouble for anyone who opposed them. As the liberators of China who had come to expedite the departure of the hated Japanese, the Americans received a tumultuous welcome in every port.[37]

While agreeing to tolerate a temporary occupation, Yenan was more concerned with how the Americans would exercise their powers in the region. After what must have been careful consideration, the Communists spelled out their terms for cooperation in an important editorial published on October 4:

Following [on] the heels of the American troops, some units of KMT army plan to move into Peiping and Tientsin, from where they will "recover" the democratic areas which have long been liberated from the hands of the enemy and in which the rule has been already returned to the people. . . . Since the entry of American troops in Peiping and Tientsin is to disarm the Japanese troops there, their stay consequently will be temporary and regional. They certainly will not extend to places which have already been liberated and where there are no Japanese troops. Only so will the actions of the American troops not damage the interests, honor and international friendship of the Chinese nation.[38]

As soon as the Marines were in place, the airlift of Nationalist forces from central to northern China began. By the end of October, two armies totaling 56,000 men had been deployed from the

Yangtze Valley into Hopeh. The main units settled in Peiping and Tientsin; one regiment each garrisoned Tangshan and Tangku; a full division took charge of Chinwangtao. The U.S. embassy noted that these moves angered the Communists, but in keeping with the declaration of October 4, the CCP press held its fire.[39] As long as the Marines limited their operations to the areas already occupied and concentrated on the rapid repatriation of the Japanese, they would enjoy continued Communist cooperation. If they allowed Chiang Kai-shek to use Japanese and puppet forces to hold the major cities and lines of communication and assisted a Kuomintang attack against the liberated areas, however, the Americans along with their Nationalist allies would meet a determined Communist resistance. While waiting to see which course the Americans would take, Yenan muted its propaganda, and Communist forces in the field made every effort to fulfill their part of the bargain.

The most celebrated encounter between American and Chinese Communist forces during this period occurred at Chefoo (Yentai), a port on the north coast of Shantung, in early October. Previous accounts of the Chefoo Incident assert that the Americans withdrew from the region in the face of Communist threats to resist a landing with force.[40] But the records on both sides demonstrate that this was not the case.

On October 4 the captain of an American transport ship anchored off Chefoo delivered a message to the Communist mayor of the city, informing him that the Marines would occupy Chefoo and requesting the withdrawal of Communist forces, which had controlled the city since late August.[41] The mayor temporized, saying that he would have to check with Yenan and warning that the Americans would be "held accountable" for any conflict, but he made no threat to resist. Two days later, Yenan cabled the U.S. military headquarters in China, requesting that the Americans withdraw from Chefoo and repeating that "U.S. Forces will be solely responsible" for any incident that might occur. Again, there was no mention of Communist resistance. When American officers entered Chefoo for talks on October 7, the mayor reversed his previous stand and offered to permit the Marines to occupy the city, provided that no Nationalist forces accompanied them and that the existing CCP administration remained intact. Finding neither Japanese nor Allied POWs in Chefoo and wishing to avoid interference in the Chinese civil conflict, the Americans concluded that a landing would be ill-advised.[42] They proceeded to Tsingtao, where the Marines disembarked along with the rest of the Sixth Division.

The outcome of the Chefoo Incident suggested that the Americans would remain within the narrow definition of their mission—to disarm the Japanese, but not to assist the Nationalist challenge to CCP "liberated areas"—and the Communists were duly gratified. *Chieh Fang Jih Pao* gave prominent coverage to friendly encounters between Communist and American forces along the coast of Shantung; Communist officials in Yenan, Chungking, and Weihaiwei, another important Shantung port held by the Reds, expressed satisfaction over the defusing of what could have become an ugly affair.[43] The example of Chefoo, moreover, was indicative of the conciliatory attitude adopted by Communist units wherever they came into contact with the Marines.

Communist forces had surrounded Chinwangtao and were sporadically attacking Japanese and puppet troops within the city, when a battalion of the First Marine Division landed there on October 1. Marines replaced the puppet sentries and the hostilities stopped. Spokesmen for the Eighth Route Army stationed in the vicinity assured the Americans that they favored cooperation.[44] After three weeks in Chinwangtao, the Marine commander described the attitude of the local Communists as "cordial and friendly" and concluded that they respected the Americans as "great allies in the war against Japan."[45]

Similarly, when the Sixth Division landed at Tsingtao, the city was teeming with armed Japanese and puppet forces and surrounded by units of the Eighth Route Army. A representative of the local Communist commander approached Marine headquarters with an offer to cooperate in disarming the Japanese and restoring order, but the Americans rejected the proposal and refused to permit Red forces to enter the city. Thereafter, the Communists abided by this decision and the Marine occupation of Tsingtao proceeded without incident.[46]

The End of the Chungking Talks

Against the backdrop of these events in Manchuria and north China, the peace talks in Chungking crept forward. When the talks adjourned on October 10, a vast gulf remained between the two sides. A bargain was struck on the make-up of the projected unified national army, but this reform would have to await an overall political settlement.[47] Mao agreed to withdraw Communist forces from south China, but in fact Yenan had already recalled these units, which were weak and dangerously isolated.[48] Only the agreement to reconvene the Political Consultative Conference saved the two sides from having to admit that six weeks of intensive and well-publicized negotiations had produced nothing.

Despite the inconclusive nature of the talks, Mao faced criticism for his policy of conciliation when he returned to Yenan. In the middle of October the chairman went before a meeting of Party cadres to answer his critics: "Some comrades have asked why we should concede eight Liberated Areas [in south China] . . . Does this mean that we are going to hand over our guns to the Kuomintang. . . ? Some cadres can't understand why we should be willing to negotiate with Chiang Kai-shek, who has always been anti-Communist and against the people."[49]

While the origin of this criticism is obscure, one source suggests that Mao may have been under pressure from Chu Teh and other army commanders who were anxious to get on with military expansion.[50] The chairman agreed that the armed struggle—"to give tit for tat, to fight for every inch of land"—must continue. But he insisted that a number of factors, including the international situation, mitigated against renewal of open warfare:

> The capitalist and the socialist countries will yet reach compromises on a number of international matters, because compromise will be advantageous. . . . The world is progressing, the future is bright and no one can change this general trend of history. . . . At the same time, we must tell the people and tell our comrades that there will be twists and turns in our road. There are still many obstacles and difficulties along the road of revolution.[51]

For the moment, the arguments of the chairman prevailed, and with good reason. Mao's sojourn in Chungking had provided the time needed for Communist forces to cross the Great Wall and a diplomatic cover for Moscow while the Soviet army aided the Communist build-up in Manchuria. These facts were appreciated in Yenan, where Colonel Ivan Yeaton, Barrett's successor as head of the Dixie Mission, found an "open expression and hint of future Soviet help [which] is a complete reversal of past [CCP] propaganda."[52] Meanwhile, the successful denouement of the Chefoo incident suggested that the Marines would confine their activities within the limits Yenan had proposed. Communist officials throughout China roundly applauded the American withdrawal from Chefoo. If the repatriation of the Japanese proceeded apace, the Americans might be out of China before a conflict with Yenan occurred.

By the end of October the Communists had a firm grasp on the Northeast, while government forces had yet to set foot in the region. Until one or both of the great powers changed its course, Yenan would continue to pursue gradual expansion behind the façade of conciliation and national unity. When the Nationalists finally arrived at the threshold of Manchuria, the Communists would bar the door—or so Mao must have thought until November, when both great powers betrayed him and his diplomatic strategy collapsed.

CHAPTER EIGHT

Setbacks in the Northeast
(November–December 1945)

If in October Mao could claim success for his strategy of conciliation and gradual expansion, November brought news of setbacks
on both Soviet and American fronts. Instead of concentrating on
repatriating the Japanese army, the Americans began to support
Nationalist advances against Communist positions on the Manchurian border and in Shantung. Meanwhile, Moscow withdrew its
support from the Communists in the Northeast, ordered Chinese
Reds out of the cities, and began to aid the government takeover
of the region. Denied its urban base in the Northeast and facing a
Kuomintang offensive backed by both great powers, Yenan could
not risk a conventional military defense of Manchuria. Red forces
withdrew to the countryside, and Yenan returned to the negotiating table in an effort to stem the Soviet and American drift toward
Chungking.

Clash with the Marines

Despite offers of cooperation from Yenan and from Communist
forces in the field, the Americans did not limit their role in China
to reoccupying the cities and repatriating the Japanese. Washington ordered the Marines to stay out of a "fratricidal war," but in
part by circumstance, in part by design, they failed to obey.[1] The

clash came at Shanhaikuan, the narrow passage between China proper and Manchuria where the Great Wall meets the sea.

By the end of October Communist forces had occupied Shanhaikuan and lined the railroad running north to Shenyang. To the south, one battalion of Marines and one division of the Nationalist army held Chinwangtao. Yenan protested alleged attempts by the Marines to "forcefully repair" the railroad from Chinwangtao to Shanhaikuan and warned that the Americans would have to assume "full responsibility for all serious consequences which develop."[2] Despite these protests, on October 30 the Nationalist Thirteenth Army, which had been denied entry at the Manchurian port of Hulutao, disembarked from American ships at Chinwangtao and immediately pushed north. An American journalist reported the scene:

The Chinese were well equipped and well armed. Every man carrying a rifle. American cargo ships also streamed into Chinwangtao unloading vehicles and heavier weapons. United States Marines protected the beach-head for the landing. The Chinese moved out of Chinwangtao under an agreement designed to avoid involving the Marines in any hostilities.[3]

The Communists reacted swiftly to this new threat. On the night of the Nationalist landing, Red forces blew up two bridges on the Peiping–Chinwangtao line and reinforced their defenses along the Great Wall. Meanwhile, according to a report from the Dixie Mission, the mood in Yenan had hardened: "Prevailing local sentiment seems welcoming of American-Communist incident as soon as possible in order to flare U.S. and world public opinion and thereby stop increased American participation which would inevitably result in large scale fighting."[4]

The behavior of Communist forces in the field, however, suggests that their objective was still to separate the war against the Kuomintang from incidental involvement with the Marines. During the first week of the fighting, Red units captured five American officers, allegedly "sightseeing" near the Wall, but released them with apologies the following day. In another incident, local Communist forces warned Marine guards stationed near a Japanese garrison of a planned attack. And 4000 Communist troops blocked an American reconnaissance patrol near Peiping in a tense encounter, but after a roadside parley they allowed the Americans to pass.[5]

Meanwhile, American involvement in the Nationalist offensive continued to mount. On November 1 U.S. aircraft initiated flights over the Peiping–Chinwangtao railroad to "show strength" and deter further Communist attacks. On the seventh, a second battalion of Marines reinforced the garrison at Chinwangtao. During the following week another Nationalist army, having been turned back at the Manchurian port of Yingkow, alighted from American ships at Chinwangtao and marched north.[6] Government forces captured Shanhaikuan on November 16.

In Shantung the story was much the same. On November 14 the 24,000-man Nationalist Eighth Army disembarked from U.S. transport ships at American-occupied Tsingtao. On the same day the local Communist commander sent a second emissary to the U.S. headquarters seeking cooperation with the Marines. Again the Americans rejected the offer. As government units moved out of the city toward the provincial capital of Tsinan, the Marines reported on the condition of the railroad and fortified defense works around the airfield, providing at least ancillary support to the offensive. The Nationalists met with unexpectedly stiff resistance and soon ran out of ammunition. Despite the prohibition against intervening in China's "fratricidal war," Wedemeyer approved a request to refill the empty Kuomintang guns.[7]

Finally, while American and Nationalist forces were preoccupied with the Communists, the job of repatriating the Japanese ground to a halt. On November 16, the day Shanhaikuan fell and over three months after V-J Day, Wedemeyer announced that of the more than 1 million Japanese soldiers in China exactly 907 had been shipped home.[8]

By joining the Nationalist assault on Communist-controlled areas, the Americans had violated the limits of acceptable behavior set down by Yenan in the October 4 editorial. Flushed with the success of their enterprise in Manchuria, the Communists had little patience with the obnoxious course of American policy. True to their earlier warning, the editors of *Hsin Hua Jih Pao* demanded the immediate evacuation of all American forces from north China. Offers of cooperation, which had been the hallmark of Communist policy toward the Marines in October, gave way to constant harassment of the Americans in November.[9]

The Ghost of Manchurian Autonomy

The adverse turn of events south of the Great Wall made Soviet support in the north that much more vital to Yenan. In the next section we shall return to this story. But first we must examine more closely the development of the Chinese Communist movement in the Northeast. For the ghost of Manchurian autonomy haunted policymakers in Yenan in the fall of 1945, just as it promised the Russians greater leverage over this region.

In the middle of September a Soviet plane landed in Yenan, the first since 1942, bringing an official delegation to discuss postwar strategy in the Northeast. According to the returned student Ch'in Pang-hsien, the Russians requested the withdrawal of Eighth Route Army regulars from Manchuria during the Soviet occupation, while assuring Yenan that Stalin would support a "Manchurian People's Movement" in their stead.[10] The implied menace—the emergence within Manchuria of a leadership more responsive to Moscow or to local interests than to Yenan—was unmistakable. The dominant position of the Soviet army made this possible; Stalin's record in such places as Poland made it plausible; and the arrival in the Northeast of several figures who could lead a separatist or pro-Soviet movement made it a credible threat to Yenan's authority.

Before the defeat of Japan, the Communists had no significant organization of any kind in Manchuria. Despite the rapid influx of cadres into the region after the war, there was still no single organ to provide direction for the movement in the Northeast as a whole. Finally, at the end of September, P'eng Chen led a high-level team from Yenan to Shenyang, where he set up the Party's Northeast Bureau.[11] Until the final victory in 1949, the bureau would remain the nerve center and command post of the CCP in Manchuria.

Yenan invested heavily in the Northeast. Beginning in the fall of 1945, almost a quarter of the Seventh Central Committee (nine of the 44 full members and ten of the 33 alternates) transferred to the region.[12] Given Mao's supremacy at the Seventh Party Congress, it is not surprising that the direction of this enterprise should pass to

P'eng Chen, a protégé of Liu Shao-ch'i, or that the group should include several figures who had emerged during the Rectification Campaign: P'eng himself, Ch'en Yun, Kao Kang, Lin Piao, and others. The complex problems of governing the Northeast fell to men with a variety of technical skills: economics (Ch'en Yun and Li Fu-ch'un), security (Tsou Ta-p'eng), logistics (Yeh Chi-chuang). A host of professional military units trained in Yenan in artillery, engineering, and mechanized warfare joined Lin Piao in building the new Northeast Democratic Allied Army.[13]

Yenan also made a special effort to promote and use natives of the region. Three of the four Manchurians on the Seventh Central Committee—Lin Feng, Lü Cheng-ts'ao, and Wan I—returned to their homeland. (The fourth, Kuan Hsiang-ying, had to remain in Yenan because of ill health.) Only two Manchurians—Lin Feng and Tsou Ta-p'eng—ever served on the Northeast Bureau, but Yenan was careful to stock its governmental apparatus with an indigenous leadership. Of the fifteen men who held the position of chairman in a Communist Provincial government in the Northeast from 1945 to 1949, nine were natives of the region. In the category of deputy chairman, the figures were five out of seven.[14]

It is less certain how much previous experience in dealing with the Russians may have weighed on the selection of Communist personnel to serve in Manchuria. Almost a third (6 out of 19) of those Central Committee members sent to the Northeast had had some education in the Soviet Union, but this fraction approximated the experience of the Central Committee as a whole (25 out of 77).[15] Two of them—Chang Wen-t'ien and Wang Chia-hsiang—were among the Russian returned students who had retained their seats on the Central Committee as a result of Mao's intervention.[16] Wang spent some of the postwar years as the CCP representative in Moscow.

The principal threat to Yenan's domination over leftist forces in Manchuria came from ostensibly Communist leaders who might be persuaded to join a movement toward regional autonomy backed by the Russians. The first such figure was Chou Pao-chung, who had combined a career in the Nationalist army with at least one (1923–25) and perhaps a second (1928–31) period of study in the Soviet Union. He joined the CCP in 1927 and went to the Northeast in

1931 to recruit and lead a force to resist the Japanese invaders. This enterprise reached its high-water mark in 1936–37 but was effectively crushed following the outbreak of war. In the winter of 1940–41, Chou and a handful of followers sought refuge on the Soviet side of the border. Sheltered by the friendly Soviet army, Chou commanded and trained a small force which returned with the Russians in August 1945 and gained a firm foothold along the Soviet border in northern Manchuria.[17]

Another potential Russian ally was Chang Hsüeh-shih, son of the famous warlord Chang Tso-lin, brother of Chang Hsueh-liang, and heir to the most illustrious name in Manchurian politics. Apparently embittered by the generalissimo's arrest of his brother following the Sian Incident (in 1936), the younger Chang organized a guerrilla band in Hopeh and joined forces with the Communists. After serving for a time as chief of staff to another Manchurian, Lü Cheng-ts'ao, he emerged at the end of the war as one of the commanders of the Hopeh-Jehol-Liaoning Military Region. According to one report, Mao invited the 30-year-old general to take command of all non-Communist forces in the Northeast, possibly an attempt to coopt the most likely candidate to lead a movement for Manchurian autonomy. Chang won broad public support in Manchuria for his severe punishment of traitors. In November he planned, apparently with Russian encouragement, to organize an independent regime. He was dissuaded from doing so only after the last-minute arrival of a message from Moscow. According to one report in November 1945, the Russians were attempting to prop up separatist elements in the Northeast, including Chang Hsüeh-shih, whose "purposes are primarily of local origin and are not directly connected with Yenan or Mao Tse-tung."[18]

Finally, in early 1946 Moscow dispatched Li Li-san to Manchuria. After his ouster from the top CCP post in 1930, Li had gone on trial in Moscow, confessed his errors, and spent the next fifteen years in the Soviet capital, where he held a series of insignificant positions and was largely ignored. While his original problems had been with the Russian returned students, Li enjoyed little support among the Maoist leadership. His was one of the few names cited with contempt in the "Resolution on History," and his election to the Seventh Central Committee, like that of the returned students, may have come only as a result of Mao's intervention. Just what role Li played following his return to China is uncertain. After flying to Yenan for a brief reunion with Mao, he proceeded to Manchuria, where he took a seat on the Northeast Bureau and served (at least ostensibly) as a political adviser to Lin Piao.[19] A number of western scholars have attributed considerable importance to Li, and one American who met him in the summer of 1946 noted that he was "always alert to rationalize any situation that might imply any shortcomings on the part of the Soviets."[20]

Whatever fears Yenan may have had about the allegiance of these men, they never materialized. Chang Hsüeh-shih, whose idea of forming a separate regime was apparently short-lived, settled easily into the chairmanship of the Liaoning Provincial Government and reportedly told one listener that without the leadership of the CCP, "I am afraid that even now I would not have been able to return to the Northeast, much less could we have won the War of Resistance."[21] Robert Rigg, an American official in Manchuria whose patent anti-Communism often led him to overestimate the strength of ties between Moscow and Yenan, claimed that Chou Pao-chung had a "concealed favoritism toward America" and felt that the Chinese could do "without too much Soviet assistance."[22] Chou served as one of three deputy commanders in Lin Piao's army, and there is no evidence that he was ever disloyal. Finally, while it is unclear just what influence Li Li-san may have had, it is unlikely that he ever used it on behalf of Stalin.[23] Touted by many as the Soviet agent in Manchuria, it is ironic that Li should be the one Chinese Communist to call on Moscow to restore to China the $2 billion he claimed were lost due to Russian extractions of "war booty" from the Northeast.[24]

If, after ousting the Japanese, Stalin hoped to exploit a separatist movement in Manchuria, he was disappointed. Relations between the Soviet Union and the CCP's Northeast Bureau were never very good; the dismissal of P'eng Chen in the spring of 1946 may have been due to his alleged anti-Soviet activities.[25] No movement for an autonomous Manchuria attracted significant support, and this left the Russians to choose between Chungking and Yenan. During the first three months of the postwar era, they favored the Communists. Then, after the middle of November, Stalin switched sides.

Betrayal in Manchuria

To return to our story: After November 1 the Communists faced a growing government offensive, which passed through north China en route to Manchuria and enjoyed various forms of American support. The Communist press sharply criticized American aid to the Nationalists, but policymakers in Yenan may also have seen the advantages of the new situation. At least, Washington had shown its true colors; meanwhile, Soviet aid to the Communists north of the Great Wall continued. The Seventh Party Congress had tried to promote just such a division between the great powers in China. In early November the Russians were still doing their part.

Chungking's difficulties in penetrating Manchuria were due largely to the machinations of the Soviet army. In the middle of October, after Moscow had denied the Nationalists entry into Dalren, General Malinovsky told them that he would not oppose a landing at Hulutao or Yingkow on the Liaotung Peninsula. When American transport ships bearing government troops arrived at Hulutao (on October 27) and Yingkow (on November 2), however, they found their entry blocked by a combination of Russian and Chinese Communist forces. Reports by American landing parties show that there was close cooperation between CCP and Soviet officials in both cities.[26] Turned back from these ports, Nationalist troops had to fight their way into Manchuria through Shanhaikuan.

Similarly, Soviet authorities in Changchun helped establish Communist domination of that city. After the arrival of the Nationalist Northeast Headquarters in the middle of October, the Russians denied Chungking's requests to fly regular troops into Changchun and to recruit police and militia units from among the local populace. Meanwhile, rebel forces encircled the airfield and prevented a planeload of government officials from landing. When the Soviet army began to withdraw from Changchun on November 12, Chinese Communist forces appeared in great numbers, the CCP-dominated *Kuang Ming Jih Pao* began publication, and a Communist mayor took over as head of the city administration. Communist forces surrounded the Nationalist headquarters and turned off the water and electricity. Reports that the Russians would withdraw from all areas south of Harbin by November 20, suggested that within a few days the Communists would control the capital of Manchuria and much more.[27]

This was the situation when, on November 17, Chiang Kai-shek recalled his Northeast Headquarters. This maneuver shifted the onus for breach of the Sino-Soviet Treaty onto the Russians, an embarrassing position for the hosts of the Big Three Foreign Ministers Conference about to open in Moscow. If the generalissimo hoped by this move to elicit better cooperation in restoring Nationalist control over Manchuria, his plan worked. Soviet forces stayed their departure from Changchun and adopted a friendlier attitude toward the remaining members of the Nationalist headquarters. Soviet officials hastened to assure the Chinese government that they had no intention of aiding the Communists. From Moscow came Stalin's personal invitation to meet with a Kuomintang envoy.[28]

All of this was bad news for Yenan. In expectation of the Soviet departure, Communist forces were preparing to take over the cities of central Manchuria and block the Nationalist advance along the railroad from Shanhaikuan. The Communists had 30,000 men in Shenyang; according to one report, Chu Teh had flown in to help plan for the city's defense. What threatened the Communist position was the hint of a deal between Moscow and Chungking which would enable the government to airlift forces into Changchun. Mao wired P'eng Chen, to "ask our friends to put off the . . . arrival in Manchuria of the Kuomintang troops as long as possible."[29] On November 27 an editorial in *Hsin Hua Jih Pao* urged Moscow to take a stronger stand against the Nationalist onslaught:

The Fascist remnants and their imperialistic sponsors are resorting to all means to prepare to make another anti-Soviet and anti-people world war . . . The most obvious and important evidence is found in the Northeast question. They emphasized strongly on national independence and territorial integrity and hinted that the Soviet Union is carrying out aggression on our Northeast. . . .
The strength of the people of China, of the people of the world and of the strong Soviet Union will be able to suppress the outbreak of a third world war.[30]

Despite these efforts, Yenan again suffered a capricious twist in Soviet policy. On November 27 Moscow and Chungking announced an agreement to provide for the smooth transfer of power in the Northeast.[31] The Russians promised to remove Communist forces from Shenyang and Changchun. Nationalist officials would return to the latter city immediately; an airlift of Chinese forces would follow. Finally, to assure the government time and a secure atmosphere in which to set up its political and military apparatus, the Soviet army would remain in Manchuria until January.

Retreat to the Countryside and to the Table

The November 27 agreement forced Yenan to reverse both its military and diplomatic strategies. Rather than meet the government head-on in a battle for Manchuria, Communist forces withdrew to the countryside to surround Nationalist-held cities and harass their supply lines. Rather than sharpen the conflict with the Americans, Yenan softened its propaganda and agreed to return to the negotiating table—now attended by General George Marshall, who replaced Hurley as the chief American representative in China. The Moscow-Chungking accord changed the whole military situation in Manchuria. If the Russians had withdrawn on schedule, the Communists were prepared to meet the Nationalists at Shenyang and fight for control of the urban Northeast. Malinovsky's order to evacuate CCP troops from Shenyang and Changchun torpedoed these plans. The Communist withdrawal began the day the agreement was announced.[32]

During the next two months, the Russians cooperated fully with Chungking in carrying out their part of the bargain. In late December they helped set up Kuomintang-controlled governments in Changchun, Harbin, and Shenyang. Nationalist regulars flew into Changchun in early January and entered Shenyang overland at the end of the month. Meanwhile, government forces landed in the now pacified port of Hulutao, whence they moved north to Shenyang and west toward Chengteh, capital of Jehol. By the beginning of the new year, the government had extended its control throughout Liaoning Province, and while its only link with Changchun was by air, that city too seemed well within the Nationalist grasp. A *Ta Kung Pao* reporter who witnessed the transfer of power in Manchuria called the Soviet army a "great help" in maintaining peace and order. Chiang Ching-kuo, the Russian-educated son of the generalissimo, left for Moscow on Christmas Day and returned with a personal invitation from Stalin to meet with the senior Chiang in the Russian capital or somewhere on the Sino-Soviet border.[33]

The Communists offered no resistance to the movement of Chungking's armies into Manchuria. As the Central Committee directive issued to the Northeast Bureau at the end of 1945 shows, Yenan had decided to bide its time, deepen its roots on all sides, and wait for a more propitious moment to recoup its losses:

> Our Party's present task in the Northeast is to build base areas, stable military and political base areas in eastern, northern and western Manchuria. . . .
> It should now be made clear that these base areas are not to be built in the big cities or along the main communication lines that are or will be occupied by the Kuomintang; under present conditions this is not practicable. . . . the regions in which to build stable bases are the cities and vast rural areas comparatively remote from the centres of Kuomintang occupation.[34]

Meanwhile, on the diplomatic front, Yenan renewed its offer to seek peaceful reunification. In a lead article in *Chieh Fang Jih Pao* on November 30, Chu Teh explained that the Communists had never opposed "in principle" the entry of Nationalist forces into Manchuria and called for a compromise settlement which would lead to a coalition government.[35] A similar message was issued to Communist units in the field. In late November Liu Lan-t'ao, deputy secretary of the Shansi-Chahar-Hopeh Party Committee, told an important gathering at Kalgan that the movement had entered a "transitional period" in which they must wage a "defensive war" while seeking "peace, democracy, unity." Despite the recent setback in the Northeast, Liu called on Party members to "propagate the inestimably great contribution of the Soviet Union and the Soviet Red Army for the peace of mankind." Stepping back from the sharp criticism of the Americans which had followed the clash at Shanhaikuan, he told his listeners that "under the condition that the American Army respects our rights and interests, we will welcome cooperation with it."[36]

The Moscow-Chungking agreement of November 27 seems quite sufficient to explain Yenan's actions in the days that followed, and there is no evidence of a causal connection to other developments—the resignation of Patrick Hurley and the appointment of George Marshall as the President's personal representative in China—that occurred the same day. These events dovetailed, however, in the formation of Chinese Communist policy. Stalin's reversal in Manchuria forced the Communists to consider efforts aimed at reducing Soviet and American aid to Chungking, while the departure of the hostile and prejudiced Hurley seemed to improve Yenan's chances for diplomatic success.

Following the announcement of the October 10 agreement and the return of Mao to Yenan, the terms for a cease-fire became the central issue in the discussions which continued in Chungking. The government asked for freedom of movement on the railroads in exchange for a commitment to leave Communist forces elsewhere alone. Yenan agreed to halt the fighting only on the condition that troops of both parties stay off the rails—in effect, a standstill cease-fire.[37] As the fighting spread, chances for ending hostilities and opening talks aimed at a political and military settlement receded.[38] Still, the question of how to define a cease-fire remained at the heart of the Communist-Kuomintang parleys well into December.[39]

Hurley's resignation and Marshall's appointment offered Yenan an opportunity for securing American support on this and other issues. On November 30 editorials in both major Communist papers contrasted the sad record of Ambassador Hurley with the persistent friendship of the Chinese and American peoples and expressed the hope that General Marshall would "consolidate and develop" that friendship. Once again, Yenan opened the door to cooperation with Washington. Having been rebuffed in their two previous attempts, however, the Communists made this third, and in the end final, offer with somewhat greater caution. The Communist press warned its readers that the success of the Marshall mission would depend on "the immediate evacuation of all U.S. troops from China."[40]

This new expression of friendship was also reflected in the behavior of Communist forces in the field. Beginning in late November, the Marine headquarters in north China reported "a sharp decrease in the hostile attitude and activities of Communist forces toward the Americans."[41] In December, bad weather forced several American reconnaissance planes down over Hopeh and Shantung, and with a single exception local Red units cooperated fully in caring for and returning the airmen.[42] Similarly, in late December the American consul at Tsingtao reported that "the Communists' attitude [has] recently changed to friendliness toward the U.S.A."[43]

The news from Washington seemed to favor Yenan's moderate line. On December 15 President Truman made public his instruction to Marshall.[44] The President called for the "prompt arrangement for a cessation of hostilities." In Communist parlance this could mean only a "standstill cease-fire," Yenan's chief objective at this time. Whether by accident or by design, Truman placed the broadening of the current "one-party government" ahead of nationalization of forces as the goals which Marshall and the United States would seek in China. This chronology matched the Communists' insistence that they receive a share of political authority before abandoning control of their armies to the Kuomintang. On both major issues Washington appeared to side with Yenan against the recognized government in Chungking.

The Communist response to Truman was prompt and positive. *Hsin Hua Jih Pao* predicted that the President's statement would "produce good influence on the situation in China." In a long interview with Colonel Yeaton, Chu Teh expressed optimism about Truman's speech and the prospects for American policy in China. Finally, the Communists invited General Wedemeyer, long a persona non grata in Yenan, to visit the Red capital.[45] "A slight hint of change in the United States policy," reported Yeaton,

has quickly brought out a desperate cry to stop the civil war at the earliest and successfully conclude negotiations. I detect a new low in assurance within the Communist camp and believe the Communists are ready to make greater concessions than ever before. At the same time, if General Marshall's reactions toward the China problem are favorable and he appreciates the Communist point of view, the Communists will throw themselves in the lap of the United States.[46]

On December 16 Chou En-lai returned to Chungking to await the arrival of Marshall and announced that the Communists favored an unconditional cease-fire, a call for peace which would undoubtedly appeal to the American envoy. In an editorial welcoming Marshall to China, Yenan retreated from its earlier insistence on immediate withdrawal of American troops, agreeing that they might first complete the task of disarming and repatriating Japanese forces in China.[47]

The enthusiasm for Truman's announcement and the arrival of Marshall did not dull Yenan's senses to less friendly American actions, however. On December 13 *Chieh Fang Jih Pao* issued its most bitter attack to date on the Marines in connection with the alleged shelling of a village in Hopeh.[48] During the following week, Washington announced that it would continue to move Nationalist forces to Manchuria, and another batch landed at Hulutao.[49] Determined to weigh discrete American actions, Yenan charged that this practice of transporting Kuomintang troops "has long constituted a factor in promoting and enlarging the Chinese civil war."[50]

The Moscow-Chungking agreement of November 27, like the Sino-Soviet Treaty of August, forced Yenan to reverse its diplomatic and military line. On both occasions the Americans had swung behind Chungking in what appeared to be the first stages of civil war. On both occasions Yenan resolved to stand and fight and counted on the Russians to play a neutral to friendly role in the coming battle. And on both occasions Moscow sided with the Kuomintang, prompting Yenan to retreat on the battlefield and join talks aimed at finding a peaceful solution. Foreign power and influence in China were too great to be ignored. Divided, the great powers would leave Yenan a chance to reach for military victory. United behind Chungking, they left the Communists no choice but to continue gradual expansion behind the charade of negotiation.

As the new year began, Yenan would proceed on the basis of a familiar strategy. On one hand, the Soviet reversal in Manchuria made the arrival of Marshall and the prospect for greater American flexibility most welcome. In the short run the great powers might favor a standstill cease-fire which would retard the build-up of Nationalist forces in the Northeast. In the long run the negotiations might enable the Communists to prove their commitment to "unity and democracy" and erode the base of Soviet and American support for Chungking. Despite earlier disappointments, the united front approach might finally pay off.

On the other hand, there were limits to Yenan's patience. Previous hints of change in American policy had not borne fruit. Even before Marshall's arrival, news of the decision to continue transporting Nationalist troops to Manchuria preceded him. The Communists had proven their ability to disrupt communications in north China, and they could do the same in the remote Northeast. Finally, Soviet policy in China remained an unsettled question. During the Foreign Ministers Conference in Moscow (December 16–26), the Soviet press openly sided with "democratic elements" who sought a role in the Chinese government and attacked the Americans for keeping the Marines in north China. The final communiqué committed all sides to support political reform in China and withdraw their forces from that country.[51] Despite the Moscow-Chungking agreement, if American policy failed to change, the alternative of protracted war and the patient pursuit of Soviet assistance remained open.

The mood in Yenan did not bode well for the success of Marshall's mediation. During the last year and a half, Mao had twice stepped forward to promote compromise with Chiang Kai-shek and his foreign supporters: first, in seeking American aid at the end of 1944; and again, when he traveled to Chungking for peace talks after the end of the war. Both initiatives failed to produce the desired results, and the latter met with sharp criticism in Yenan. After the November 27 agreement, it was Chu Teh rather than Mao who defended Yenan's decision not to oppose the Nationalist takeover of Manchuria. From this time on, the chairman withdrew as spokesman for efforts to restore the united front at home and win favor abroad.

Finally, the success of the peace talks depended on the continued presence of foreign power in China. The Moscow-Chungking agreement delayed the Soviet departure from Manchuria and the day when the naked force of Communist and Kuomintang armies would collide in that vital region. The Marines retained control of the key links in north China, deterring an open clash for that narrow passageway to the north. American aid to the government provided some leverage over both parties and helped keep them apart. Foreign power, real and perceived, weighed heavily on events in China. While it remained, both sides avoided an open clash; when it declined, so did the chances for peace.

CHAPTER NINE

Last Chance for Peace
(*January–March 1946*)

The first round of talks in Chungking produced the results Yenan had hoped for: a cease-fire, an agreement to form a coalition government, and the first solid evidence that the Americans had had a change of heart. The moderate approach aimed at broadening Yenan's appeal at home and abroad was never more richly rewarded than in early 1946, but stronger forces within the Communist movement overrode this diplomatic success. Red commanders in Manchuria wanted to fight rather than wait on the peace talks; radical land reform in the outlying base areas pressed Yenan to adopt a more aggressive line; and Mao, who had been criticized for seeking elusive concessions through the united front, would not stand against this tide toward civil war.

Marshall's Plan for China

After only six weeks in China, George Marshall achieved the seemingly impossible task which had eluded his predecessor: he arranged a cease-fire and secured Chiang Kai-shek's commitment to form a coalition with the Communists. Yenan greeted these results, and the Communist press roundly applauded the performance of Truman's envoy. The agreements still had to be ratified by both parties, but whatever course Chungking adopted, the new direction of American policy in China promised Yenan the long-sought rewards of working through the united front.

The Communists had welcomed Marshall from the outset, for they needed his cooperation, and they hoped he would reverse Hurley's pernicious line. After his arrival on December 21, Yenan waited patiently as Marshall sounded out the various parties and silently mapped his strategy. When he informed Chou En-lai that the United States would continue to move Nationalist troops into Manchuria, Chou promptly replied that Yenan would accept this practice and the exception of Manchuria from the scope of the cease-fire.[1]

Yenan's patience paid off, for Marshall backed the Communists on the first important issue, the terms of the cease-fire itself. The chief obstacle to conclusion of an agreement was a dispute concerning control of two cities, Chihfeng in Jehol Province and Tolun in Chahar. To cut Yenan's line of communication to the Northeast, the Nationalists had sent two columns toward these cities. Chungking maintained its right under the Sino-Soviet Treaty to restore sovereignty over any place previously occupied by the Russian army and refused to call off the attack. Yenan countered that the treaty covered only Manchuria (which did not include Jehol or Chahar) and that in any case Communist forces now held the cities in question. The Communists insisted that the cease-fire must cover both provinces; the government said no. On the evening of January 9 Marshall persuaded Chiang to halt his troop movements in Jehol and Chahar.[2] The following day the agreement was signed.

The January 10 cease-fire met all of Yenan's basic demands.[3] It halted the government offensive in Jehol and ordered the cessation of "all movements of forces" north of the Yangtze, except in Manchuria where the Nationalist army might enter "for the purpose of restoring Chinese sovereignty." While prohibiting the "destruction of and interference with all lines of communication," it permitted the Communists to retain control of the places they had already occupied. As long as the government honored the standstill, Yenan had no need to "interfere" with communications. If, on the other hand, Nationalist forces resumed their advance, the Communists could repulse the attack and declare the agreement void.

In exchange for these assurances, Yenan agreed to permit the entry of the Nationalist army into Manchuria—an important provision, but hardly a concession by the Communists. Moscow had agreed to the restoration of Nationalist sovereignty in Manchuria as a part of the package linked to the Sino-Soviet Treaty. The Communists could not oppose a government takeover of the Northeast without Russian cooperation, and this had been precluded by the Moscow-Chungking agreement of November 27. At the same time, the cease-fire specified that the Nationalist occupation of Manchuria was to be "for the purpose of restoring Chinese sovereignty." Yenan may have foreseen that this phrase sanctioned the transfer of authority only from Soviet to Nationalist hands *directly*, excluding government expeditions through areas held by the Communists. Recognizing that Moscow had already given away most of the pie, the January 10 agreement enabled Yenan to preserve at least one crucial slice.

The Communists applauded the cease-fire. An editorial in *Chieh Fang Jih Pao* credited Truman and Marshall with reversing Hurley's policy and helping to "usher in a new era of peaceful reform and peaceful reconstruction unprecedented in the history of China." Meanwhile, a secret Central Committee directive told Party cadres that a democratic faction had emerged in the United States to "oppose the Hurley policy" and put forward an alternative acceptable to Yenan.[4]

Conclusion of the cease-fire agreement laid the foundation for discussion of the next major topic, governmental reform, the focus of the Political Consultative Conference (PCC) which opened in Chungking on January 10. Membership of the PCC included representatives of the Kuomintang, the Communists, the Democratic League, and the Youth Party, as well as several prominent nonparty figures. The PCC had no independent authority; its decisions would have to be ratified by the various parties. The Americans played no role in this purely Chinese affair, but Truman's new interest in China, the signing of the cease-fire, and Marshall's presence in Chungking had created a momentum that carried the PCC toward a program of sweeping governmental reform.

The final resolutions of the PCC, passed on January 31, laid out the blueprint for creation of a coalition government. The National

Assembly would convene on May 5 to adopt a new constitution. Pending the establishment of constitutional government, authority was to rest with a reorganized State Council, half of whose members would come from outside the Kuomintang. Until all of these plans took effect on the national level, the local status quo would be maintained—a crucial guarantee to the integrity of the liberated areas. Finally, a three-man military subcommittee (one Kuomintang member, one Communist, one American) was charged with finding a solution to the problems of demobilizing forces on both sides and reorganizing them into a single nonpartisan national army.[5]

The Communists were delighted with the PCC resolutions. The long-sought coalition had at last received formal sanction, thanks largely to American influence. *Hsin Hua Jih Pao* hailed the "New Historic Direction" mapped out at the Conference. Yenan's "person in authority" announced that "from this moment China has doubtlessly entered a new stage of peace, democracy and reconstruction." Mao wrote Marshall promising continued cooperation, and Chou told him that the chairman still hoped to visit the United States.[6]

Policing the Cease-Fire

Distrust between Yenan and Chungking and divisions within the Communist movement itself made implementation of the cease-fire difficult. In Chungking, Chou En-lai tried to make the machinery set up under the January 10 agreement work. In Peiping and in the field, however, Communist military men were more protective of the gains already made and less willing to risk them in exchange for paper promises. Initially, these differences were resolved, but the signs of conflict boded ill for the future of the fragile cease-fire accords.

The setting for Chinese Communist–American relations during 1946 was the elaborate structure erected in accordance with the January 10 agreement to supervise the cease-fire and its related provisions. At the top was the Committee of Three—Marshall, Chou En-lai, and the Nationalist representative, Chang Chih-chung—located first in Chungking, later in Nanking. This committee was to conclude agreements which carried the approval of the three governments and issue instructions to an executive arm, the Peiping Executive Headquarters (PEH), which was similarly headed by three commissioners—Walter Robertson (US), Yeh Chien-ying (CCP), and Cheng Kai-ming (KMT). These commissioners operated through a combined chiefs of staff—Generals Henry Byroade (US), Lo Jui-ch'ing (CCP), and Ts'ai Wen-shih (KMT)—and thence to tripartite truce teams, forty in all, which made contact with field units on both sides, issued orders, and reported on results. The structure was a pyramid of three-man committees, with unanimous agreement required at every level. Their functions included supervision of the cease-fire, separation of forces, restoration of communication, and repatriation of Japanese. In theory the system would work; in practice it worked hardly at all. For in the absence of unanimity (and it was conspicuously absent during most of 1946) the PEH was more an instrument of propaganda and manipulation than of common policy.

The creation of the cease-fire machinery enhanced the position of Chou En-lai. During most of the war, neither Chou nor his liaison office in Chungking had occupied an important place on the spectrum of Yenan's concerns. It was not until 1944 that the prospect of major gains, and specifically diplomatic gains, in Nationalist China first arose. Even then, Mao himself handled the most important talks, with Hurley and the Americans in Yenan, and later with Chiang Kai-shek in Chungking. The problem of dealing with Marshall, by contrast, passed to Chou.[7]

In this role, Chou advocated cooperation with the Americans and warned Yenan against becoming too closely identified with the Russians. In part, this can be explained by his position. It was Chou's task to persuade the Americans that Yenan wanted peace and to inch them toward a more even-handed policy in China. Located in Chungking, he was particularly sensitive to the mounting criticism of Soviet actions in Manchuria. In part, it also reflected his relationship with Marshall. In contrast to Hurley, Marshall was intelligent, conscientious, and honest. Chou, as well as virtually everyone else who dealt with Marshall, appreciated these qualities. According to Carsun Chang, who worked closely with both men, Chou had complete confidence in Marshall's impartiality. "Marshall's personality had much to do with his success," Chang later recalled. "Chou En-lai told me many times that General Marshall never once attempted to deceive him. . . . Chou En-lai had always shown great confidence in General Marshall."[8]

Communist military leaders did not share Chou's optimism or his patience. The differences between them were evident in the first of many disputes that shook the Executive Headquarters as it sought to apply the cease-fire orders at Chihfeng. The story of this affair illustrates a number of problems inherent in the peace-keeping machinery and the divergent perspectives within the Communist camp.

On January 14 the Committee of Three in Chungking instructed the PEH to dispatch a truce team to Chihfeng to report on conditions in that city, which had been the focus of recent conflict. Three days later, reportedly due to obstruction by Communist Commissioner Yeh Chien-ying, the team had still not left Peiping. The Americans protested to Chou, who immediately wired Yeh reminding him of his orders, and the team departed. The situation in Chihfeng was complicated. One thousand Soviet soldiers controlled the city in cooperation with the Communist Peace Preservation Corps (approximately 1200 strong), which occupied Chihfeng and five surrounding hamlets. Regular Communist units were 15 miles west of the city. Nationalist forces, located 8 to 12 miles to the east, had been instructed to occupy Chihfeng after the Soviet evacuation—a move which would violate the cease-fire agreement. When the Russians withdrew on January 23, a struggle for Chihfeng appeared imminent. By this time, the truce team had made its findings and ordered the Peace Preservation Corps to withdraw from the hamlets surrounding the city. The commander of the corps balked; it was not until January 26 that his troops removed to Chihfeng. Meanwhile the Nationalist commissioner of the PEH agreed to join an order halting the advance of government forces. By the end of January the situation in Chihfeng was under control.[9]

The case of Chihfeng demonstrates how vulnerable the cease-fire machinery was to conflict between the Communists and the Kuomintang. Perhaps because this was a test case in which both sides wanted to prove their good intentions, the dispute was resolved. As relations between Yenan and Chungking soured, however, the ability of the PEH to reach agreement and elicit compliance from forces in the field first wavered, then collapsed.[10]

Viewed from another angle, Chihfeng reveals divisions within the Communist movement itself. Yeh Chien-ying, whose experience tied him more closely to the problems of Communist forces in the field, did not share Chou En-lai's regard for the value of foreign entanglements. Despite Yenan's strong public support for the Marshall Mission, on his arrival in Peiping, Yeh told reporters that "all problems should be settled between ourselves [Communists and Nationalists] and I can't see why there must be need of any foreign mediation." In Yeh's view, the Communists had not yet decided what role Marshall would play in keeping the peace. Similarly, the work of the truce team at Chihfeng was obstructed by what the Americans saw as the "unwillingness of [the] Communist representative to assume any authority" and the attitude of the commander of the Peace Preservation Corps, "who took [the] position that Executive Headquarters had no authority to give him orders and that he recognized only those orders which came from [the Communist] Governor of Jehol." As these reports suggest, recalcitrant Communist military officials could block the work of the PEH from above, or simply ignore the orders of the truce teams from below.[11]

At Chihfeng the line pressed by Chou En-lai won out, perhaps as a result of intervention by Yenan. After the dispute was resolved, control over Communist forces in the area passed from the governor of Jehol to the regional military commander, suggesting that Yenan may have wanted to assure compliance with PEH directives and opted for the more reliable channel of direct army command.[12] If so, this merely underlines the difficulty of maintaining control over a diverse and widespread guerrilla movement, while attempting to coordinate military and political objectives. Any commitment made by Chou En-lai in Chungking had to pass through an intervening network of sometimes skeptical officials and be made to stick with local commanders who faced their own problems and opportunities. In all of this, Yenan alone could play the arbiter. But the Party leadership itself was open to influence from all these sources—a fact which became increasingly evident when the focus shifted to Manchuria.

Conflict over Manchuria

Conflict over Manchuria was the opening wedge of the Chinese civil war. In the early part of 1946, Soviet actions in the Northeast prompted a massive outcry in Nationalist China against the "rape of Manchuria." Communist representatives in Chungking saw Moscow's behavior as a threat to the settlement pieced together under Marshall's supervision. But Yenan refused to break with the Russians, even at the expense of substantial support at home and abroad, and by the end of February the agreement to form a coalition government began to come undone.

Before the ink on the January agreements had dried, hard-line anti-Communists in Chungking tried to destroy them. Tai Li's secret police heckled and threw stones at mass public gatherings called to discuss the work of the Political Consultative Conference. After the PCC resolutions were announced, "organized hoodlums," whom virtually all observers agreed were Kuomintang extremists or their agents, broke up a meeting to celebrate the move toward unification and beat up several of its organizers.[13] Failure of the government to punish the perpetrators of these crimes cast doubt on the willingness of the Kuomintang to ratify the work of the PCC and carry forward the program of peaceful reform.

Soviet behavior in the Northeast played into the hands of those who opposed a settlement with the Communists. Russian looting of Manchurian industry, the prolonged military occupation, and Stalin's transparent attempts to hold the area hostage in exchange for further economic concessions provoked resentment throughout China. Publication, on February 11, of the secret Yalta protocol brought anger against Russian encroachments to the surface.[14] Right-wing elements within the Kuomintang helped turn mass anti-Soviet demonstrations against all Communists at home and abroad. These protests were no mere fabrication, however. They were real; they were widespread; and they posed a serious problem for those charting the course of the Communist movement in China.

In Chungking, Chou En-lai was frankly aghast at Soviet behavior in Manchuria, which was undermining his efforts to win the confidence of foreigners and Chinese moderates. As he told one group of correspondents, "Our position is the sooner [the Russians] evacuate the better."[15] On the night of February 22, following student demonstrations which led to an attack on the office of *Hsin Hua Jih Pao* and several of its employees, John Melby, a Foreign Service officer, found the Communists in a mood of deep despair:

That night the atmosphere at Communist headquarters was grim, only candles for light, the gates barred, and armed guards mounted on the wall. They were an angry group of people, declaring their readiness again to take to the caves and ditches if necessary, and fully aware that for the moment they must take what happens here without striking back openly. Their anger was laced with frustration. They resent the growing signs of Russian reluctance to get out of Manchuria, especially since they are so far not allowed to get in any more than is anyone else. Chou En-lai was bitter: "After all these years this is too much!"[16]

In Yenan, however, Communist leaders took a quite different view. Chu Teh told one foreign correspondent that Chou En-lai was "mistaken" in calling for the withdrawal of Soviet forces. Ch'in Pang-hsien staunchly defended the Soviet role in the Northeast.[17] Finally, in a lengthy interview in *Chieh Fang Jih Pao* on February 14, a "spokesman for the Central Committee" praised the Russians for their support of popular forces in Manchuria. The "spokesman" recognized the government's right to "restore sovereignty" in the Northeast, but insisted on certain democratic reforms in that region and a limitation on Nationalist troops to a "stipulated" number, two new conditions which drew into question Yenan's support for the original cease-fire agreement. He admitted, for the first time publicly, the presence of 300,000 Communist troops in Manchuria and warned that "if the Kuomintang refused to recognize the status of the democratic forces and Chinese Communist Party in Manchuria and is unwilling to cooperate and work sincerely with them, it would also commit a grave mistake."[18]

This line—staunch in defense of the Soviet army, bellicose on the future disposition of Manchuria—continued throughout the next few turbulent weeks. Alone among the Chungking papers, *Hsin Hua Jih Pao* denounced criticism of the Russian occupation as "anti-alien." *Chieh Fang Jih Pao* reprinted Moscow's reply to the "slanderous rumors" emanating from Chungking and echoed the Soviet attack on the "Chinese Fascists" who fomented them. "Why do these lowly Chinese Fascists view the Soviet Union as an enemy?" asked the official organ in Yenan. "Why do they slander Stalin? Clearly it is because the power of the Soviet Union under the leadership of Stalin is the main strength of anti-Fascism in the world, because the Soviet Union and Stalin defeated Fascism."[19]

Yenan's vigorous defense of the Russians had its costs. Success of the Communist movement in China rested largely on its record of resistance to foreign aggression. In failing to apply this same robust nationalism to the Soviet intrusion into Manchuria, Yenan was risking collapse of one major pillar of its popular appeal. Chou En-lai saw this danger, but his advice was rejected. By early March, the American embassy concluded that after building up a "vast fund of good will among non-Communists" during the war, "At the present time the Communists appear to be alienating this good will because of their silence concerning Russian activities in Manchuria and playing directly into the hands of the [rightist] CC Clique or other Chinese elements who are disgruntled with the PCC and military reorganization programs."[20]

Yenan's record in these events is puzzling. By February 1, the united front approach had at last begun to yield results: the cease-fire was in place; Chiang had agreed to form a coalition; the commitment of the American government and of moderate Chinese to both measures would play in Yenan's favor if the Kuomintang failed to carry out these agreements. Chou En-lai warned Party leaders that their association with Moscow was alienating this same constituency. Yet Yenan's response, the incendiary article of February 14, contributed precisely to that end. Why, after their ejection from Manchurian cities by the Russians at the end of 1945, and now, in early 1946, appearing to win more favorable treatment from the Americans, did the Communists adopt such a provocative stance?

Yenan Leans to One Side

The available evidence points to three possible answers. First, Communist military commanders opposed American mediation and saw the advantages of courting Soviet cooperation in Manchuria. Second, spontaneous, radical land reform in the outlying base areas created pressure on Yenan to raise its commitment to class struggle. Third, by this late date, Mao, who had led earlier moves toward the united front and the Americans, was no longer willing to risk his power and prestige on behalf of a perennially losing cause. News from all three fronts pointed to a mounting struggle for control of China, and Yenan moved with the tide.

In his talks with Marshall, Chou En-lai often cited Manchuria as the center of Communist opposition to efforts to reach a negotiated settlement.[21] Evidence from the battlefield supports this contention. Acting against the advice of Yenan's December 28 directive, which called for the dispersal of Communist forces across the Manchurian countryside, Red commanders in the Northeast pressed the attack. In the middle of February, Lin Piao struck and, despite heavy losses, captured the Nationalist stronghold of Hsiushuihotzu. As he explained to one subordinate, "Under the present wartime situation we must use seventy, eighty or even ninety percent of our forces to attack the enemy—this is what we mean by concentrating the main force to solve the main contradiction!" When Lin's forces reached Hsiushuihotzu, they found the streets littered with American war materiel and enemy bodies clad in American uniforms.[22]

Experience such as this helped turn Communist military leaders against American mediation. In the spring of 1946, CCP sources in Manchuria told U.S. intelligence that "a large section of the Communist Party is violently opposed to the peace negotiations in Nanking." The leader of this group was said to be Chu Teh, who has "so far gone along with the party line and accepted the peace proposals." Also in the ranks of the opposition were military leaders from the principal base areas of north China outside Yenan and, notably, Lin Piao and Chang Hsüeh-shih in Manchuria.[23]

While increasingly alienated from the Americans, Communist leaders in the Northeast could appreciate the importance of Soviet cooperation at this time. Politically, widespread hostility toward the Russians in Manchuria made Communist efforts to mobilize mass support difficult.[24] Militarily, a Soviet withdrawal would favor the Communists, whose forces lined the railroads and surrounded the major cities, against the Nationalists, who had only token units in the cities north of Shenyang and insufficient troops from that point south. A departure of the Soviet army at any reasonable speed and without special provisions to hand over control to the Nationalists would leave all of Manchuria above Shenyang to the Chinese Reds. It was on this final condition, however, that Communist strategy in the Northeast must have turned: the Russians had to go, but they had to go in a manner conducive to the Communist takeover. At a time when everyone else in China was castigating the Soviets, Yenan could help secure their much-needed assistance.

Further pressure on Yenan to move from compromise to conflict came from the spontaneous, radical land reform which began to well up in the base areas east of the Yellow River. After the war, Yenan continued the policy of "reduction of rent and interest," restricting confiscation to land held by proven collaborators and traitors. This policy may have been appropriate to the Shensi-Kansu-Ninghsia Border Region, which was never occupied by the Japanese and where the Communists had already achieved a substantial leveling of wealth and income, but a different situation prevailed in north China and Manchuria. Here, the population had suffered from Japanese and puppet exploitation; the desire for revenge was strong; and once unleashed, the forces of revolution burst the limits of Yenan's moderate guidelines.[25]

During the winter slack season of 1945–46, a campaign to "settle accounts" provided the opening wedge for a general attack on property. According to William Hinton's description of one county in Shansi, by February 1946 virtually all concentrations of wealth in this part of the province had been redistributed. The campaign assumed anti-imperialist overtones, for a major target of the radicals was the Catholic Church, which had huge land holdings and was closely identified with the wartime collaboration. Similar excesses may have occurred in such cities as Kalgan, where the Communist-dominated government authorized generous labor settlements and outright confiscation of property. In Manchuria, where virtually all land belonged either to Japanese or to Chinese who had cooperated with them, the campaign to "settle accounts" had much broader implications. In the middle of April the Northeast Bureau issued a directive calling for the confiscation and redistribution of all Japanese- and puppet-owned land.[26] Party leaders east of the Yellow River were discovering that the exploitation of class conflict was the best means of mobilizing mass support.

If this was the message reaching Yenan from Manchuria and north China in early 1946, then Mao and other Party leaders were better prepared to accept it than at any time in the past two years. On the whole, the chairman's role during this period remains obscure. No documents written during the first three months of 1946 appear in the *Selected Works*. Mao made no public statements and refused to see foreign journalists. There was some speculation that he might be ill, but after he reappeared Colonel Yeaton found him "entirely rested and in perfect health."[27]

While subject to closer examination, disclosures made during the Cultural Revolution suggest at least one possible explanation for this mysterious behavior. As mentioned above, there is no evidence to suggest that through the end of 1945 Liu Shao-ch'i was anything but a loyal supporter of Mao and his program of Party Rectification. Unlike the returned students, the new spokesman for the urban areas never pressed for the united front with the government or its foreign supporters. If we are to believe his latter-day critics, however, Liu's attitude began to change after the January 1946 accords. In a speech delivered on February 1, Liu allegedly warned against the sectarian deviation of "closed doorism" and favored a peaceful transition to socialism through "parliamentary struggle."[28] Mao, on the other hand, purportedly wanted "to conserve our strength and train our armed forces."[29] Given the line which prevailed during the Cultural Revolution, it is not surprising that these allegations place Mao on the side of militant struggle and Liu for accommodation. But this interpretation may contain a kernel of truth, for it squares with what we know about the chairman's role in this period as a whole.

In 1944 Mao had taken the lead in a diplomatic offensive aimed at securing American assistance, and this policy had failed. After the war he agreed to join the talks in Chungking and was criticized in Yenan for offering too many concessions. According to Lin Piao, from this point on Mao rejected the advice of "some well-intentioned friends at home and abroad," and instead "put forward the thesis that all reactionaries are paper tigers."[30] Thereafter, Chu Teh emerged to explain the retreat from an aggressive line in Manchuria at the end of November 1945 and to welcome closer cooperation with the Americans in December. While Liu's call for accommodation was no heresy in early 1946, it came against the background of leftist gains in the campaign to "settle accounts" and rightist reaction against the peaceful reforms worked out in Chungking. The chairman's disappearance during this period may have been designed to avoid identification with policies which had failed him in the past.

Clutching the American Connection

Whatever its domestic motivations, Yenan's defense of the Russians did not reflect a reassessment of the international situation or the role of foreign power in China. The Americans continued to play an important and positive role on the mainland. The Communists responded by cooperating with Marshall and withholding criticism from Washington—despite the signs of growing Soviet-American conflict.

Until Marshall's departure from China on March 11, Yenan continued to support his program for peaceful unification. Following the close of the PCC, the Military Subcommittee took up the next item on Marshall's agenda, an agreement to demobilize forces on both sides and integrate the remainder into a new national army. The major sticking point in the deliberations was the pace of this change: Yenan favored a gradual process; Marshall wanted to speed it up. With the news from Manchuria running against him, Chou En-lai must have sensed that he needed a breakthrough on this issue to keep Marshall's confidence alive. On February 19 he made a special trip to Yenan to put his case to the Party leaders, and they agreed. This compromise paved the way to the signing, on February 25, of the Military Reorganization Agreement.[31]

At the same time, Yenan spared Marshall and the Americans from criticisms levelled against the "Chinese Fascists." On March 4 the Committee of Three visited Yenan as part of an extended tour meant to advertise the success of the cease-fire (which had held remarkably well) and to campaign for compliance with the agreements reached in Chungking. Proclaiming "Welcome to General Marshall," the editors of *Chieh Fang Jih Pao* heaped effusive praise on the American and Kuomintang negotiators and reaffirmed the need for "continued support of the American people and especially the support of General Marshall." Privately, Mao gave Marshall "every assurance of cooperation," and Marshall went away buoyed by the success of his visit.[32]

A final indication of Yenan's determination to retain American friendship was its handling of the crisis in U.S.-Soviet relations which broke that spring. The western powers were annoyed by the Soviet presence in Manchuria and the failure of Russian forces to withdraw from Iran by the deadline (March 2) that both London and Washington thought had been agreed to during the war. Finally, on March 5, they hammered Moscow with a series of apparently coordinated attacks. In Washington the State Department made public protests against the Soviet presence in both areas. In Chungking the Chinese government broke a long silence by rejecting what it claimed were excessive and illegal Soviet claims in Manchuria. And in Fulton, Missouri, Winston Churchill, in the company of President Truman, delivered his seminal "Iron Curtain" speech.[33]

In contrast to its handling of the Manchurian question as a dispute between Moscow and Chungking, Yenan responded cautiously to these attacks. Initially the Communist press simply ignored Washington's charges. Later, as Moscow blew first hot then cold on the American protests, Yenan stuck closely to the most conciliatory line, concentrated its criticism on Churchill, and absolved Truman as an enlightened and progressive statesman whose good deeds had been twisted by reactionary forces in Washington.[34] The imagination of Yenan's propagandists was spared any further test by the Soviet withdrawal from both Manchuria and Iran and the defusing of these sources of East-West tension. Through the end of March, Yenan's public commitment to unity among the Big Three remained credible and intact.

Yenan's diplomacy in early 1946 reflects a careful assessment of Communist interests in China. The impending departure of the Soviet army from Manchuria and the opportunities this would pose for Communist forces in that sector argued for a strong public defense of the Russians. At the same time, right-wing Kuomintang attacks on the January peace agreements and the emergence of radical land reform in the outlying base areas prompted Yenan to take a tougher stance with Chungking. The logical extension of this line pointed toward renewed attacks on the Americans, who belonged (in an ideological reading of these events) on the side of the "reactionaries" and against the "revolutionary" forces of Communist China and the Soviet Union. But Yenan did not reduce the problem to such ideological simplicity, because its real interests lay in continuing pursuit of the American connection. Marshall's mediation offered hope that the Americans would play an even-handed role in China; if Chungking were found responsible for the failure of the Marshall Mission, Washington might cut its aid to the Kuomintang. Thus, despite the signs of Soviet-American conflict and despite American transport of Nationalist forces to Manchuria, the Communist press held its fire and Yenan's diplomacy remained on course.

CHAPTER TEN

The Road to War
(*March–July 1946*)

In the spring of 1946, both parties in China opted for civil war and the Chinese Communists resumed their attacks on American "imperialism." The controlling factor in these events was not foreign power, but the lack of it. The Soviet withdrawal from Manchuria removed the last obstacle to an open struggle for that region. The American presence in north China was declining, and Washington proved unable to control its "client" regime. With the Russians gone and the Americans going, Chinese on both sides decided to settle the dispute among themselves. In the heat of civil war, Yenan shifted to a policy of promoting class struggle at home and opposing "imperialism" abroad.

The Decision To Fight

Within ten days of Marshall's departure from China, Yenan resolved to fight for control of the Northeast. The precipitous Soviet withdrawal from Manchuria left the cities and railroads north of Shenyang in Communist hands. Upset by these events, Kuomintang support for the January agreements wavered. The Americans, rather than calling the Chinese government to account, continued to move Nationalist forces north and appeared to acquiesce in the drift toward civil war. The partial withdrawal of the Marines, meanwhile, reduced American leverage on both parties. For the Communists, the time had come to complete the move "from the countryside to the cities."

Departure of the Soviet army from Manchuria in the spring of 1946 (whatever its manner and motivation) was certain to benefit the Communists, who alone were prepared to fill the expanding vacuum in the Northeast. In addition, the pattern of Russian behavior during this period revealed a conscious effort to facilitate the Communist takeover. Despite the Moscow-Chungking agreement of November 27, the Soviet army had not cooperated with the restoration of Nationalist authority in Manchuria. The Russians refused to put down local resistance forces or to provide liaison officers to accompany government takeover teams, and in some cases they even suppressed armed groups friendly to the Kuomintang. When the February 1 deadline for the Soviets' withdrawal passed, Chungking urged them to leave and sought a schedule of their departure dates. The schedule was crucial, because it would indicate when and where a vacancy was to occur and give the government time to fill it before the Communists arrived. Moscow refused to provide a schedule until early April, and by then it was too late.[1]

On March 7, without prior notification, the Soviet army pulled out of Shenyang. Government troops, in Shenyang since January, fought to block a takeover by Chinese Communist forces in the surrounding countryside. After a brief skirmish, the Nationalists established control, but the Communists destroyed the bridge leading north out of the city, creating a serious obstacle to any further government advance. The Russians, monopolizing all rolling stock in their rapid retreat, refused to permit Nationalist forces to travel north by rail. Meanwhile, on the fifteenth, the Soviets withdrew from Ssupingchieh.[2] Again the departure was unannounced. Government forces had no chance to reach the city, and the Communists moved in the following day.

Shockwaves from the Northeast reverberated in Chungking. Hoping to block ratification of the PCC resolutions, rightist elements in the KMT attacked government policy in Manchuria, charging those responsible for permitting a hasty Soviet withdrawal and the Communist takeover. Under intense pressure from the generalissimo, they agreed to ratify the resolutions. At the same time, however, Chiang was forced to table, rather than risk passage of, a set of counterproposals which would have effectively nullified this decision.[3] By the middle of March, the Kuomintang commitment to the January agreements was very much in doubt.

In the Communist view, Chungking was reneging on its promise to form a coalition government. Chou En-lai called its work a "fraud," while Yenan charged that a "Fascist clique" had gained the upper hand within the Kuomintang. Pending clarification of Chungking's position, both the Communists and the Democratic League refused to submit their lists of candidates for the new coalition state council.[4] A meeting of the CCP Central Committee, originally called for March 31 to ratify the January resolutions, was postponed.

As the achievements of Marshall's mediation began to unravel, the Americans gave no sign to dispel fears that they would back Chungking in the coming civil war. Even though seven months had passed since the defeat of Japan, the flow of lend-lease supplies to the Nationalists and the transport of government troops to Manchuria continued. Marshall's replacement, Lieutenant General Alvan Gillem, evinced a prejudice against the Communists which upset Yenan's confidence in the objectivity of the American side.[5] Finally, the Americans remained silent as Chungking's support for the PCC resolutions wavered. Michael Lindsay, a man with long experience in Yenan and close ties to the CCP, later cited Washington's failure to protest at this juncture as "responsible for the change in the Communist party line from conciliation and readiness to accept American mediation to its present [1947] uncompromising anti-American attitude."[6]

While Washington continued to favor the Nationalists, American power in China was declining, and this also contributed to Yenan's decision to fight. Postwar demobilization eroded the size and strength of American forces everywhere. From a peak of 53,000, the number of Marines in north China shrank to 46,553 at the end of January 1946, and to 30,379 at the end of April. Throughout this period, veterans were replaced by men fresh from boot camp, and the long, cold winter, punctuated by incidents of violence, made most of them anxious to leave.[7] Americans on both sides of the Pacific wondered why the troops could not come home now that the war was over. Their role in China was unclear and increasingly unpopular. All observers could see the decline of American might in China, and this enabled Yenan to act with greater impunity.

Expanding opportunities in the Northeast; a belligerent mood in Chungking; an unfriendly, but declining, American presence: news from all three fronts encouraged Yenan to take a harder line. In an unusual interview, Chou Pao-chung, deputy commander of Communist forces in Manchuria, revealed the timing of Yenan's decision to fight. He recalled that after the seizure of Ssupingchieh (on March 16), the Communists were prepared to yield the Shenyang–Harbin railroad to the Nationalists. "Between 15 and 20 March we were told repeatedly by Yenan that there was hope for peace," Chou Pao-chung confided, "but on 21 March we received a telegram saying that peace was hopeless."[8]

While there is no evidence that this decision followed assurances of Russian support, the departure of the Soviet army during the next few weeks facilitated the Communist takeover of much of Manchuria. By the middle of March it was clear that the Russians would soon evacuate Changchun, which lay north of Communist-controlled Ssupingchieh. If the Nationalist army did not reach Changchun quickly, Chungking's token representation there would be stranded and seizure of the city by the Communists certain. The Russians refused government requests to delay their departure and to help move Nationalist troops into Changchun along the railroad from Shenyang, which was still under Soviet control.[9] The Russians left Changchun on April 18; the Communists moved in behind them. This pattern was repeated at Harbin and Tsitsihar. By the beginning of May the last Soviet soldier had left Manchuria, and Communist forces held all of the Northeast from Ssupingchieh to the Russian border.

The Diplomatic Stalemate

With the departure of the Russians from Manchuria and the decision that peace in that quarter was "hopeless," the Communists (and the Nationalists as well) ended their cooperation with American mediators. Opposed by both parties, the Peiping Executive Headquarters could not enforce the cease-fire. In Chungking, Chou En-lai tried to work out a compromise which would convince the Americans that his side wanted peace. Yenan overruled its chief diplomat, however, for after their decision to fight, the Communists' principal aim was not to appease the Americans but to keep them out of the Northeast.

"Immediately upon the departure of General Marshall from China," the American branch of the PEH reported, "the situation began to deteriorate."[10] Field commanders of both Chinese factions ignored instructions issued by the truce teams. In fact, Communist and Kuomintang members of the truce teams refused to sign orders which had not first been approved by their respective military commanders in the region. Both sides adopted delaying tactics when it suited their purposes and issued false reports to prevent investigation of real conflicts.

While the Communist military had always been hostile to the peacekeeping efforts, Chou En-lai looked for a way to keep American mediation alive. On the eve of his departure, Marshall had secured Chiang's approval for a plan to send truce teams into Manchuria, an area excluded from the original cease-fire and now the eye of the gathering storm. In their meeting in Yenan, Mao had told Marshall he would support this proposal.[11] Chou En-lai tried to work out acceptable terms.

Marshall's proposal contained five points. The first three set forth the teams' powers: they were to deal solely with military matters, keep clear of the Russians, and try to arrange a cease-fire. Point four authorized the government to reestablish sovereignty in Manchuria; point five called on the Communists to withdraw from those places necessary for this purpose and to refrain from occupying areas vacated by the Russians. In short, Marshall proposed a Nationalist military takeover of the Northeast, without any provision for applying the political reforms foreseen in the PCC resolutions. Yenan's press statement of February 14 had already rejected this option. Knowing that Communist officials in Manchuria would never accept the plan, Chou told Marshall that he would have to go to the Northeast personally "to consult and work out some concrete measures with the local people on our side," and invited the Americans to accompany him.[12] In the end, neither party made the trip.

Despite the delicacy of his situation, Chou tried to arrange a compromise. The crux of his offer was to permit government troops to occupy those areas being evacuated by the Soviet army. In no case, however, could the Nationalists pass through Communist territory without prior agreement. Given the situation in Manchuria at this time—the Russian and Nationalist armies were separated by a wide strip of Communist property—Chou's offer, which denied the government right of passage, was meaningless. The Nationalists understood this, for they immediately declined his proposal. Of greater interest for our story, Yenan also rejected Chou's compromise.[13]

On March 20 Chou left for Yenan, promising to return "in a day or two" and to bring back information on the demobilization of Communist forces, information required by the February 25 agreement and already overdue. Despite his promise, however, and despite two urgent pleas from General Gillem, Chou did not return in "a day or two." It was five days later and only after radio messages confirmed that the agreement would be limited to the first three points of Marshall's draft (omitting altogether the question of Nationalist sovereignty in Manchuria) that Chou rejoined the talks in Chungking.[14] He did not bring the lists required by the Military Reorganization Agreement. They were never submitted, nor were the lists of CCP members to the State Council.

The timing of Chou's recall (March 20) coincides with instructions to Communist forces in Manchuria that "peace was hopeless" (March 21) and suggests that by offering too much in the talks in Chungking, Chou had fallen out of step with the dominant mood in Yenan. One American observer in the Communist capital reported that Chou was "bitter" about criticism from some Party members over his failure to demand greater concessions from the government. A later report confirmed this view.[15] When Chou returned to Chungking, the nature of his mission had changed: he was no longer to appease the Americans, but to keep them out of Manchuria, where Lin Piao was preparing for war.

The agreement authorizing truce teams to enter the Northeast was signed on March 27, but both Chinese factions made sure that it never took effect. Nationalist forces obstructed movement of the teams to Shenyang, and after their arrival in that city on March 30, government officials forcibly detained the Communist members. When the first team ventured out of Shenyang in the middle of April, its Communist members were held prisoner by the commander of the Nationalist unit which the team had been sent to inspect. Not to be outdone, Chou En-lai claimed that government forces in Manchuria had exceeded the number authorized by the February Agreement on Military Reorganization and that the truce teams could not go to work until this situation was rectified.[16] The text of the agreement did not bear Chou out, but the effect was the same. Opposed by both sides, the truce teams played no role in the Northeast.

During the next few weeks, fighting in Manchuria intensified, the talks in Chungking ground to a halt, and the Communist press resumed its attacks on the United States. After his return from Yenan, Chou reopened the issue of American transport of Nationalist troops to the Northeast (which the Communists had tacitly accepted since the beginning of the Marshall Mission) and warned of "countermeasures" if the practice was not stopped. The Communist press lashed out at this and other transgressions by the Americans, both real and imagined.[17] Finally, when Marshall returned to China on April 18, the editors of Hsin Hua Jih Pao greeted him in terms decidedly different from those offered on his previous arrival: "If the United States Government resumes Hurley's policy of an anti-Soviet, anti-Communist, anti-democratic character . . . then not only will full-scale civil war result, but also world peace will be seriously menaced and grave consequences will follow."[18] On the day of Marshall's return, Lin Piao's forces occupied Changchun. One reporter found that even the mood of the Communist liaison office in Chungking, hitherto a model of diplomatic discretion, had changed to "cocky, confident." According to one Party spokesman, "control of Manchuria would be settled by force."[19]

Marshall made one last bid to stop the fighting, but it was too late. He proposed that the Communists withdraw from Changchun and permit an advance section of the Executive Headquarters to enter the city. Chou rebuffed the offer.[20] The Communists wanted no more American mediation and no more interference by the truce teams. Confident of their hold on the cities of the Northeast, they had decided to meet the Nationalists in a set-piece battle at Ssupingchieh.

The Battle of Ssupingchieh

The test of Yenan's decision to meet the Nationalists head-on came at Ssupingchieh. Occupied by Lin Piao's forces when the Soviet army withdrew on March 15, Ssupingchieh was the southernmost Communist-held city in Manchuria. Nationalist forces moving north from Shenyang would have to pass through this key railroad juncture en route to Changchun. In the past—at Shanhaikuan, for example—the Communists had avoided pitched battles with better-equipped government units, a strategy confirmed in the December 28 directive to withdraw from major cities and lines of communication in the Northeast and build base areas in the countryside. Earlier in the year, Lin appeared to ignore this directive when he concentrated his forces and struck at Hsiushuihotzu. The decision to stand and fight at Ssupingchieh was a more serious affair; in this case, the order came from Yenan.[21]

On March 21 Yenan notified Lin Piao's headquarters that "peace was hopeless." Within two weeks Lin amassed 40,000 men and promptly overran a Nationalist division located 40 miles southwest of Ssupingchieh. An observer on the government side described the Red assault as a "human sea": "Communist units of company size were dashing at Nationalist machine gun positions. No matter how many of them got killed, there was always another horde coming behind them." The effort was gallant but misguided. Lin's essay at large-scale mobile warfare, prepared under his direction in Yenan during the previous year, ended in defeat. After suffering more than 2500 casualties, he withdrew his remaining forces to Ssupingchieh.[22]

Government troops reached the gates of the city on April 16. With perhaps 70,000 men on each side, the battle at Ssupingchieh was the largest engagement in China since 1937. For five weeks they exchanged blows in what one observer described as a "toe-to-toe slugfest." Casualties ran high. The Communists were outgunned, and Lin's officers found it difficult to move divisions rather than the battalions they were used to.[23] In the end, victory and defeat turned on the question of firepower.

With the tide running against him, Lin wanted to sue for peace. In a confidential report to Yenan, he explained that Marshal Malinovsky had been dissatisfied with the Communist military effort and advised Moscow against providing further assistance. The Russians had decided to pull out and leave the Chinese Reds "to shift for themselves."[24] In the short run, the Soviet departure had helped the Communists seize Ssupingchieh. In the long run, the weight of Nationalist arms, which included American heavy artillery and airplanes, was more than the Communists could handle. Lin urged Mao to resume peace negotiations immediately.

Policymakers in Yenan refused to give up. Mao acknowledged that the Soviet Union could not help much, "because it does not feel capable of challenging the U.S. at present." But he explained to Lin that the talks must be postponed for another month to give the Communists time to recoup their strength. Throughout May, the editors of *Chieh Fang Jih Pao* underlined the importance of defending Ssupingchieh. They reported that members of one company had taken an oath to "fight to the death to hold this place, fight to the death to stop the enemy." On May 19, the very day that Lin Piao led his forces hastily out of the city, a front-page editorial praised the Democratic Allied Army for its defense of Ssupingchieh.[25]

This message to hold the line in Manchuria reflected a mood of growing belligerency in the Communist capital. In the middle of April, Mao issued a circular calling for "resolute, effective struggles by all the democratic forces of the world against the reactionary forces of the United States, Britain and France." The editors of the *Selected Works* have explained that this circular was written "to counter a pessimistic appraisal of the international situation at that time" and to combat the "erroneous thinking" of those comrades who dared not meet with force the "armed attacks of the U.S.– Chiang Kai-shek reactionary gang." Another sign of the temper in Yenan was the May 4 directive on land reform, the first official authorization by the Party center to move beyond the "reduction of rent and interest" to redistribution of land. This was on the whole a moderate document, which fell far short of the radical attack on property already underway in Communist areas east of the Yellow River.[26] But it was nonetheless a significant first step toward sharpening class struggle to mobilize support for the coming civil war.

Despite these exhortations, the Communist position at Ssupingchieh caved in. On the morning of May 19 Lin Piao led his forces out of the city, marching north in scattered units to avoid the pursuit of Nationalist aircraft.[27] Once on the move, they also abandoned Changchun and did not stop until they reached the far shore of the Sungari River in early June.

The Last Cease-Fire

After the defeat at Ssupingchieh, the Communists at first appeared ready to sue for peace. Chou En-lai told Marshall that Yenan would accept his proposal to withdraw from Changchun in exchange for a cease-fire. The Communist press halted attacks on the United States and expressed "great sympathy" for Marshall's efforts to restore peace. In Peiping and in the field, Communist commanders evinced a new willingness to stop the fighting.[28]

Weeks earlier the Communists might have swapped Changchun for a cease-fire as Marshall had suggested. After they abandoned that city, the bargaining chip was lost. With Lin Piao in full retreat, the generalissimo proceeded to the Northeast. On the day of his arrival (May 23), Nationalist forces occupied Changchun. Marshall urged Chiang to call off the offensive and return to Nanking (site of the Nationalist capital after May 1). Chiang refused.[29]

Despite efforts by Marshall and Chou to restore the cease-fire, Yenan's patience had lapsed.[30] On June 1, after a week of silence and without apparent provocation, Chieh Fang Jih Pao renewed its criticism of American policy in China. Four days later, just forty-eight hours after Chou had informed Yenan of Marshall's most recent proposal, the official Party organ printed its harshest attack on the United States since the summer of 1945.[31]

Finally, Marshall persuaded both sides to accept a temporary cease-fire, which was later extended to the end of June, but by this late date events had moved beyond the control of the diplomats.

In the Northeast, where Communist and Nationalist forces were separated by the wide Sungari, the cease-fire served to formalize an already existing quiet. South of the Great Wall, however, in Shantung and Kiangsu, the announcement of the truce coincided with the onset of the most intense fighting to date. Policymakers in Yenan were convinced that the United States was encouraging the government to prosecute the civil war. At the same time, the instruments of American power in China continued to decline: on May 1 the China Theater was deactivated; in early June the United States announced further reduction of the Marines in north China, lowering their number to 25,252.[32] By the end of June the last cease-fire had run its course. Fed up with American behavior and with less reason to fear American retaliation, on July 7 Yenan announced its final break with the United States:

> Let us ask how did the reactionary group of our country sustain its dictatorship and civil war after the war. The answer is the world-known fact of armed intervention on the part of [the] American reactionary clique and its so-called "aid to China." If it were not for this intervention, we would have achieved democracy [a] long time ago and the civil war could not have survived. . . . American imperialism is far more dangerous than the Japanese imperialism as the former has a more "civilized" and "legal" outlook and the tools it uses are the capitalism of anti-fascism and the asset of traditional friendship between the people of the United States and China. It breeds traitors and bears potential danger.[33]

Soon Yenan escalated its attacks from words to deeds. At the end of July, Communist forces ambushed a Marine convoy near the village of Anping, 35 miles southeast of Peiping. The commanding officer and three other Americans were killed. One Marine observer noted that firing had been exchanged at that spot three days earlier, so the ambush may have been a retaliatory strike.[34] In any case it was well planned, for the scene lay midway between Peiping and Tientsin, out of range of radio contact with either city.[35] As General Marshall later told a congressional investigation, the incident at Anping was a "definite departure" from previous Communist behavior and a "deliberate break" in relations between the two sides. Attempts by Communist members of the Executive Headquarters to block an investigation of the affair prompted a press statement by Marshall and the new American ambassador,

Leighton Stuart, which was widely regarded as a declaration that American mediation was at an end. This suited Yenan, which responded on August 14 with its first direct attack on Marshall himself.[36] The following day, Marshall confided to a top aide: "This is it. It's all over. We're through in China."[37]

Civil war came to China when the foreign powers, whose intervention had temporarily delayed the final reckoning, got out of the way. The Soviet withdrawal from Manchuria opened up an area which both Chinese factions were confident they could control. The American military presence in north China was rapidly declining, and Washington's ability to grant or withhold aid to the National government was not sufficient to induce cooperation from either side. Both great powers had urged the Chinese to settle their differences peacefully, and when their power appeared great, their words were heeded. When that leverage disappeared, however, Communists and Nationalists got on with the business of war.

The resumption of civil war led to Yenan's attack on the Americans. Some Communists, notably Chou En-lai, must have pointed out that American-Kuomintang relations were badly strained and that Yenan could hasten a rupture by continuing to cooperate with Marshall while pinning the onus for conflict on Chiang Kai-shek. Policymakers in the Communist capital did not see it that way. The Americans were arming Nationalist troops, transporting them to the battlefield, and assisting the government in countless other ways. Yenan was at war, and the Americans were aiding the enemy. Mobilizing for civil war meant abandoning the united front for a struggle against class enemies at home and "imperialists" abroad.

Conclusion

This work has presented the case that during its inception, Chinese Communist foreign policy followed the dictates of circumstances more than ideas. The Communists acted not according to some ideology or vision of world order, but simply in response to the limits and opportunities of the situation they found themselves in. Three major factors constrained the choices of policymakers in Yenan. First, there was the environment in China: opportunities for military expansion were good, those for political settlement with the government were poor. Second, there were the forces within the Party: the military commanders wanted to fight, few members of the post–Cheng Feng leadership opposed them with efforts to restore the united front. Both these factors hastened the coming of civil war and strained relations with the great powers. Third, there was the behavior of the Russians and Americans themselves. The power of the foreigners in China was great, and for the most part they used it to support national unification under the leadership of Chiang Kai-shek. The Communists had to maneuver around this situation: now mollifying, cooperating, trying to edge the foreigners in their direction; then fighting, seeking to divide Moscow and Washington and win Russian support in the coming conflict. Neither strategy met with much success. In the end, it was the departure of foreign power that freed both parties in China from unwanted interference and set the course toward civil war.

Throughout this period, events on the battlefield and opportunities for military expansion dominated Yenan's options in all areas. In 1944 the Ichigo Offensive prompted remobilization of Red forces and invited them to push south into Kuomintang territory and east to meet the Americans on the coast. In 1945 the sudden collapse of the Japanese sent Communist troops hurtling toward the cities of north China and over the Great Wall into Manchuria. In 1946 the withdrawal of the Soviet army left Lin Piao in command of northern Manchuria and persuaded the Communists to make their stand at Ssupingchieh. Admist this chaos, clubs alone were trump. Yenan had either to lead the armed advance or let the centrifugal force of spontaneous local initiative tear the Communist movement apart.

The attraction of these military opportunities was enhanced by knowledge that Yenan could make no comparable gains through peaceful negotiation. By the end of World War II the Communists and Nationalists had little confidence in one another. During the war Chiang squelched plans for a unified Chinese army under Stilwell's command, which would have sent American arms to the Communists, and flatly rejected any formula for sharing power with Yenan. He offered no concessions at the Chungking talks in the fall of 1945. Finally, when he did agree to the sweeping reforms worked out in early 1946, these were overturned by right-wing forces determined to destroy Communism in China. Without absolving the Communists of responsibility for the failure to achieve peace, the fact remains that the government was never willing to accept Yenan's minimum demand for a coalition or some sort of autonomy within a divided state.

The balance of forces within the Communist movement hastened the drift toward civil war. Military commanders in Yenan and the outlying base areas were determined to seize the opportunities on the battlefield and take the offensive. They made no secret of this fact in talking to American observers with the Dixie Mission. Throughout the last year of the war, Mao's speeches and internal Party documents, such as the "Resolution on History," reveal pressures for stepped-up military operations. The commanders may have criticized Mao for the concessions he made at the Chungking talks in the fall of 1945; they certainly criticized Chou for his dealing with Marshall. Communist forces refused to cooperate with the

Peiping Executive Headquarters. In Manchuria, Lin Piao seems to have gone beyond his instructions in launching large-scale attacks against the Nationalists in early 1946.

On the other side, there is little evidence of support within Yenan for a strategy of broadening the Communist appeal at home and abroad through efforts to restore the united front. Only Mao and Chou made a substantial commitment in this direction. Both were criticized for doing so. With the single exception of Liu Shao-ch'i (and here the evidence is tainted by its Cultural Revolution provenance), no one supported their efforts. The harsh lesson of Cheng Feng seems to have quenched enthusiasm for the line once championed by Wang Ming.

All of this left Yenan with little room to maneuver in dealing with the great powers. During the war, both Washington and Moscow urged the Chinese to settle their differences and concentrate on resisting Japan. The Communists, led by Mao and Chou, tried to persuade the Allies that they would restore the united front, but after the spring of 1945 even this pretense was dropped as fighting between the two factions intensified. Again that fall, following announcement of the Sino-Soviet Treaty, Mao joined talks aimed at forestalling the conflict, but the Communist move into Manchuria and the government assault on Shanhaikuan provoked renewed hostilities. Finally, the Moscow-Chungking agreement to restore Kuomintang sovereignty in the Northeast and the arrival of the Marshall Mission led to another cease-fire, but the conviction shared by Communists and Nationalists that they could seize power in Manchuria destroyed this last chance for peace. However much they may have wanted foreign support, policymakers in Yenan were outpaced by the momentum toward civil war.

Finally, Yenan's foreign policy was a response to the behavior of the great powers themselves. During the period of this study, the Chinese Communists were an ill-equipped insurgent group seeking to take control of a poor and backward country. Foreign power loomed large in China; however they dealt with it, the Communists could not ignore it. For the most part, Yenan found itself at odds with Moscow and Washington. When the Russians and Americans united behind Chungking and a program of peaceful reunification, when there was reason to hope that a show of moderation might be rewarded by support from abroad, Yenan sought cooperation with the foreigners and peace with the Kuomintang. At times, however, Washington openly backed Chungking against the Communists, while Moscow appeared to tilt toward Yenan. When American support for the Nationalists proved obnoxious and when there was reason to hope that the Russians might agree to change their tack, Yenan broke with the government, attacked American "imperialism," and sought Soviet support in the coming civil war. In either case, the foreigners were mostly a hindrance; on only a few occasions were they (especially the Russians) much of a help. In the end, the decline of foreign power in China convinced the Communists that they could cast off the burden of courting the outsiders and settle the matter by force.

After the middle of 1944, American power in the Far East mounted, while the disposition of this power on the mainland grew less certain. The dispatch of the Dixie Mission, the plans for Stilwell's command, the initiatives by Hurley and Wedemeyer—all these actions indicated that Washington might adopt a more even-handed policy in China. Hoping to minimize U.S. aid to Chungking and perhaps to win a slice of that aid for themselves, the Communists did their best to accommodate the Americans. They cooperated with American officials in Chungking and Yenan, offered a "democratic" plan for unifying China, and moved forces toward the coast where they might link up with an Allied landing party. They may even have delayed for a time the advance of Red forces to the south in order to avoid conflict with the Kuomintang. Despite the evidence that Washington would not in fact reverse its policy—the recall of Stilwell, the intransigence of Hurley and Wedemeyer, the confirmation of Hurley's views in the April 2 press conference—Yenan continued this friendly line through the spring of 1945. With Nationalist defenses collapsing, with the first signs of Japan's demise, with the Russians tied down in Europe, American power was a significant factor in China and one which the Communists could not ignore.

The shift of Yenan's policy at the Seventh Party Congress—the move toward open civil war and connectedly the attack on American "imperialism"—was prompted by perceived changes in American behavior. News of a possible settlement between Washington and Tokyo which would enhance American influence in postwar China; the OSS-KMT project to aid puppet forces north of the Yellow River and pave the way for a Kuomintang return; the arrest of John Service on charges which suggested an anti-Communist witch hunt; all these signs helped persuade Yenan that the Americans would continue to back Chungking, come what may. Yenan's attack on the "imperialists" was part of a campaign to mobilize popular support, drive a wedge between the United States and the Soviet Union, and win Russian aid in the coming civil war.

During most of the war, Moscow was preoccupied with events in Europe and wielded little influence over Yenan. The Russians, like the Americans, advised the Communists to support the united front. Mao was apparently solicitous toward Soviet agents in Yenan, and the ostensible offers to reach a settlement with Chungking were undoubtedly aimed at Moscow as well as Washington. Until the very end of the war, however, there were no Russian troops in China, and the Communists saw no reason to follow the dictates of what was then only a "paper" ally. Instead, in the summer of 1945 Yenan offered Moscow its own advice: The Soviet Union should recognize that the Grand Alliance against Fascism was giving way to a postwar struggle between capitalism and socialism and join the battle in China.

Two events persuaded Yenan to change its tune: the entry of the Russian army into Manchuria and the signing of the Sino-Soviet Treaty. After the end of the war both great powers occupied cities and lines of communication adjacent to Communist strongholds: the Americans in north China, the Russians in Manchuria. Both recognized the Nationalist government and urged Yenan to seek a settlement. Facing the combined strength of the victorious Allies, the Communists were left with little choice. Mao agreed to join the talks in Chungking; and in the field, Yenan's forces sought cooperation with foreign troops in an effort to slow the Kuomintang advance north and expand the area of Communist control. Above the Great Wall this strategy worked well, as the Russians cooperated with the Communist takeover of large portions of Manchuria. It failed in north China, where the Americans refused the Reds entry into the cities, moved in Nationalist troops, and finally supported the government offensive against Shanhaikuan.

The second shift of Communist foreign policy, at the end of October 1945, followed the same pattern as the first. Again, American behavior prompted the change. When the Marines backed the Nationalist assault on Shanhaikuan, they crossed the line of acceptable behavior and forced the Communists to respond. On this occasion, more than during the war, there was reason to believe the Russians might side with Yenan. The war was over, the Grand Alliance dissolved; Soviet-American conflict had begun to surface; and the Russians were tilting in favor of Communist expansion into Manchuria. Again, Yenan attacked American "imperialism" and sought Soviet support in preparation for civil war.

As on the previous occasion, however, the Russians rejected Yenan's advice. The Moscow-Chungking agreement of November 27 removed Communist forces from the cities of Manchuria and promised support for a Nationalist takeover of the region. Moscow would not challenge Washington in China; both powers remained wedded to the Kuomintang regime. Again, the Communists were forced to retreat a step, resume the talks, and try to edge the foreigners to their side.

Throughout early 1946, Yenan sought cooperation on both foreign policy fronts. In Chungking, Marshall oversaw agreements to halt the fighting and form a coalition government. The Communists encouraged this trend, which promised to erode American support for the Central government. In Manchuria the Russians refused to cooperate with the Nationalists as agreed, and the impending departure of the Soviet army pointed toward a Communist takeover of much of the region. At a time when almost everyone in China was critical of the Russians, Yenan came out enthusiastically in their defense.

As this late date, however, the decline of foreign power had reduced the influence of both Moscow and Washington over events in China. The Russian departure from Manchuria left Communist and Nationalist forces to fight for control of Ssupingchieh. The Marine presence in north China was shrinking, and while American aid to the Kuomintang continued, it was apparent that the Americans could no longer control Chiang Kai-shek. Yenan, and Chungking as well, had heeded the foreigners because they recognized the importance of foreign power on the mainland. Now the Russians were gone and the Americans were going. Left to their own devices, Chinese on both sides agreed to fight.

If ideology, Mao's "view of the world," played such a small role in this story, it is because the Chinese Communists were weak and the forces surrounding them—the reality of China, the divisions within the Party, the role of the foreign powers on the mainland— were strong. Yenan lacked the muscle to apply a master plan. The Communists did the only thing they could do: push here, pull there, inch their way toward victory.

Proponents of the "lost chance in China" school might welcome this picture of a pragmatic Yenan. These students of Sino-American relations have argued that during the 1940s, there was a chance for Americans and Chinese Communists to reach an understanding which would have prevented much of the pain and bitterness of the subsequent decades.[1] Was there a "lost chance in China"? What does the evidence of the mid-1940s show?

First, it shows that the United States could have acted differently. Within the limits imposed by its formal relations with the National government, Washington could have pursued an even-handed policy in China: aiding all parties willing to resist Japan; aiding no party which would use American arms in a civil war. During the war, this would have required some assistance to Yenan along the lines favored by Barrett, the Foreign Service officers, and others. After the war, it would have meant cessation of aid to the Nationalists when it became clear (as it did at least as early as October 1945) that they would use this aid to fight the Communists. There is no reason to believe that the United States could have prevented the Chinese civil war or significantly altered its outcome. At best, the Americans might have acted as the Russians did: withdrawn their forces, stepped aside to await the outcome of the conflict, and made their peace with the winner.

The evidence also suggests that Yenan would have responded favorably to such behavior. Despite the gains made during the war, the Chinese Communists were still weak in both resources and experience (especially experience in running the cities, railroads, and "modern" sectors of the economy). The Americans had a great deal to offer, and Yenan tried to play ball with them. There is no evidence that Communist ideology prohibited cooperation with the United States. Rather, it was *after* the Americans had turned against the Communists—first in May 1945, again in October 1945, and finally in the spring and summer of 1946—that Yenan used ideology as an instrument to mobilize public opinion and appeal for Soviet support. If the American military had aided the Communists, cooperation between the two sides might have developed its own momentum. If the Americans had halted aid to the Nationalists, Yenan would have had no reason to view the United States as an enemy.

Would this have prevented the Cold War in Asia? The evidence provides no answer to this question. When the civil war ended and the Communists took charge of Peking, they entered a dangerous and sharply divided world. Their earlier experience must have made them suspicious of the Americans and contributed to the decision to "lean" to the side of the Soviet Union. It does not follow, however, that a different, more positive experience would have been sufficient to overcome the fear and hostility engendered by global Soviet-American confrontation of the late 1940s. We have noted, after all, that during the mid-1940s the Russians behaved as wisely as any foreign power in China could—namely they got out and let the Chinese settle matters on their own. Yet this did not prevent a bitter confrontation between Peking and Moscow when other times and circumstances set them at odds. As this study shows, circumstances rather than perceptions have been the dominant force in shaping Chinese Communist behavior. If there was a "chance" for Sino-American rapprochement, it must be found in a similar examination of the events of 1949 and 1950.

Our story also sheds light on the relationship between foreign policy and the internal politics of the Chinese Communist Party. Some scholars have noted the persistent conflict between "internationalist" and "nativist" factions within the Party—the former more, the latter less sympathetic to Moscow—with Mao consistently ranged on the "nativist" side.[2] This basic cleavage, they argue, contributed to Mao's successive purges of rivals identified with the Soviet Union: Wang Ming, Kao Kang, P'eng Teh-huai, Lo Jui-ch'ing, Liu Shao-ch'i, Teng Hsiao-p'ing, Lin Piao. Stuart Schram goes even further to forge the link between the foreign and domestic aspects of Mao's ultranationalist impulse:

Mao's conviction that the countryside, though it must assimilate modern knowledge, is not inferior to the city, is intimately linked to his belief that the Chinese need not regard themselves as inferior to the foreigners. Here lies the nub of his rebellion, not only against Soviet domination, but against the whole Europe-centred logic of Marxism.[3]

In precisely this manner, the Rectification Campaign shaped the political environment in which Yenan's foreign policy was made. Mao used this Intra-Party struggle to crush his opponents by identifying them with the shortcomings of urban man, especially his submission to foreign influence. The threat of Wang Ming lay in his ties to Moscow and the potential for Soviet interference in Chinese Communist affairs. But the message of Cheng Feng cut a wider swath, razing all notions of compromise with the urban bourgeoisie, represented by the Kuomintang, and its foreign supporters.

It would be wrong, however, to picture Mao or Yenan as trapped in the confines of a narrow "nativist" vision. As we have seen, after the middle of 1944, Mao, the erstwhile champion of independence and rural revolution, led successive moves, apparently against internal opposition, toward restoring the united front and connectedly winning American and Soviet support. Recognizing the reality of foreign power, Mao acted not on the basis of prior perceptions but in response to hard and stubborn facts. That he had helped shape the internal political environment which made this diplomatic shift more difficult was an irony of his situation.[4] Still, circumstances more than ideas dominated Yenan's behavior.

Finally, we might ask, What was the legacy of the Yenan experience? What did the Chinese Communists learn from their first attempts to deal with the great powers? What did they learn about the world and about China's place in It? Answering such questions is a matter for speculation. So let us speculate.

First, these events must have confirmed the suspicions of Mao and at least some of his colleagues that the Soviet Union was not a reliable ally. On two occasions—first in the fall of 1945, again in the spring of 1946—the Soviet army gave aid, passive at least, active at best, to the Communist takeover of Manchuria. But just as often—in the Sino-Soviet Treaty and the Moscow-Chungking agreement of November 1945—the Russians tilted toward the Kuomintang. In the end, the Soviet departure left the Communists with no foreign ally to offset the considerable help Chiang was getting from the Americans. The zig-zag course of Russian policy made sense only as Stalin's attempt to get the most he could out of Manchuria, to keep China divided and weak, and finally to induce Washington to withdraw its forces from the mainland of Asia. Yenan could count on Moscow only when their interests happened to coincide. The Soviets had no consistent policy of helping a fraternal Communist Party.

Similarly, this first experience in dealing with the Americans must have helped persuade the Communists that the United States was an enemy. During the war, Washington clung to the moribund and ineffective Kuomintang regime which contributed so little to the defeat of Japan, while refusing to aid Communist forces who at least promised to fight. After the war, the Americans continued to arm and transport Nationalist troops long after it became clear that their only purpose was to crush the opposition at home. If Marxist ideology prepared the Communists to see the United States as an enemy, the experience of these years proved the ideology right.

Ultimately, the Communists must have learned that the only sensible strategy was to rely on themselves, expand their power, and deal with all outsiders from a position of strength. "Self-reliance" is a phrase which runs throughout the documents of this period, those written both by the Communists and about them. Again and again during the next three decades, Mao returned to the theme of tzu-li keng-sheng or "regeneration through our own efforts." Some scholars have traced the roots of this theme to the Yenan experience.[5] It had much to do with the early formation of Chinese Communist foreign policy and with the lessons the Communists would later draw from it.

"Self-reliance" was a virtue born of necessity. As an insurgent movement, the Communists lacked foreign recognition, and the Nationalist government for the most part succeeded in blocking their contacts with the outside world. As a rural movement, tucked away in the remote hinterland, hemmed in by Kuomintang and Japanese armies, the Communists lacked access to the cities, the coast, the points and lines of international communication. The exigencies of war left Yenan with no choice except to create a network of self-sufficient economic and military cells, linked by a common ideology and a disciplined but slender organization. This was in the first instance a domestic strategy, a means of survival in a lonely, hostile environment, and largely as a result of Yenan's isolation, it was applied to foreign policy.

"Self-reliance" is an accurate description of the way Yenan made its decisions. Western scholars have differed on whether the Chinese Communists were prone to take directions from Moscow. This study confirms the view that Yenan made up its own mind. The best evidence for CCP independence comes from the periods before August 1945 and after March 1946. In both cases Moscow advised Yenan to seek a peaceful settlement with the Kuomintang, and the Communists opted for civil war. During the nine-month interim, Russian influence on the Communists was important, in some cases even decisive. This had nothing to do with Moscow's organizational or ideological hold over Yenan, however. It simply reflected the Communists' appreciation of Russian power in China. Decisionmakers in Yenan called the shots; they weighed the Soviet factor like any other.

"Self-reliance" did not mean autarky. On the contrary, the Communists were acutely aware of foreign power in China and did their best to attract support from the Americans and the Russians. The slogan describes rather the means by which Yenan went after foreign aid. The Communists knew that their military might had drawn American observers to Yenan; they appealed for aid by showing their visitors what they had accomplished. If persuasion failed, they would try to capture a portion of the coast and barter support for an Allied landing in exchange for American arms. Similarly, after the war Communist forces pushed into Manchuria not on the assumption that the Russians would offer aid freely, but in the knowledge that a foreign army would need the cooperation of whoever controlled the countryside. Red forces followed the same strategy with the Marines in north China. In both cases, the sympathy of the foreigners was inconstant, and the Communists fell back on their own resources.

"Self-reliance" was most of all a psychological and political weapon. The Central Committee directive "On Diplomatic Work" set the tone for Yenan's attitude toward the outside world. The Communists would welcome foreign visitors and what they brought with them, but the Chinese people were never again to supplicate for favors from abroad. "We must intensify the feeling of national self-respect and faith in ourselves," Yenan decreed. "This is what constitutes the correct national platform, this is what constitutes the essence of the prototype of the new man in new democratic China."[6] This message was meant to kindle pride and stiffen backbones among the Party faithful. It was also a selling point, a reason for following the Communists rather than the flaccid and sycophantic Kuomintang. "We are not like Chiang Kai-shek," Mao boasted. "No nation needs to prop us up. We can stand erect and walk on our own feet like free men."[7]

The theme of "self-reliance" is an important part of the Yenan legacy. It has placed no limits on subsequent Chinese foreign policy. After the victory in 1949, Peking was quick to turn to the Soviet Union for assistance in defending China and rebuilding its economy. Today, the outside world is still a source of capital and expertise for China's modernization. But "self-reliance" has been evoked during those periods, such as the Great Leap Forward and the Cultural Revolution, when Mao sought to rekindle the Yenan spirit. It serves as a reminder that China is a poor country, caught between the two "super-powers" and subject to the whims of decisions over which the Chinese have no control. And it remains a part of the myth of how the Communists liberated China from the twin scourge of feudalism and imperialism. When the Yenan myth is revived, when it is brought forward as a symbol of the wisdom of the founding fathers, its lesson will be that reliance on the elemental force of the Chinese peasant is a more reliable means of restoring the unity and greatness of China than a course which depends on the cities and the foreign interests imbedded therein. This myth need not dictate the future course of Chinese foreign policy, but it remains a powerful instrument in the hands of those who choose to assert Chinese independence and national pride.

Notes

Abbreviations

Barbey Papers	Personal Papers of Admiral Daniel E. Barbey
CCP	Chinese Communist Party
CFJP	*Chieh Fang Jih Pao*
CPR	*Chinese Press Review*
FRUS	U.S. Department of State, *Foreign Relations of the United States: Diplomatic Papers*
HHJP	*Hsin Hua Jih Pao*
HHLY	Hsing Huo Liao Yüan (A Single Spark Can Light a Prairie Fire)
JPRS	Joint Publications Research Service
MTtC	Mao Tse-tung Chi (Works of Mao Tse-tung)
NRC	National Records Center
R&S	Charles F. Romanus and Riley Sunderland, *U.S. Army in World War II: The China-Burma-India Theater*
SCMM	*Selections from China Mainland Magazines*
SCMP	*Survey of the China Mainland Press*
SCMP/Sup	*Survey of the China Mainland Press*/Supplement
SW (London) / SW (Peking)	*Selected Works of Mao Tse-tung*, London or Peking edition
URI	Union Research Institute
USMC	United States Marine Corps

Introduction

1. In addition to the works mentioned below, the most recent attempts to explain CCP foreign policy during the 1940s in terms of Communist perceptions of international relations are Okabe Tatsumi, "The Cold War and China," Franz Schurmann, *The Logic of World Power* (New York: Pantheon, 1974), pp. 214–15, and articles by Steven Goldstein and Michael Hunt in forthcoming book on Chinese-American relations, 1947–50, edited by Waldo Heinrichs and Dorothy Borg and published by Columbia University Press.

2. Tang Tsou, *America's Failure in China*, p. 213.

3. John Gittings, *The World and China*, pp. 8–9, 12, 213, 260. For a similar treatment of CCP statements on international affairs during the late 1930s see Steven M. Goldstein, "Chinese Communist Perspectives on International Affairs."

4. See, for example, Robert G. Sutter, *China-Watch*, ch. 2; and Donald Zagoria, "Mao's Role in the Sino-Soviet Conflict."

5. John S. Service, *The Amerasia Papers*, p. 183.

6. Some notable examples are David Mozingo, *Chinese Policy toward Indonesia, 1949–67* (Ithaca, N.Y.: Cornell University Press, 1976); Robert Simmons, *The Strained Alliance: Peking, Pyongyang, Moscow and the Politics of the Korean Civil War* (New York: Free Press, 1975); and Allen S. Whiting, *The Chinese Calculus of Deterrence: India and Indochina* (Ann Arbor: University of Michigan Press, 1975).

7. For a description of the Bureau of Investigation holdings see Peter Donovan, Carl E. Dorris, and Lawrence Sullivan, *Chinese Communist Materials at the Bureau of Investigation Archives, Taiwan* (Ann Arbor: Center of Chinese Studies, University of Michigan, 1976).

1. The Politics of War (1935–1943)

1. Edgar Snow, *Red Star over China*, p. 152.

2. Stuart Schram, *Mao Tse-tung*, pp. 41, 53.

3. *Wang Ming Hsüan-chi*, 1:7, cited in Tetsuya Kataoka, *Resistance and Revolution in China*, p. 24. Unless otherwise noted, the following discussion of the debate between Mao and Wang is based on Kataoka and on Gregor Benton, "The 'Second Wang Ming Line' (1935–38)."

4. *M Tt C*, 5:34, in Kataoka, p. 31. This quotation is from the Wayaopao Resolution of December 1935.

5. Kataoka, pp. 59–60; Benton, "The 'Second Wang Ming Line' (1935–38)."

6. Mao Tse-tung, "On the New Stage," in Stuart Schram, *The Political Thought of Mao Tse-tung*, p. 288.

7. Mao Tse-tung, *SW* (Peking), 2:366.

8. Pyotr P. Vladimirov, *China's Special Area*, p. 72, notes: "The 'dogmatists' are accused of the desire to shift the brunt of the revolutionary struggle from the village on to the town and win victory 'through the towns.' According to Mao Tse-tung, this is the basic mistake of the 'dogmatists.' " Vladimirov was a TASS agent in Yenan from 1942 to 1945. His diary will be discussed further in ch. 5. Benton states that Wang "envisaged an end to the land revolution in the interests of national unity" (p. 66).

9. Lo Fu, "K'ang-Jih min-tsu t'ung-i chan-hsien-chung ti tso-ch'ing wei-hsien" (Left deviation danger in the anti-Japanese national United Front) (August 10, 1940), in *Kung-fei Huo-kuo, 3*:452–53, cited in Kataoka, p. 198.

10. Cited in *Amerasia* (May 1941), 5(3):113.

11. For the debate between Mao and the military opposition during the Encirclement Campaigns see Schram, *Mao Tse-tung,* pp. 156 ff. For the debate at the Ningtu Conference of 1932 see James Harrison, *The Long March to Power,* p. 229. And at the Lochuan Conference of 1937 see Harrison, pp. 283–84; Kataoka, pp. 57–61; William Whitson, *The Chinese High Command,* pp. 67–68; Chang Kuo-t'ao, *The Autobiography of Chang Kuo-t'ao,* pp. 526–41; SCMP, no. 4007, p. 9; *SCMP/* sup, no. 175, p. 2.

12. Mao's most important works on military strategy were published in 1938: "Problems of Strategy in Guerrilla War against Japan," "On Protracted War," and "Problems of War In Strategy." All appear in *SW,* (Peking) vol. 2. They are discussed in Kataoka, pp. 75 ff.

13. Kataoka, pp. 69–71.

14. Kataoka (pp. 59–60) reports that the Kuomintang proposed to attach its officers as cadres of Communist forces. Mao opposed this move as a compromise of Yenan's independence. Chou En-lai and Chu Teh favored the offer. Chang Wen-t'ien worked out a compromise (see also Benton, p. 75).

15. Kataoka, p. 70.

16. For P'eng's role in the Hundred Regiments Offensive see Donald W. Klein and Anne B. Clark, *Biographic Dictionary of Chinese Communism,* 2:737; JPRS, no. 49826, p. 10; URI, *The Case of P'eng Teh-huai,* pp. 2, 33 ff., 190–93. For Chu's role see *SCMP/*sup, no. 175, p. 3. These materials assert that Mao was ignorant of the planning of the offensive, but I agree with Kataoka (p. 216) that it is more likely that Mao knew of the plan but opposed it.

17. Whitson, pp. 70–71.

18. *Ibid.,* p. 74; Harrison, p. 316.

19. A. M. Dubinsky, *The Far East in the Second World War,* pp. 120–21.

20. Ngok Lee, "The Chinese Communist Bases in North China," p. 110, cited in Whitson, p. 74, n. 92.

21. This is confirmed in the official history of the CCP: Ho Kan-chih, *A History of the Modern Chinese Revolution,* p. 377. For evidence from contemporary sources see Boyd Compton, *Mao's China,* p. 37.

22. For criticism of the military in the *Cheng Feng* Documents see Compton, pp. 26, 151, 161, 166, 221–22. For specific reference to "warlordism" see Whitson, pp. 76, 166. Criticism of P'eng Teh-huai during *Cheng Feng* is noted in URI, *Case of P'eng Teh-huai,* p. 193, and *SCMP/*sup, no. 175, p. 11.

23. Compton, p. 221.

24. The text of this resolution is in Compton, p. 161.

25. Chang Kuo-t'ao, p. 521, and Harrison, p. 321, give details on these students.

26. Compton, p. 55.

27. *Ibid.,* pp. 16–17.

28. *Ibid.,* p. 37.

29. *CFJP* May 28, 1943, translated in Schram, *Political Thought of Mao Tse-tung,* pp. 422–23.

30. Lowell Dittmer, *Liu Shao-ch'i and the Cultural Revolution* (Berkeley: University of California Press, 1974), pp. 20 ff.

31. Snow, *Red Star over China,* p. 406.

32. Jack Belden, *China Shakes the World,* p. 68.

33. *Ibid.,* p. 67.

2.   Fight or Talk *(January–July 1944)*

1. For details on the Stilwell-Chennault debate see Charles F. Romanus and Riley Sunderland, *Stilwell's Mission to China,* part 1, pp. 176, 279–82, 320. This is the first of three parts dealing with the China-Burma-India Theater in the series *United States Army in World War II,* vol. 9 (cited hereinafter as R&S, 1).

2. Barbara Tuchman, *Stilwell and the American Experience in China,* pp. 357–60.

3. In April 1944 it was reported that shipping from Japan to Southeast Asia, which passed through the Formosa Straits, had been reduced by one-third *(New York Times,* April 20, 1944, p. 18:2).

4. The following discussion of the Ichigo Offensive is based on Charles F. Romanus and Riley Sunderland, *Stilwell's Command Problems,* part 2, pp. 316–28, 364–74, 405–9, 433–36; and Romanus and Sunderland, *Time Runs out in CBI,* part 3, pp. 49–56, 164–70 (cited hereinafter respectively as R&S, 2, and R&S, 3).

5. R&S, 1, p. 320.

6. Hu Hua, *Chung-kuo Hsin-min-chu chu-i ke-ming shih,* p. 249, places Nationalist losses at 600,000–700,000 soldiers; 2,000,000+ sq. km.; and 60,000,000+ people. For a slightly different estimate see John Hunter Boyle, *China and Japan at War,* p. 319.

7. *FRUS,* 1944, 6:199–200, 207, 724.

8. Whitson, p. 76; Lyman P. Van Slyke, ed., *The Chinese Communist Movement,* pp. 114–15, 119; R&S, 2, p. 319.

9. For confirmation of this point by General Okamura, commander of the Japanese China Expeditionary Army in 1944, see Samuel B. Griffith, *The Chinese People's Liberation Army,* p. 75.

10. Van Slyke, *The Chinese Communist Movement,* p. 119; Michael Lindsay, "China, 1937–1945," p. 168.

11. Parris Chang, "Honan," in Edwin Winkler, ed., *Provinces of China* (Stanford, Calif.: Stanford University Press, forthcoming).

12. *FRUS,* 1944, 6:100, 193, 384; *FRUS,* 1945, 7:164–68; *New York Times,* October 31, 1944, p. 4:3.

13. Yeh Hu-sheng, *Jen-min ti Sheng-li,* pp. 105–7. For the CCP version of the events in Honan during 1944 see *ibid.;* Hu Hua, pp. 252–53; Ch'i Wu, *I ke Ke-ming Ken-chü-ti ti Ch'eng-chang,* pp. 239–40; *FRUS,* 1945, 7:164–68.

14. Ch'i Wu, p. 239; Ho Kan-chih, *A History of the Modern Chinese Revolution,* p. 409; *K'ang-jih Chan-cheng Shih-ch'i ti Chung-kuo Jen-min Chieh-fang-Chün,* pp. 176–80. Yeh Hu-sheng (p. 99) gives the same figures for the period July 1943–July 1944, but I prefer the former sources and think that the claims are more likely sustained for the calendar year 1944.

15. Harrison, p. 307.

16. *Ibid.; K'ang-Jih Chan-cheng* . . . , p. 180; Hu Hua, p. 253; Yeh Hu-sheng, pp. 106–8, 109; Van Slyke, pp. 180–82; Harrison, p. 307; Klein and Clark, 2:805, 866.

17. *FRUS,* 1945, 7:248; Edgar Snow, *Random Notes on Red China,* p. 128.

18. That the Communists were aware of Nimitz's statements is demonstrated by reporting of these statements in CCP press. See for example, *Chieh Fang Jih Pao*, August 22, 1944, p. 1. One source with access to Nimitz's thinking on this subject claims that the statements to the press were made for the purpose of distracting Japanese attention from the real target, which was the Philippines (R&S, 2, p 457).

19. Mao Tse-tung, "Our Study and the Current Situation," *SW*, (Peking) 3:171 72.

20. *Ibid.*, p. 166.

21. Harrison, pp. 229, 283; Whitson, pp. 68, 156.

22. John S. Service, Report no. 19, August 31, 1944, in U.S. Congress, Senate, Committee on the Judiciary, *The Amerasia Papers*, 1:818 (cited hereinafter as Service, report number, date, and page in *Amerasia Papers*. A complete list of these reports and where they can be found in various publications appears in Service, *The Amerasia Papers*, pp. 193 ff.).

23. Service, Report no. 7, August 4, 1944, p. 735.

24. Service, Report no. 19, August 31, 1944, p. 820.

25. *Ibid.*, p. 821.

26. For details on the Li Chi-shen faction and its activities during this period see *FRUS*, 1944, 6:318, 414, 419, 490, 491.

27. For details on the activities of the minor parties during the war see Lyman P. Van Slyke, *Enemies and Friends*, pp. 168–84, and *FRUS*, 1944, 6:414, 458, 475.

28. *FRUS*, 1944, 6:414, 418–19, 428–29, 497, 507, 512 ff., 590.

29. R&S, 1, pp. 279, 329–33, 358–60.

30. For example, see reports by Service and Davies in *FRUS*, 1943, *China*, 193 ff., 258 ff.

31. Kenneth Shewmaker, *Americans and Chinese Communists*, pp. 142–44. This book contains the best available account of the visits by foreign observers to the Communist areas during these years.

32. Tuchman, *Stilwell*, p. 401; R&S, 2, pp. 297–302, 306–14.

33. Lyman P. Van Slyke, ed., *The China White Paper*, 2:549, 554–57.

34. In the original agreement of 1937 creating the Second United Front, the government recognized the two Communist armies and two of the Border Regions and agreed to support them with a generous monthly stipend (see Harrison, pp. 278 ff.).

35. Discussion of the Yugoslav model and its relevance for China can be found in *FRUS*, 1944, 6:431, 473, 639, 710.

36. For details on the biographies of these individuals see Klein and Clark, and Donald W. Klein, "The Management of Foreign Affairs in Communist China," pp. 307–10.

37. For details of Chou's life see Hsü Kai-yu, *Chou En-lai*.

38. Harrison, pp. 229, 283; Klein and Clark, 1:208 9; *CFJP*, August 6, 1943, cited by Hsü Kai-yu, p. 141. See also Klein and Clark, 1:211.

39. Chang Kuo-t'ao, p. 497.

3. *The American Connection (August–October 1944)*

1. David D. Barrett, *Dixie Mission*, p. 24.

2. Warren I. Cohen, "The Development of Chinese Communist Policy toward the United States, 1922–1933," pp. 220 ff., and "The Development of Chinese Communist Policy toward the United States, 1934–1945," pp. 553 ff. See also Schram, *Mao*

Tse-tung, pp. 214 ff., and Goldstein, "Chinese Communist Perspectives in International Affairs."

3. For a description of the foreign journalists who visited Yenan during the 1930s see Shewmaker, *Persuading Encounter.*

4. See, for example, *FRUS,* 1942, *China,* p. 227; see also Shewmaker, p. 125.

5. Barrett, p. 13. This discussion of the Dixie Mission is based on the extant papers of the Mission contained in three collections: *Yenan Observer Group: Dixie Mission,* 4 vols., microfilm (1 roll), Modern Military Records Division, National Archives; "Barrett Reports" file, National Records Center, Suitland, Md.; special OSS file. The last of these consists of 41 sheets of OSS material which was turned over by the Central Intelligence Agency to the Modern Military Records Division of the National Archives circa 1973. A search by the OSS of its complete files carried out at my request revealed no further useful material. These three collections will be refered to hereinafter respectively as Dixie Mission Papers; "Barrett Reports"; OSS/CIA.

6. Barrett, pp. 29, 43–45. Reports on trips to the areas behind Japanese lines are contained in U.S. Congress, Senate, Committee on the Judiciary, *Amerasia Papers,* 2:1004, 1329, 1342.

7. *CFJP,* July 4, 1944, translated in Schram, *Mao Tse-tung,* p. 226.

8. Report from Colonel David D. Barrett to Commanding General, U.S. Forces, China Theater, August 14, 1944, in "Barrett Reports." Barrett's recommendation to aid the Communists came in this passage: "If the Communists are willing to fight and have the people on their side, it would appear that they are worthy of the support of the United States. I believe that a small amount of aid in the way of ammunition, automatic weapons, pack artillery, and signal equipment would bring immediate results. If it did not, we would have lost very little. I am in favor of giving this aid now, not to wait until we have sent out observers to cover areas from which reports cannot be received for a long time."

9. See for example *CFJP,* August 15; September 25, 28, 30; October 9, 11, 16, 18, 20, 25; November 11, 20, 29 (all p. 1).

10. Service, Report no. 48, October 18, 1944, p. 1115; *FRUS,* 1944, 6:754.

11. Barrett, pp. 49–51.

12. *FRUS,* 1944, 6:505; Service, *Amerasia Papers,* pp. 67–74; U.S. Congress, Senate, Committee on the Judiciary, *Amerasia Papers,* 1:768–69, 776–78.

13. Klein and Clark, 2:890–92; Ma Han-ping, *Wang Chen Nan-cheng Chi,* p. 4.

14. Joseph Esherick, ed., *Lost Chance in China: The World War II Despatches of John S. Service* (New York: Random House, 1974), p. 291. Mao Tse-tung, "Talk at the Chengtu Conference," March 10, 1958, in Schram, *Chairman Mao Talks to the People,* pp. 97–98; and Michael Lindsay, "China: Report of a Visit," p. 26.

15. "CPC Central Committee Directive on Diplomatic Work."

16. *Ibid.,* p. 11.

17. Service, Report no. 15, August 27, 1944, p. 787.

18. For Mao's presentation of CCP domestic policy to foreign journalists, see interviews with Gunther Stein and Maurice Votaw, in Service, Report no. 3, July 30, 1944, pp. 691–702.

19. *Ibid.,* p. 692.

20. Service, Report no. 15, August 27, 1944, p. 796.

21. *Ibid.*

22. *Ibid.,* pp. 796–97 (italics in original).

23. Chiang's analysis of China's past and his plans for China's future were spelled out in *China's Destiny* and *Chinese Economic Theory*, first published in Chinese in 1943. For a translation of both works see Bibliography.

24. Service, Report no. 15, August 27, 1944, p. 790 (italics in original).

25. *Ibid.*, pp. 791, 792.

26. Van Slyke, *China White Paper*, 1:53–55.

27. Service, Report no. 15, August 27, 1944, pp. 790, 793, and Report no. 3, July 30, 1944, p. 703; *FRUS*, 1944, 6:590, 593.

28. Service, Report no. 3, July 30, 1944, pp. 707, 716, 717, and Report no. 15, August 27, 1944, pp. 794–95; *New York Times*, December 7, 1944, p. 16:2–3; *CFJP*, September 15, 1944, p. 1.

29. For statements by Chou En-lai, Chu Teh, and Ch'en I see U.S. Congress, Senate, Committee on the Judiciary, *Amerasia Papers*, 1:705, 716, 820, 902, and *FRUS*, 1944, 6:591. For another statement by Mao showing interest in the American landing see John Paton Davies, *Dragon by the Tail*, p. 347. For statements in the CCP press see *CFJP*, August 22, p. 1; September 15, p. 3; September 18, p. 1; October 3, p. 3; October 19 and 21, p. 1. Vladimirov (*The Special Region of China*, p. 273) states in the entry for November 23, 1944: "Mao Tse-tung has declared that the paramount task is to deprive Chiang Kai-shek's troops of the possibility of advancing to the sea coast. 'The most important task for the CPC forces is to block the area of our future joint operations with the Allies. . . .'"

30. *FRUS*, 1944, 6:160–62.

31. *Amerasia* (April 20, 1945), 9(8):120.

32. Tang Tsou, p. 174; *FRUS*, 1944, 6:662.

33. Van Slyke, *Enemies and Friends*, p. 182.

34. R&S, 2, pp. 383–07, 413–18, 422.

35. Tuchman, *Stilwell*, p. 158.

36. R&S, 1, p. 368; R&S 2, pp. 380, 429–31; Tuchman, *Stilwell*, pp. 388, 469, 485, 495.

37. One possible source of information on this and other important matters may have been Chi Ch'ao-ting, a covert CCP agent working as confidential secretary to H. H. Kung, the Nationalist's top economic expert and brother-in-law to Chiang Kai-shek. See Klein and Clark, 1:161.

38. *CFJP*, September 15, 1944, p. 1; Service, Report no. 3, July 30, 1944, pp. 697, 705, 707–9; *FRUS*, 1944, 6:591. Vladimirov noted in his entry of September 24, 1944. "Stilwell's forthcoming visit has raised great hopes in Yenan. He is being very much awaited here" (p. 241).

39. Tuchman, *Stilwell*, p. 485; *FRUS*, 1944, 6:589.

40. Service, Report no. 3, July 30, 1944, p. 705.

41. *Ibid.*, pp. 697, 707.

42. *FRUS*, 1944, 6:636.

43. Report by Brooks Atkinson in *New York Times*, October 31, 1944, p. 4:2.

44. *CFJP*, November 10, 1944, p. 1.

45. Service, Report no. 8, March 11, 1945, p. 1392.

46. Ma Han-ping, pp. 5–6. For further details on the departure of Wang Chen's expedition see Chou Li-p'o, *Nan Hsia Chi*, pp. 1–4.

47. Lindsay, "China: Report of a Visit," p. 26; Schram, *Chairman Mao Talks to the People*, pp. 97–98.

48. Barrett, pp. 31–32; *FRUS*, 1944, 6:752.
49. Chou Li-p'o, p. 4; Ma Han-ping, p. 6.

4. The American Initiatives (November 1944–February 1945)

1. Barrett, pp. 56–57; *FRUS*, 1944, 6:589, 655; *FRUS*, 1945, 7:193; *Ch'ün Chung* (The Masses) (September 30, 1944), vol. 9, no. 18, cited in Cohen, "Communist Policy," p. 563; *New York Times*, November 1, 1944, p. 4:1.
2. *New York Times*, October 8, 1944, p. 31:3.
3. The record of this meeting kept by the American side is in *FRUS*, 1944, 6:674 ff. No CCP version of the meeting with Hurley is available.
4. *Ibid.*, pp. 679–82.
5. *Ibid.*, p. 685; Barrett, p. 60.
6. *Ibid.*, p. 62.
7. *FRUS*, 1944, 6:688.
8. Colonel Barrett, who witnessed the signing of the Communist Five Point Proposal, notes that Hurley told Mao that "although I consider these fair terms, I cannot guarantee the Generalissimo will accept them." But Barrett also reports that Hurley was acting "with his eyes open and fully aware of the significance of his act . . ." (Barrett, pp. 64, 76). Hurley himself later acknowledged his role in drafting these Five Points (*FRUS*, 1944, 6:733).
9. Mao to Roosevelt, November 10, 1944, in *FRUS*, 1944, 6:688; Roosevelt to Mao, November 14, 1944, in General Wedemeyer Radios File, books 1 and 2, items nos. 201–422, part IV (Wedemeyer Files, RG 322, box 5, NRC).
10. *FRUS*, 1944, 6:693, 699. When he first saw the Communist Five Points, Nationalist Foreign Minister T. V. Soong told Hurley: "You have been sold a bill of goods by the Communists. The National Government will never grant what the Communists have requested" (*FRUS*, 1945, 7:195).
11. *FRUS*, 1945, 7:196; Barrett, p. 68. Chiang had urged the President to assign Hurley to China "on a more permanent basis" even before the resignation of Ambassador Gauss. Hurley accepted the appointment immediately and may have felt beholden to Chiang for the promotion he obviously wanted (*FRUS*, 1944, 6:170, 700).
12. *FRUS*, 1945, 7:196.
13. *FRUS*, 1944, 6:727, 728–29, 730.
14. *Ibid.*, p. 730.
15. *Ibid.*, p. 729.
16. *Ibid.*, p. 730.
17. *Ibid.*, p. 731.
18. Barrett, p. 75.
19. *FRUS*, 1944, 6:724.
20. Barrett, p. 75; *FRUS*, 1944, 6:732–33.
21. *FRUS*, 1944, 6:725.
22. R&S, 2, p. 316; *FRUS*, 1944, 6:199, 207, 724; *New York Times*, December 4, 1944, p. 1:6.

23. Ch'i Wu, p. 240; *FRUS*, 1944, 6:193–94. The information on Wang Chen is in Ma Han-ping, p. 19.

24. For contemporary claims see "A Year of Great Victories behind Enemy Lines," *CFJP*, December 31, 1944, p. 1; December 22, 25, and 30 (all p. 1); *New York Times*, December 6, p. 1:6; and *FRUS*, 1944, 6:754. For a later account of the move from Kiangsu to Chekiang by a Communist historian see Yeh Hu-sheng, p. 108; and on events in north, central, and south China, Hu Hua, pp. 252–54.

25. "Communist Plans for Expansion," report by Raymond P. Ludden, February 16, 1945, in U. S. Congress, Senate, Committee on the Judiciary, *Amerasia Papers*, 2:1343.

26. *Ibid.*

27. Mao Tse-tung, *"I-chiu-ssu-wu nien ti jen-wu"* (Our Task in 1945), *MTtC*, 9:142–43. The passages quoted are taken from a full and accurate translation of this speech in OSS/CIA.

28. *MTtC*, 9:141.

29. "Chinese Communist Viewpoints on Chinese Political Situation," an undated and unsigned report from OSS agent in Yenan to Major General William J. Donovan, head of the OSS, in OSS/CIA. Based on internal and circumstantial evidence, I believe this report was written by Captain Charles C. Stelle in late January 1945.

30. *MTtC*, 9:146.

31. For Lin's support of Mao in Kiangsi see Dieter Heinzig, "The Otto Braun Memoirs and Mao's Rise to Power," pp. 283–85, and Snow, *Random Notes on Red China*, pp. 26–31. For Lin's role during the War of Resistance see Kataoka, pp. 64–66; Whitson, p. 293; Harrison, p. 325; Klein and Clark, 1:562.

32. Yang Ch'eng-wu, *"Ts'eng-ts'eng huo chen shao yeh niu,"* *HHLY*, 7:130.

33. T'ieh Chen, *"Jen-min chun-tui hsiang ch'ien chin"* (The people's army advances), *HHLY*, 7:68.

34. T'ang Che-ming, *"Kung-ping tsai ch'eng chang"* (The growth of the engineering corps), *HHLY*, 7:71; Sun San, *"Hu pei sheng yi"* (Wings on the back of a tiger), *HHLY*, 7:74.

35. Davies, pp. 347–48, 361. The original report of November 3, 1944, summarizing the plan drawn up in Yenan, is contained in OSS/CIA.

36. R&S, 3, pp. 72 ff., 249 ff.

37. "Plans for Operations in Communist Territory," a report by Major General Robert B. McClure written in conjunction with the investigation into the Bird and Barrett missions; Telegram of January 27, 1945, from Lieutenant General Albert C. Wedemeyer to General George C. Marshall.

38. Letter from Colonel Willis H. Bird to Major General Robert B. McClure, January 24, 1945, in OSS/CIA; letter from Colonel David D. Barrett to Major General Robert B. McClure, January 18, 1945; Barrett, p. 76.

39. *FRUS*, 1944, 6:739–40, 740–41.

40. *FRUS*, 1944, 6:744–45.

41. Barrett, p. 77; Barbara Tuchman, *Notes from China*, p. 86.

42. Barrett, p. 78.

43. Message no. 322, Captain Upshur Evans to Lieutenant General Albert C. Wedemeyer, January 9, 1945; Message no. 324, Evans to Wedemeyer, January 10, 1945.

44. Message no. 322, p. 2.

45. *FRUS*, 1945, 7:175–76, 208–10; Barrett, p. 76.

46. *FRUS,* 1945, 7:181.

47. R&S, 3, pp. 64, 164–65; *New York Times,* December 12, 1944, p. 1:6.

48. *New York Times,* January 2, 1945, p. 10:5–7; January 16, p. 1:8.

49. R&S, 3, pp. 141, 14.

50. *HHJP,* December 5, 1944, cited in *New York Times,* December 6, 1944, p. 1:6 (for further details on CCP press comment see n. 24 above); *HHJP,* January 17, 1945, in *CPR,* 1945, 16:7. Ma Han-ping, pp. 24–28; Yeh Hu-sheng, p. 108.

51. *FRUS,* 1945, 7: 223–30; Service, Report no. 1, February 14, 1945, p. 1337; *New York Times,* February 16, 1945, p. 5:1.

52. Stelle report cited in n. 29 above; *FRUS,* 1945, 7:222, 232–33; R&S, 3, pp. 253–54.

5. From the Countryside to the Cities (February– April 1945)

1. Mao Tse-tung, "We Must Learn To Do Economic Work," *SW* (Peking), 3:190.

2. *Ibid.,* p. 191. I have chosen to use the translation from *SW* (Peking) because it is readily available, authoritative, and in this case substantially correct. The first sentence of this paragraph, however, has been subjected to some deletions, which do not bear on the point in question. For the original see *MTtC,* 9:161–62.

3. For the text of the Soviet-Japanese Neutrality Pact see Jane Degras, ed., *Soviet Documents on Foreign Policy* (London: Oxford University Press, 1953), 3:486–87.

4. Charles B. McLane, *Soviet Policy and the Chinese Communists,* pp. 157–58; *World News and Views,* December 19, 1942, cited in McLane, p. 159.

5. Vladimirov, pp. 37, 38, 79, 143. Pyotr P. Vladimirov was chief agent for TASS News Agency and the Comintern in Yenan from 1942 to 1945. His diary, cited here and below, has been subjected to deletions, additions, and rewriting to serve Moscow's current purpose of discrediting Mao and his leadership. Still, most of this document is consistent with our general understanding of the Chinese Communist movement during this period, supported by independent evidence in many of its specifics and both plausible and provocative in several of its unverifiable assertions. Radio contact between the Chinese Communists was restored in the summer of 1936, when a technical unit sent by the Comintern crossed Mongolia to the CCP headquarters then in Paoan (see Dieter Heinzig, "The Otto Braun Memoirs," pp. 284–85). There is no evidence of when the first TASS or Comintern agents arrived in Yenan, but Vladimirov (p. 4) states that there were three other Soviet agents there when he and his two companions arrived in 1942. According to Vladimirov (pp. 7, 18, 21, 29, 39, 100, 101, 125, 126, 232, 350), during 1942–43 Mao kept his distance from the Soviet delegation, which was obliged to work through K'ang Sheng and Ch'in Pang-hsien. O. Vladimirov and V. Ryazantsev (*Stranitsy politicheskoi biograffii Mao Dze-dung* [Moscow, 1969], pp. 52–53) assert that the Maoist leadership viewed the Soviet agents in Yenan with extreme suspicion and kept them surrounded with security personnel (see Steven I. Levine, "Soviet-American Rivalry in Manchuria and the Cold War," in Chün Tu-hsueh, ed., *Dimensions of China's Foreign Relations* [New York: Praeger, 1977], p. 32).

6. Vladimirov, p. 376. In its broadcast of May 10, 1970, Radio Moscow asserted that in July 1941 the Comintern requested Yenan to undertake "concerted action to

prevent Japan from attacking the Soviet Union," and that "Mao Tse-tung openly boycotted these proposals . . ." (cited in Richard C. Thornton, *China: The Struggle for Power*, p. 351). Vladimirov and Ryazantsev [p. 54] and S. Sergeichuk, *SShA i Kitai 1948–1968* [Moscow, 1969], p. 7, assert that in the first days of Barbarossa Moscow appealed to Yenan for coordinated military action in case of a Japanese attack on Siberia, that Chu Teh assured the Soviet mission in Yenan that the CCP would cooperate, but that nothing was done to fulfill this promise (see Levine, "Rivalry," p. 32).

7. McLane, pp. 166–69.

8. Herbert Feis, *The China Tangle*, pp. 137–40.

9. McLane, pp. 170–71.

10. *Ibid.*, pp. 171–75.

11. *War and the Working Class*, December 1, 1944, no. 23, quoted in "Situation Report: USSR," OSS, Research and Analysis (R&A), February 24, 1945, no. 1785.38, p. 6.

12. *FRUS*, 1944, 6:799. For Molotov's comments of August 1944 see Van Slyke, *China White Paper*, 1:72.

13. Vladimirov, pp. 170–77.

14. *Ibid.*, pp. 170, 222, 225–26. For similar allegations bearing on the role of K'ang Sheng in the Rectification Movement see Warren Kuo, *Analytical History of the Chinese Communist Party*, Book Four (Taipei: Institute of International Relations, 1971), pp. 373–74, 401, 412, 583–88, 622.

15. Vladimirov, p. 239.

16. *CFJP*, September 6, 1944, p. 3 (on United Nations); August 22, 1944, p. 3 (on the western front); August 14, 1944, p. 3, and September 9, 1944, p. 3 (on Poland).

17. *CFJP*, November 7, 1944, p. 1.

18. Robert J. C. Butow, *Japan's Decision to Surrender*, p. 86.

19. *CFJP*, December 3, 1944, p. 1; December 13, 18, 25 (all p. 3); Vladimirov, pp. 286, 290, 294, 301, 315.

20. Van Slyke, *China White Paper*, 1:113–14; "Private Papers of President Chiang Kai-shek, Some Aspects of the Secret Yalta Agreement Concerning the Negotiations of the Sino-Soviet Agreements" (unpublished; in Chinese), cited in Chin-tung Liang, "The Sino-Soviet Treaty of Friendship and Alliance of 1945," p. 375.

21. In 1951 Patrick Hurley told a Senate investigating committee that he learned of the Yalta protocol "through the Chinese armed Communists," presumably before his departure from China on February 19, 1945 (see U.S. Senate, 82nd Cong., 1st Sess., *Hearing before the Committee of Armed Services and the Committee on Foreign Relations, Military Situation in the Far East* [Washington: Government Printing Office, 1951], 4:2883). I find this statement of dubious validity; there is no contemporary evidence to support it. Similarly I know of no evidence that the Communists learned of the Yalta agreements before their implications became clear with the signing of the Sino-Soviet Treaty in August, though such a negative statement cannot be proved.

22. *HHJP*, February 15, in *CPR*, 1945, 41:2.

23. For selections from the Soviet press during the period February to April see OSS, R&A Reports: February 24, 1945, no. 1785.38, pp. 5–6; March 24, 1945, no. 1785.40, pp. 12–14; April 21, 1945, no. 1785.42, pp. 5–6.

24. McLane, p. 171.

25. *War and the Working Class*, April 15, 1945, cited in McLane, p. 182.

26. *Chung Yang Jih Pao*, February 14, in *CPR*, 1945, 40:1–2; *Ta Kung Pao*, February

15, in *CPR*, 1945, 41:4; *HHJP*, February 15, in *CPR*, 1945, 64:1; *CFJP*, February 17, 1945, p. 1; Vladimirov, pp. 322–24, 328–32.

27. Vladimirov, p. 328. The creation of a federation of trade unions had been the subject of an editorial in *CFJP* on February 7.

28. Vladimirov, pp. 240, 281, 327, 328–29; Service, Report no. 18, March 18, 1945, pp. 1423–25.

29. Service, Report no. 11, March 14, 1945, pp. 1405–8.

30. *FRUS*, 1945, 7:214.

31. Service, Report no. 11, March 14, 1945, pp. 1405–6.

32. For details on the confrontation between Hurley and the State Department see *FRUS*, 1945, 7:242–54, 260–64.

33. *HHJP*, March 10, in *CPR*, 1945, 64:1.

34. *FRUS*, 1945, 7:235, 266–67, 268–69; Service, Report no. 8, March 11, 1945, p. 1391.

35. *FRUS*, 1945, 7:307, 308. A different view was taken by Charles Stelle ("Conditions in Dixie," April 12, 1945, p. 2, in OSS/CIA), who reported that the Communists felt that they had been "neatly euchred" by Chiang on the United Nations delegation matter.

36. Service, Report no. 26, April 1, 1945, p. 1577.

37. Ch'i Wu, p. 241; Ma Han-ping, pp. 24–28; *FRUS*, 1945, 7:238–39; Van Slyke, *Chinese Communist Movement*, pp. 103, 104; R&S, 3, pp. 275–76; *New York Times*, April 1, 1945, p. 18:1; April 4, 1945, p. 4:7.

38. *FRUS*, 1945, 7:254, 255, 257–58, 265–66.

39. Service, Report no. 8, March 11, 1945, p. 1390.

40. Mao Tse-tung, "Resolution on Some Questions in the History of Our Party," *SW* (London), 4:178, 190, 193, 198.

41. *Ibid.*, pp. 196–97 (italics added).

42. *MTtC*, 9:161–62, 165; Mao Tse-tung, *SW* (London), 4:202–3.

43. Service, Report no. 8, March 11, 1945, p. 1392; Vladimirov, p. 331; P'eng Teh-huai, "How We Fought for Six Years in North China," in Stuart Gelder, *The Chinese Communists*, p. 162; URI, *The Case of P'eng Teh-huai*, pp. 193–94.

44. Vladimirov, pp. 418–21; Whitson, p. 111.

45. *Ibid.*, p. 79.

46. Liu Shao-ch'i, *On the Party*, pp. 46–48, 109; Yang Hsiu-shan, " 'Ch'i-Ta ti kuang-mang" (Radiance of the Seventh Party Congress), *HHLY*, 7:431–32 (see also Vladimirov, p. 427).

47. Mao Tse-tung, "Address at the Opening of the Ninth National Congress," in Schram, *Chairman Mao Talks to the People*, p. 281; *JPRS*, no. 49826, p. 11; Vladimirov, pp. 350, 354, 357, 360, 366, 368, 425, 430, 448.

48. In December 1944 Chou told Davies that "he favored such a step but that Chairman Mao was more cautious and wanted to delay such action" (*FRUS*, 1944, 6:753). Vladimirov (p. 413) says that in debate at the Seventh Party Congress Chou led proponents for immediate formation of a separate government.

6. The Seventh Party Congress and the Civil War (April–July 1945)

1. Harrison, p. 284; Kuo, *Analytical History*, p. 566; Yang Hsiu-shan, *HHLY*, 7:429.

2. Mao's political report appeared in *CFJP*, May 2, 1945, pp. 1–6. An English ver-

sion, which Stuart Schram calls "the translation from the original text" (*Mao Tse-tung*, p. 231), appears in Stuart Gelder, *The Chinese Communists*, p. 2. Chu Teh's military report appeared in *CFJP*, May 9, pp. 1–4, and was later published under the title *On the Battlefronts of the Liberated Areas.* Liu Shao-ch'i's report was not made public at the time but was later published under the title *On the Party.* For an English text of the Party constitution and a list of the Seventh Central Committee see Conrad Brandt et al., *A Documentary History of Chinese Communism*, pp. 284 ff, 419 ff. The speeches by Chou, Lin, Jen, and Okano Susumu appeared in *CFJP*, May 1, 1945.

3. Ho Kan-chih, *A History of the Modern Chinese Revolution*, p. 424, cites the following figures for the Chinese Communist movement as of April 1945: regular army, 910,000; militia, 2.2 million; self-defense forces, 10 million; liberated areas, 19; area, 950,000 sq. km.; population, 95.5 million.

4. Mao Tse-tung, "Lun lien-ho cheng-fu" (On coalition government), *MTtC*, 9:198–99, 223–24, 244–45, 267–68. For an English version see Gelder, pp. 10–11, 26–27, 40–41, 56. These and other points taken from "On Coalition Government" are corroborated by the only extant notes on Mao's oral presentation of the speech, taken by Vladimirov. These notes appear only in the Russian version of the diary. They have been translated and summarized by Steven I. Levine, "Mao Tse-tung's Oral Report to the Seventh Party Congress of the CCP: Summary Notes" (Santa Monica: RAND Corporation, September 1977).

5. *MTtC*, 9:265–66, 268, 274; Gelder, pp. 53–55, 56, 59.

6. Service, *Amerasia Papers*, pp. 113–16; *FRUS*, 1945, 7:318.

7. *HHJP*, April 5, in *CPR*, 1945, 90:2. *CFJP* did not report the Hurley press conference until May 8, when it ran a short announcement and the texts of the *HHJP* editorials of April 5 and 8. Vladimirov (p. 365) states that a decision to reply to Hurley was made and reversed in Yenan during April 3–6.

8. *CFJP*, April 14, 1945, p. 1; *HHJP*, April 14, in *CPR*, 1945, 99:2, and April 19, in *CPR*, 1945, 104:1.

9. *MTtC*, 9:259; Gelder, p. 50.

10. *CFJP*, May 4, 5, 10, 15, 1945 (all p. 1).

11. See *New York Times*, May 11, 1945, p. 10:2; May 20, p. 1:7; June 19, p. 1:6; July 29, p. 1:2. Also R&S, 3, pp. 350–53.

12. *FRUS*, 1945, 7:386, 397, 406–7.

13. *HHJP*, March 30, in *CPR*, 1945, 84:1–2.

14. Van Slyke, Chinese Communist Movement, pp. 103–4, 123.

15. *Ibid.*, pp. 122–23; "Summary of Monthly Military Situation behind Enemy Lines," *CFJP*, January 9, 1945, p. 1; "Welcoming the New Situation," *CFJP*, May 15, 1945, p. 1; "Summary of Military Situation during the Past Month on the Battlefield of the Liberated Areas," *CFJP*, June 8, 1945, p. 1.

16. "Summary of the Military Situation behind Enemy Lines during the Past Month," *CFJP*, January 15, 1945, p. 1; *ibid.*, April 13, 1945, p. 1; "Military Situation during the Past Month on the Battlefield of the Liberated Areas," *ibid.*, May 5, 1945, p. 1.

17. Yeh Hu-sheng, p. 108; Van Slyke, *Chinese Communist Movement*, p. 103; "The Military Situation during the Past Month on the Battlefield of the Liberated Areas," *CFJP*, May 6, 1945, p. 1; *New York Times*, May 25, 1945, p. 2:2, June 7, 1945, p. 3:1; "Welcoming the New Situation," *CFJP*, May 15, 1945, p. 1.

18. Van Slyke, *Chinese Communist Movement*, p. 125. For further evidence of Japanese respect for Communist forces see *ibid.*, p. 106.

19. Vladimirov, p. 414; "The Enemy Strengthens Its 'Decisive Battle Measures' along the Coast of Central China," *CFJP*, May 25, 1945, p. 1; "Military Situation during the Past Month on the Battlefield of the Liberated Areas," *ibid.*, June 8, 1945, p. 1.

20. "Impasse at Dixie," report by Captain Charles C. Stelle, June 6, 1945, in CIA/OSS.

21. See, for example, *HHJP* editorials during April and May in *CPR*, 1945, 92:1, 98:1, 101:3, 104:1, 117:2, 119:4, 124:3, 145:2.

22. *Ta Kung Pao*, May 10, in *CPR*, 1945, 125:1. This is not far from the facts as recorded by Butow, pp. 91, 121, 126–29, 150. Butow states that former Japanese Premier Hirota first approached the Soviet ambassador to Tokyo, Jacob Malik, on June 4, to discuss the maintenance of peace between the two countries following Moscow's decision not to renew the Neutrality Pact, announced on April 5. During the rest of the war, the Japanese sought both in Tokyo and in Moscow to persuade the Russians to arrange a peace settlement on something less than the Allied terms of "unconditional surrender." Stalin refused all such overtures and informed Truman of them at Potsdam.

23. *HHJP*, May 15, in *CPR*, 1945, 130:2.

24. *Ta Kung Pao*, May 29, in *CPR*, 1945, 144:4. According to Butow (pp. 104–11), on April 23 Japanese officials in the embassy in Switzerland attempted to open discussions with the Americans through the OSS. Washington authorized the OSS in Switzerland to listen to the offers, but Tokyo, which was concentrating on reaching the Russians, never approved these contacts.

25. For a detailed discussion of this subject see Goldstein, "Chinese Communist Perspectives."

26. *HHJP*, June 1, in *CPR*, 1945, 148:2, 149:8–9.

27. See reports from Captain Charles C. Stelle to Colonel Richard Heppner, "Conditions in Dixie" (April 12, 1945, p. 1) and "Affairs in Dixie," (May 1, 1945, p. 3). Both reports are in OSS/CIA.

28. For the Communist version of the May 29 incident see "Impasse at Dixie," report of Stelle to Heppner, June 6, 1945, p. 3. Also letters: Peterkin to Dickey, June 4, 1945, and Chu to Wedemeyer, September 5 and 17, 1945, in *Dixie Mission Papers*. For confirmation by American officials see letters: Yeaton to Mao, August 5, 1945, and Wedemeyer to Mao, August 8, 1945, *Dixie Papers*. Also "Historical Summary of Yenan Liaison Team: Shensi Province, China," 1, in CIA/OSS, and "Excerpts from *History of the Clandestine Branch, G-5 Section, Headquarters, United States Forces, China Theater*," by Major Martin F. Sullivan, November 15, 1945, III, Office of Strategic Services, in *Dixie Papers*.

29. *MTtC*, 9:212–13; Gelder, p. 20. The Gelder version does not mention Scobie by name. This is the only discrepancy I have found between Gelder and the original. For details on the role of Scobie see Gabriel Kolko, *The Politics of War*, pp. 183–89, and *SW* (Peking), 3:268.

30. Vladimirov, pp. 417, 437, 454; *FRUS*, 1945, 7:372.

31. Stelle report of June 6, p. 3.

32. *CFJP*, June 17, 1945, p. 1. In an interview on August 3, 1945, General Yeh Chien-ying told Colonel Ivan D. Yeaton, commanding officer of the Dixie Mission, "Reports submitted by American observers and correspondents have been almost always criticised by officials in Washington, and in some instances, even the observers were 'punished,' as in the Service case." This report is in *Dixie Papers*.

33. "When Is a Secret Document Not a Secret Document," I. F. Stone, *PM*, June 10 (reprinted in *CFJP*, June 17–18, 1945).

34. *SW* (Peking), 3:271–72.

35. *CFJP*, June 14, 1945, p. 1.

36. *CFJP*, June 17, 1945, p. 1. The "*NCNA* Correspondent" was a pen name which has been described in some instances as belonging to Mao (*SW* [Peking], 3:281n., 285n.). The "Correspondent" was quoted regularly in *CFJP* in June, July, and August concerning important policy issues. In the absence of evidence to the contrary, it seems likely that the name was used invariably by Mao.

37. Telegram of the Preparatory Conference of the CLAPRC in *CFJP*, July 14, 1945, p. 1. See also *FRUS*, 1945, 7:435.

38. *SW* (Peking), 3:273.

39. "The Case of Six Men: A View of the Two Roads in American Policy toward China," *CFJP*, June 25, 1945, p. 1.

40. These two articles have been included in *SW* (Peking) (3:281, 285), which identify Mao as the "NCNA Correspondent." I have checked these translations against the original articles which appeared in *CFJP* and they are identical.

41. *Hsin Hua Jih Pao*, July 29, in *CPR*, 1945, 204:2–3.

42. Tso Shun-sheng, *Chin san shih nien chien-wen tsa-chi* (Interesting events in the past thirty years) (Hong Kong: Freedom Press, 1954), p. 90, cited in Schram, *Mao Tse-tung*, p. 232.

43. Another view of Soviet policy at this time cites the attack by Jacques Duclos, a major figure in the French Communist Party, on Earl Browder, head of the American Communist Party, as Moscow's signal to foreign Communist parties to abandon the wartime united front and shift toward a more aggressive and sectarian line in the postwar era (see Arthur Schlesinger, Jr., "Origins of the Cold War," *Foreign Affairs* (October 1967), 46:43). I argue that Moscow's message to Yenan was precisely the opposite, and that if Yenan had read and understood the Duclos article in these terms, the CCP would have been delighted. The evidence, however, suggests that the Chinese Communists never got the message, at least as Schlesinger has interpreted it. Rather than joining the attack on Browder, which would have been consistent with the "anti-imperialist" line emerging from the Seventh Party Congress, Yenan gave Browder a good press long after the Duclos article appeared in April (see *CFJP*, April 25, 1945, p. 1; June 25, p. 1).

44. McLane, pp. 172, 176. *Izvestia*, June 3, 1945, cited in *New York Times*, June 4, p. 2:6.

45. Van Slyke, *China White Paper*, 1:94–96; *FRUS*, 1945, 7:376; *New York Times*, April 24, 1945, p. 1:2, and May 14, p. 8:3.

46. Robert E. Sherwood, *Roosevelt and Hopkins*, pp. 902–3; *New York Times*, June 8, 1945, p. 1:5.

47. Report, Stelle to Heppner, June 6, 1945, p. 2, in CIA/OSS. For a similar observation made much earlier see Vladimirov, p. 365.

48. *CFJP*, June 19, 1945, p. 3. For earlier analyses of economic relations with the United States which took a less ideological and more tolerant line see *HHJP*, May 19, in *CPR*, 1945, 134:7; *ibid.*, May 24, in *CPR*, 1945, 136; and *CFJP* June 17, 1945, p. 1.

49. *CFJP*, June 21, 1945, p. 1.

50. In Chungking the editors of *HHJP* were apparently late in getting the message, for during the last week in June they ran a series of editorials stressing the im-

portance of Allied unity (*CPR*, 1945, 170:4, 173:3, 174:1, 175:1). The paper carried no editorials devoted to this subject during the remainder of the war.

51. *CFJP*, July 12, 1945, p. 1, July 15, p. 1, and *New York Times*, 1–15 July; *SW* (Peking), 3:282.

52. *New York Times*, July 15, 1945. p. 1:7.

53. On July 24 (p. 1:7), for example, the *New York Times* reported that at the Potsdam Conference progress was being made and an early and successful conclusion was expected. An article in the same issue, entitled "Soviet Held Ready to Buttress China," reported that progress made in the Stalin-Soong talks had laid the basis for "a realistic and practical program in which China might find herself in the closest relationship with her powerful neighbor. . . ."

54. *CFJP*, July 23, 1945, p. 1 (italics added).

55. *SW* (Peking), 4:18; *CFJP*, August 13, 1945, p. 1.

56. The CCP order appeared in *CFJP*, August 11, 1945, p. 1. For an English translation see *SW* (Peking), 4:30n. Chiang's order appeared in *CFJP*, August 13, 1945. p. 1. The translation has been rendered, "stay where they are, pending further orders" (*SW* [Peking], 4:27).

57. *CFJP*, August 13, 1945, p. 1; *SW* (Peking), 4:27, 43.

58. *Ta Kung Pao*, August 10, in *CPR*, 1945, 215:7.

59. *SW (Peking)*, 4:21–22.

60. *CPR*, 1945, 215:7.

61. *CFJP*, August 10, 1945, p. 1; *HHJP*, August 10, in *CPR*, 1945, 215:1; *SW* (Peking), 4:21, 20.

7.   The Reoccupation of China (August–October 1945)

1. *HHJP*, August 17, 1945, in *CPR*, 1945, p. 222:1; Feis, *China Tangle*, p. 358; John F. Melby, *The Mandate of Heaven*, p. 30; E. Iu. Bogush, *Mif ob 'eksporte revoliutsii' i Sovetskaiia vneshniaia politika* (Moscow, 1965), p. 99, cited in Steven Levine, "Soviet-American Rivalry in Manchuria and the Cold War," p. 33.

2. Hu Hsi-k'uei, *Shih-chü Pien-hua ho Wo-ti Fang-chen* (*Changes in the Present Situation and Our Plan*), August 30, 1945. The text of this speech is in the Bureau of Investigation, Ministry of Justice, Republic of China. For a summary see Warren I. Cohen, "American Observers and the Sino-Soviet Friendship Treaty of August 1945," *Pacific Historical Review* (1966), 35:347. I have translated this passage from Mr. Cohen's hand-copied notes.

3. Vladimir Dedijer, *Tito Speaks*, p. 331; Milovan Djilas, *Conversations with Stalin* (New York: Harcourt, Brace and World, 1962), p. 182.

4. Schram, *Chairman Mao Talks to the People*, p. 191.

5. *Pravda*, August 31, quoted in *New York Times*, September 1, 1945, 4:1.

6. Vladimirov, p. 480; *FRUS*, 1945, 7:519–20, 789.

7. "On the Present Situation," *CFJP*, August 27, 1945, p. 1. For an accurate translation see *CPR*, 243:3–4. The original text is also in *MTtC*, 9:321–23.

8. *SW* (Peking), 4:48.

9. For details on the Communist movement in Manchuria see Klein and Clark, 1:225–27.

10. Van Slyke, *Chinese Communist Movement*, p. 123; Dubinsky, p. 353; *CFJP*, August 12, 1945, p. 1.

11. Francis Clifford Jones, *Manchuria since 1931*, p. 232.

12. The most authoritative account of Soviet extractions from Manchuria is Edwin W. Pauley, "Report on Japanese Assets in Manchuria to the President of the United States, July 1946" (Washington, D.C.: Government Printing Office, 1946). Richard Lauterbach (*Danger from the East*, pp. 279–80) quotes Chou En-lai on the subject: "No matter what I would say it would be used against us by our enemies." David J. Dallin (*Soviet Russia and the Far East*, p. 245) quotes Li Li-san: "I feel that the movement of the machinery is not an important problem at all. Of course the Soviet Union moved some machinery but not a large amount compared with its losses."

13. For Russian views of the Chinese see "Intelligence Notes on Kalgan, Sept. 1945," Report YV-30, October 5, 1945, p. 2, in CBI Theater, RG 332, Box 3, NRC; and Barbey Papers, ser. 4, no. 146, "Yingkow," p. 2 (in the Operational Archives Branch, Center for Naval History, Washington, D.C.). For Chinese views of the Russians see *New York Times*, October 31, 1945, p. 2:2; Melby, p. 39; George Moorad, *Lost Peace in China*, pp. 117, 245.

14. "Intelligence Notes on Kalgan," p. 1; *New York Times*, October 31, 1945, p. 2:2; Raymond L. Garthoff, "Malinovsky's Manchurian Campaign," *Military Review* (October 1966), 46 (10):56. Yang Yao-ts'ai, "*Chi-shang li-ming*" (Beginning of Dawn), *HHLY*, 7:439, states: "It appeared that the Soviet-Mongolian United Army had already launched an attack on Kalgan from the north. Comrades of the 40th regiment heard gunfire in the north." For another Communist account of the capture of Kalgan which makes no mention of Soviet forces in the area see Hsiao Wu, "*Shan-kuang ti hung-hsing*" (Sparkling Red Star), *HHLY*, 7:470.

15. Chai Ta-chün, "*Sung-po ch'ang ch'ing*" (Long life and good health) *HHLY*, 7:467; *New York Times*, November 5, 1945, p. 6:1; *FRUS*, 1945, 7:576; OSS R&A Report no. 3264, September 28, 1945, p. 4; *New York Times*, November 18, 1945, p. 4:4.

16. Yang Yao-ts'ai, *HHLY*, 7:438; Wang Wen, "*Tsui ch'iang yin*" (The loudest noise), *HHLY*, 7:464; *New York Times*, October 31, 1945, p. 2:2; *FRUS*, 1945, 7:579.

17. Tseng K'o-lin, "*Ta ti ch'ung-kuang*" (Recovery of a great land), *HHLY*, 7:448–49. This account is corroborated by reports in the Communist press that their forces captured Shanhaikuan between August 30 and September 1 (*HHJP*, September 8, 1945, in *CPR*, 1945, 242:5; *CFJP*, September 6, 1945, p. 1), and a report by the Domei news agency in Peiping that the Soviet army entered the city on August 31 (*New York Times*, September 2, 1945, 6:1).

18. "History of the China Theater" (manuscript, Office of the Chief of Military History), 14:9.

19. Tseng K'o-lin, *HHLY*, 7:450; Huang Jung-hai, "*K'ua-hai pei-shang*" (North across the sea), *HHLY*, 7:456–63; *New York Times*, October 31, 1945, p. 2:2; *FRUS*, 1945, 7:576, 691; III Amphibious Corps to China Theater Headquarters, November 8, 1945, and UPI release, November 17, 1945, in "History of the China Theater," 16:19; Ho Kan-chih, p. 433–34; Hu Hua et al., *Chung-kuo ko-ming shih chiang-yi* (Lectures on the History of the Chinese Revolution) (Peking, 1962), p. 263.

20. Dubinsky, pp. 354–55; Ho Kan-chih, p. 433; Huang Jung-hai, *HHLY*, 7:463.

21. *SCMM* no. 217, July 11, 1960, p. 26; *Peking Review*, February 7, 1975, p. 14, cites these figures: 110,000 troops, 20,000 cadres. See also Steven I. Levine, "Political Integration in Manchuria, 1945–1949," p. 229.

22. Feng Shu-yen, "*Nu-t'ao Ch'ung-chüan Ch'üan-yen-ho*" (Turbulent recapture of Chuanyenho), *HHLY*, 7:441–45; Dubinsky, p. 354; Huang Jung-hai, *HHLY*, 7:463; Klein and Clark, 2:647.

23. In October 1967 Radio Moscow claimed the Russians had given the Chinese Communists some 740,000 rifles, 18,000 machine guns, 800 aircraft, 800 tanks, 4,000 artillery pieces, and 600 armories (see Harrison, pp. 598–99). These are compared with slightly lower figures cited by Tang Tsou, p. 331. Tsou also provides figures on quantity of weapons recovered by the Nationalists. Lin Piao reportedly told Anna Louise Strong: "Whatever came with the Red Army into Manchuria went back when the Red Army went. No troops, no weapons, no advisers!" Other CCP spokesmen said that the Russians "destroyed on the spot all the war material that they did not take back into the USSR" (*Amerasia*, (May 1947), 11(5):137–38.

24. *New York Times*, October 30, 1945, p. 1:3; Huang Jung-hai, *HHLY*, 7:458; *CFJP*, February 14, 1946, p. 1 (For a translation of this article see *FRUS*, 1946, 9:450–53).

25. This conclusion was drawn by Pauley, p. 52.

26. Dubinsky, pp. 355–59; Tseng K'o-lin, *HHLY*, 7:450–52, 455.

27. Tung Yen-p'ing, *Su-O chu Tung-pei* (Soviet Russia in the Northeast) (Taipei, 1965), p. 7, in Levine, "Political Integration," p. 119. See also Chiang Kai-shek, *Soviet Russia in China*, pp. 142–43.

28. Chiang Kai-shek, *Soviet Russia in China* p. 143; "China Presents Her Case to the United Nations" (New York: Chinese Delegation to the United Nations, 1949), p. 13. For the text of the agreement on Dairen see Van Slyke, *China White Paper*, 2:589.

29. *CFJP*, editorials of September 10, 14, 17, and October 2, 1945, p. 1; *New York Times*, September 10, 1945, 4:2 (see also Military Attaché report for the week ending September 8 in *FRUS*, 1945, 7:552); Yeh Hu-sheng, pp. 108–9; Ma Han-ping, pp. 35–37.

30. This was first announced by Mao at a press conference on September 26 (see *CPR*, p. 261:4).

31. Ch'i Wu, p. 245; Ho Kan-chih, p. 450. An important battle in north China during the fall of 1945 occurred at Shangtang, in southeast Shansi, from September to October. For a discussion of this battle see Hu Hua, Chung-kuo ko-ming Shih Chiang-i, p. 486, and Liu Chung, "Shang-tang ta chieh" (Great victory at Shangtang) in *Hung Ch'i P'iao P'iao* (The Red Flag Waves) (Peking: Chung-kuo ch'ing-nien ch'u-pan-she, 1959), 13:119 ff.

32. *New York Times*, September 28, 1945, p. 4:6.

33. For a description of Kailan coal mines see *New York Times*, December 27, 1945, p. 4:2. Information on precisely who guarded what portions of the railroad in Hopeh is sketchy. I have drawn the above generalizations from these sources: *New York Times*, December 26, 1945, p. 5:2; Shaw, p. 9; "History of the China Theater" 15:76, 84, 113; *FRUS*, 1945, 7:599.

34. "History of the China Theater," 15:53; Benis Frank and Henry Shaw, *History of U.S. Marine Corps in World War II*, p. 545, cite these figures for forces in the area occupied by the Marines: Communists, 170,000 regulars, plus militia; Nationalists, negligible; Japanese, 116,000 regulars.

35. Frank and Shaw, pp. 547–48 (for an account of the meeting between Chou and the American advance party, see "Interview with Maj. Gen. William A. Worton," [February 10, 1959], Historical Branch, Division of Headquarters, USMC, p. 8); Henry I. Shaw, *The United States Marines in North China*, p. 1; *CFJP*, September 30, 1945, p. 1.

36. *New York Times*, September 28, 1945, p. 4:6, October 4, p. 10:1; *CFJP*, October 5, p. 1; *HHJP*, October 4, in *CPR*, 1945, 268:1–2.

37. Shaw, p. 2; *New York Times,* October 4, 1945, p. 10:1; October 16, p. 4:4.

38. *HHJP,* October 4, in *CPR,* 1945, 268:1–2 (italics added).

39. Frank and Shaw, pp. 558–68; *FRUS,* 1945, 7:580.

40. Tsou, p. 307; Feis, *China Tangle,* pp. 365–66; Vice Admiral Daniel E. Barbey, commander of the Seventh Amphibious Force, and Major General Keller E. Rockey, commanding officer of the Third Amphibious Corps, were both present at Chefoo and concurred in the decision not to land. Both men later told Marine Corps historians that the Communist mayor of Chefoo threatened to fight. For Barbey's statement see Frank and Shaw, p. 559 n. For Rockey's statement see interview with Henry I. Shaw, April 29, 1959, p. 3 (Historical Branch, Division of Headquarters, USMC). George Moorad, a journalist who was with Barbey and Rockey at Chefoo, has quoted the mayor as saying, "We'll shoot if you try to land" (Moorad, p. 91).

41. Both American (Barbey Papers, 4:28, "Chefoo") and Communist (letter from General Yeh Chien-ying to Colonel Yeaton of October 6 in *CFJP,* October 8, p. 1, and "Dixie Mission Papers") sources agree on these points. Mentioned in the CCP source but not in the American records are two additional points: first, the Americans made a previous landing on October 1, at which time they assured the mayor that the Marines would not land at Chefoo; and second, the letter presented to him on October 4 included a demand that the Communists "hand over control of the city in an orderly manner to the U.S. Forces." I have not been able to locate the original October 4 letter.

42. Daniel E. Barbey, *MacArthur's Amphibious Navy,* p. 334; Letter from Yeh to Yeaton, October 6; Commander, Seventh Amphibious Force, "Beleager Operation: Report of Operation in Korea and North China during Occupation of Japanese Held Territory," December 22, 1945, pp. 8–9, in Barbey Papers; Memo to Generalissimo, October 8, 1945, cited in "History of the China Theater," 15:117–18.

43. *CFJP,* October 11, 1945, p. 1. In Chungking, CCP representative Wang Ping-nan "expressed great satisfaction over the recent Chefoo arrangement" (*FRUS,* 1945, 7:474–75). The Communist mayor of Weihaiwei told an American reporter that he "deeply appreciated" the decision to withdraw (UPI dispatch of October 26, in Barbey Papers, 4:29, "China: News Reports"). Yeaton reported the American action in Chefoo "well received" in Yenan (Yeaton to Wedemeyer, October 6, 1945, in "Eyes Alone, Book 6-A," item 5007, Wedemeyer File, RG 332, box 6, NRC).

44. *New York Times,* October 16, 1945, p. 4:4; Memo from Headquarters, III Amphibious Corps, October 22, 1945, in "History of the China Theater," 16:17.

45. "Intelligence: Estimate of Enemy Situation," October 22, 1945, Annex A to 1st Marine Division, War Diaries, October 1945, p. 9. The details of the contacts at Chinwangtao are contained in the War Diaries, which provided the basic source for the accounts in Frank and Shaw. See also Tillman Durdin's report from Chinwangtao in *New York Times,* October 16, 4:4. These details were corroborated in a letter from Colonel John Gormley, Marine commander at Chinwangtao, to the author, October 21, 1973.

46. Sixth Marine Division, War Diaries, October, p. 6; Frank and Shaw, p. 564; Shaw, p. 5; Alan I. Shilin, "Occupation at Tsingtao," p. 35.

47. Van Slyke, *China White Paper,* 2:577 ff.; *FRUS,* 1945, 7:455–59, 470.

48. Yenan had recalled units in Chekiang which had become isolated (see T'an Ch'i-lung, *"Hsi-pieh Ssu-ming"* [Sad Parting from Ssuming], *Hung Ch'i P'iao P'iao,* 10:112). Wang Chen was not recalled until October 12, two days after the announcement of the agreement, but by this time Wang's position was extremely perilous (Ma Han-ping, pp. 35–37, 47).

49. Mao Tse-tung, "On Chungking Negotiations" (October 17, 1945), *SW* (Peking), 4:56–58.

50. *FRUS*, 7:462–63.

51. "On Chungking Negotiations," pp. 54, 59.

52. Yeaton to Wedemeyer, October 6, 1945 (see n. 43).

8. Setbacks in the Northeast (November–December 1945)

1. *FRUS*, 1945, 7:527–28. This study does not treat the Marine occupation of China from the American side, but the reader may be interested in the following documents: The directive from JCS to China Theater of August 10, 1945, provided for American forces to "secure control of key ports and communications points in the China Theater" and to "assist the Central Government in the transport of Chinese Central Government forces to key areas in China." This directive ignored the subject of repatriation, but it was assumed by China Theater that the problem would be left in the hands of the Central government (see *FRUS*, 1945, 7:527–28, and "History of the China Theater," 15:7). This interpretation is supported by Wedemeyer's memo to Chiang Kai-shek of November 5, in which he stated that upon movement of the 8th Army to Tsingtao, the American mission of transporting Nationalist forces would be complete, and therefore he had recommended that the Marines be withdrawn beginning on the fifteenth (*FRUS*, 1945, 7:604–5). Similarly, in a second memo on November 10, he told Chiang to concentrate on repatriation of the Japanese as his "first priority" and refrain from attempting to retake Manchuria (see "History of the China Theater," 15, Appendix H.) On November 20, following the clash between Communist and Nationalist forces at Shanhaikuan, which had involved the Marines on the Nationalist side, Wedemeyer recommended the withdrawal of all American forces from China on the grounds that "under the present circumstances, it is impossible to avoid involvement in fratricidal warfare or political strife, yet I am admonished by my directive to do so" (Wedemeyer memo, November 20, 1945, in "History of the China Theater," 15, Appendix F, p. 4.)

2. Yeh to Wedemeyer, October 26, 1945, in "Jih-pen t'ou-hsiang hou Chung-kung tung-t'ai tsu-liao hui-pien" (Collected materials on Chinese Communist developments after the surrender of Japan), Yushodo Bookstore Microfilms, reel 17. Also on October 26, Yeh made a similar protest against alleged American intervention in the Hupeh-Honan-Anhwei liberated area (*ibid.*).

3. *New York Times*, October 30, 1945, p. 2:3.

4. First Marine Division, War Diaries, October 1945, p. 5; *New York Times*, October 30, 1945, p. 2:3; Yeaton to Wedemeyer, November 1, 1945, in "Eyes Alone, Book 6-A," item no. 5013.

5. Third Amphibious Corps, War Diaries, November, p. 4; First Marine Division, War Diaries, November, p. 2; "History of the China Theater," 15:124.

6. Frank and Shaw, p. 588; Shaw, p. 9; "History of the China Theater," 15:118; *New York Times*, November 9, 1945, p. 2:3, and November 14, 1945, p. 1:2.

7. Sixth Marine Division, War Diaries, November, pp. 7, 9; "History of the China Theater," 15:120; Frank and Shaw, p. 579. For Wedemeyer's explanation of this decision, see memo, "China Theater to Washington," November 25, 1945, in "History of the China Theater," 15:121.

8. *New York Times*, November 17, 1945, p. 1:4. A State Department memo of November 19 asserts that by that date 6,881 Japanese, military and civilian, had been repatriated from China (see *FRUS*, 1945, 7:640).

9. *HHJP*, November 9, in *CPR*, 1945, 302:4. For a comparison of CCP treatment of the Marines during October and November see III Marine Amphibious Corps, G-3 Periodic Reports, November 1, 1945, p. 2, and December 1, 1945, p. 2, in U.S. Marine Corps Geographic File, 1941–1949, III MAC, China, National Records Center.

10. Yeaton to Wedemeyer, September 29, 1945, and October 6, 1945, in "Eyes Alone, Book 6-A," items 5003 and 5004.

11. *Wei Tung-pei ti ho-p'ing min-chu erh tou cheng* (Struggle for Peace and Democracy in the Northeast) (Ta-chung wen-hua ho-tso-she, 1946), p. 4, cited in Levine, "Political Integration," p. 232; Tseng K'o-lin, *HHLY*, 7:454.

12. Levine, "Political Integration," p. 236.

13. T'ieh Chen, T'ang Che-ming, and Sun San, *HHLY*, 7:67–74.

14. Levine, "Political Integration," pp. 236–37, 274.

15. *Ibid.*, p. 237.

16. In fact, Wang was demoted from full to alternate member of the Central Committee by the Seventh Party Congress, but this occurred despite strong support for his election on the part of Mao (see Vladimirov, pp. 437, 444, 448, 450).

17. Dallin, *Soviet Russia and the Far East*, p. 250; Carsun Chang, *The Third Force in China*, pp. 168–69.

18. Lauterbach, *Danger from the East*, p. 297; Feng Tzu-chao, *Chung-kuo k'ang-chan-shih*, pp. 237, 262; Chang, *Third Force*, pp. 164–65; Report of November 8, 1945, by Captain Colin E. Tweddell, Barbey Papers, 4:146, "Yingkow," p. 2.

19. *Eighth National Congress of the CCP* (Peking, 1957), 2:253.

20. Dallin, pp. 245, 325–26, Jones, p. 234; Pauley, "Report on Japanese Assets in Manchuria . . . ," Appendix 2-b, p. 2.

21. Chou Erh-fu, *Tung-pei Heng-tuan-mien*, p. 53. For additional information on the life of Chang Hsüeh-shih see *ibid.*, pp. 49–53, and Liu Pai-yü, *Shih-tai ti Yin-hsiang*, pp. 63–64.

22. Robert B. Rigg, *Red China's Fighting Hordes*, p. 37.

23. For a contrary view see *New York Times*, October 11, 1946, p. 10:1.

24. *New York Times*, July 20, 1946, p. 4:4; Peiping Headquarters Group, Box 3562, Peiping Executive Headquarters, 3rd qtr., 1946, section I, *Situation: General History of the China Area*, pp. 61–62. On another occasion, Li reportedly told a foreign journalist "there were instances of faulty Soviet behaviour in Manchuria," but these were "small matters compared with Russia's sacrifices in the war with Japan and with her helping the liberation of Manchuria" (*New York Herald Tribune*, September 8, 1946, cited in John Gittings, *The World and China*, p. 150).

25. Klein and Clark, 1:555, 2:715.

26. For details on the events at Yingkow and Hulutao see Barbey Papers, 4:57, "Hulutao"; 4:146, "Yingkow"; and "Chronological Report of the Action and Movements of Commander, Seventh Amphibious Force." Also Commander, Seventh Amphibious Force, "Beleager Operation: Report of Operation in Korea and North China during Occupation of Japanese Held Territory," December 22, 1945.

27. Feng Tzu-chao, pp. 262–63, Chiang Kai-shek, *Soviet Russia in China*, p. 143; *China Presents Her Case to the United Nations*, pp. 13–14; *New York Times*, November 16, 1945, p. 1:7.

28. Feng Tzu-chao, pp. 262–64; Tang Tsou, p. 333; *FRUS*, 1945, 7:798–99.

29. *New York Times,* November 12, 1945, p. 1:3; November 26, 1945, p. 2:2; Dubinsky, p. 363.

30. *HHJP,* November 27, in *CPR,* 1945, 317:2.

31. *New York Times,* November 28, 1945, p. 1:7.

32. *Ibid.*

33. Feng Tzu-chao, pp. 234–35; Chiang Kai-shek, p. 147.

34. Mao Tse-tung, "Build Stable Base Areas in the Northeast," December 28, 1945, *SW* (Peking), 4:81.

35. *CFJP,* November 30, 1945, p. 1.

36. "Mu-ch'ien ti shih-chü, jen-wu, ho ssu-hsiang wen-t'i t'ao-lun t'i-kang" (A discussion outline on problems concerning our current situation, tasks and thought) (Changchiak'ou: Chin-Ch'a-Chi Central Committee Propaganda Bureau, December 1, 1945), pp. 1–3, 5, 13, Yushodo Microfilm, reel 3.

37. *New York Times,* October 28, 1945, p. 5:4, November 2, 1945, p. 5:4; *FRUS,* 1945, 7:602.

38. For information on the fighting see *New York Times,* October 29, 1945, p. 1:6; on negotiations see *FRUS,* 1945, 7:480–83.

39. See the exchange between Chou En-lai and Shao Li-tse in *New York Times,* December 21, 1945, p. 1:2, and in *FRUS,* 1945, 7:490–91.

40. *CFJP,* November 30, p. 1; *HHJP,* November 30, in *CPR,* 1945, 320:1.

41. Third Amphibious Corps, War Diaries, November, p. 6.

42. See Frank and Shaw, p. 578; III Amphibious Corps, War Diaries, December, p. 5; First Marine Aircraft Wing, War Diaries, December, p. 3; Sixth Marine Division, War Diaries, December, pp. 9–10. On one occasion a pilot and five passengers were held for thirty-eight days, from November 10 to December 17, in a village 80 miles south of Peiping. Their release may have been timed to create an atmosphere of good will on the eve of Marshall's arrival (Frank and Shaw, p. 588).

43. *FRUS,* 1945, 7:705. For additional evidence that the Communist pressure on United States Marines in China declined after the first of December see III Marine Amphibious Corps, G-2 Periodic Report, Tientsin, January 1, 1946, in United States Marine Corps Geographic File; and letter, Shang Chen to General Randall, December 7, 1945, in "China Service Command," Office of the Commanding General, Correspondence no. 16, item no. 195, in Army Field Command, China Theater, box 937.

44. Van Slyke, *China White Paper,* 2:607–9.

45. *HHJP,* December 18, in *CPR,* 1945, p. 335:1; Yeaton to Wedemeyer, December 20, 1945, in "Eyes Alone, China Theater Policy Radios," item no. 47, in China Theater (Wedemeyer) Files, box 8; Yeaton to Wedemeyer, January 8, 1946, in "Eyes Alone, Book 6-A," item no. 5051, China Theater (Wedemeyer) Files, box 8.

46. Yeaton to Wedemeyer, December 20, 1945.

47. *New York Times,* December 19, 1945, p. 2:2; *HHJP,* December 21, in *CPR,* 1945, 338:1. This theme was repeated in *HHJP* editorials on December 24 (in *CPR,* 1945, 340:1) and December 31 (in *CPR,* 1945, 344:3).

48. "Protesting the Massacre of the American Bombing of Lulung Village," *CFJP,* December 13, 1945, 1. Among other things this editorial charged that "this lawless and godless act can only be the work of an imperialist aggressor against its colony."

49. *New York Times,* December 19, 1945, p. 2:5; December 23, 1945, p. 14:4. In a memorandum for the War Department dated December 9, Secretary of State Byrnes requested that Wedemeyer be ordered to assist the Nationalists in transporting

troops to Manchuria. Further transport to north China was to wait Marshall's approval (Van Slyke, *China White Paper*, 2:607). The key to the latter point, however, was that Marshall was told that if the talks should fail, he was to revert to the policy of aiding the Nationalist government exclusively regardless of which side bore the responsibility for failure (Feis, *China Tangle* 419). While this last provision was never revealed to any of the parties in China, it gave Chiang Kai-shek a veto on American policy and thus prevented Washington from wielding real leverage on the Chinese government.

50. *CFJP*, quoted in *New York Times*, December 23, 1945, p. 14:3.

51. *Pravda*, December 14, cited in *New York Times*, December 15, 1945, p. 7:4; *Pravda*, December 19, in *FRUS*, 1945, 7:702; *New York Times*, December 28, 1945, p. 5:6; and December 30, p. 1:4.

9. Last Chance for Peace (*January–March 1946*)

1. Melby, p. 76; *FRUS*, 1946, 9:12, 20.

2. *New York Times*, January 1, 1946, p. 12:2; January 2, p. 1:3; January 3, p. 2:3; January 6, p. 28:1; *FRUS*, 1946, 9:81–82, 129, 130.

3. *FRUS*, 1946, 9:125–26.

4. *CFJP*, January 12, reprinted in *HHJP*, January 14, translated in *CPR* (Chungking), 1946, 355:4; Report no. 229, March 11, 1946, reprinting undated document of January 1946, in Archives, Bureau of Investigation, Republic of China, cited in Warren Cohen, *America's Response to China*, p. 187.

5. Texts of the PCC resolutions are in Van Slyke, *China White Paper*, 2:610–21.

6. *HHJP*, February 1 and 2, 1946, in *Hsin Chung-kuo ti Shu-kuang*, pp. 99, 102; *CFJP*, February 1, 1946, p. 1; *FRUS*, 1946, 9:151–52.

7. For a description of Chou and his foreign affairs apparatus during this period, see Donald W. Klein, "The Management of Foreign Affairs in Communist China."

8. Carsun Chang, pp. 147, 156–57.

9. *FRUS*, 1946, 9:345, 362–64, 379–80, 381, 389–90; *New York Times*, January 24, 1946, p. 2:4; History, Peiping Executive Headquarters, 1st qtr., 1946, section II, "Truce Summaries, Record of Events," pp. 13–14, Peiping Headquarters Group, box 3562, NRC.

10. Robert Richard Kehoe, "The Ceasefire in China, 1946," p. 92.

11. *CPR* (Peiping), 1946, 11:6; *FRUS*, 1946, 9:389, 426; Kehoe, p. 92.

12. *FRUS*, 1946, 9:390.

13. Melby, p. 93; *FRUS*, 1946, 9:154; *New York Times*, February 11, 1946, p. 9:1; "Operations Report: The Executive Headquarters, Peiping, China, 1946–1947: Section I: The United States Branch," p. 3, Peiping Headquarters Group, box 3551.

14. For reports of demonstrations against the Soviet occupation of Manchuria, see *CPR* (Chungking), 1946, 350:1, 385:6, 388:5, and Melby, pp. 114–6.

15. *New York Times*, February 18, 1946, p. 1:5. For similar statements by Chou to American officials see *FRUS*, 1946, 9:440–41, 515, 534.

16. Melby, p. 115. For details on the February 22 student demonstrations see *FRUS*, 1946, 9:440, and *New York Times*, February 23, 1946, p. 4:1. In September 1946 Chou told an American journalist, "They [the Russians] made too many mistakes for us in the early days . . ." (Max Beloff, *Soviet Policy in the Far East*, p. 51).

17. *FRUS,* 1946, 9:514, 515; Freda Utley, *Last Chance in China* (New York: Bobbs-Merrill, 1947), pp. 163–69.

18. Translation of the February 14 article appears in *FRUS,* 1946, 9:450–53.

19. *New York Times,* February 19, 1946, p. 11:1; HHJP, February 24, in *CPR* (Chungking), 1946, 389:2; *CFJP* editorials of February 27 and 28, March 1 and 2, 1946 (all p. 1).

20. *FRUS,* 1946, 9:515. For a similar account by another observer see *ibid.,* p. 539.

21. *Ibid.,* pp. 792, 818, 831, 1049, 1073.

22. Liang Pi-yeh, "Ti i-ke ch'un-t'ien: Hsiu-shui-ho-tzu chien-mieh-chan ch'ien-hou" (The first spring: the circumstances of the battle of annihilation at Hsiushui-hotzu), *Hung-Ch'i P'iao-P'iao* 15:12–17; Li Shih-wen, " 'I-tien, liang-mien, san-san-chih' ti ku-shih" (The story of "One point, two sides, three-three system"), *ibid.,* 14:151.

23. "Manchurian Communist Attitudes and Opinions," War Department Strategic Services Unit, April 1, 1946, Yv-1365, Record Group 226, Box 373. This is information of March 15, 1946. The source is a Communist intelligence officer who spoke to a U.S. intelligence officer he believed to be fully sympathetic with the Communist cause in China.

24. In March 1946 a *Ta Kung Pao* reporter in Shenyang observed, "Those who have helped foreigners to remove things from the Northeast have made a bad impression upon the people" (see *CPR* [Shanghai], April 26, 1946; cited in Suzanne Pepper, "The Politics of Civil War," p. 293).

25. This is the view presented by Tanaka Kyoko, "The Civil War and Radicalization of Chinese Communist Agrarian Policy, 1945–1947," *Papers on Far Eastern History* (Australia National University), no. 8 (September 1973); and by Frederick C. Teiwes, "The Origins of Rectification."

26. William Hinton, *Fanshen,* pp. 58, 125–33, 143, 198–209; Pepper, pp. 409, 446; Tanaka Kyoko, p. 80.

27. *New York Times,* February 1, 1946, p. 3:1; February 2, p. 3:4; *FRUS,* 1946, 9;778.

28. *SCMP,* no. 3982, p. 9. In 1948 Liu reportedly favored continuing guerrilla warfare, while Chou En-lai supported a push for final victory (see C. P. Fitzgerald, *The Birth of Communist China,* pp. 106–7).

29. *SCMP,* no. 4060, p. 7.

30. Lin Piao, "The Victory of the Chinese People's Revolutionary War Is the Victory of the Thought of Mao Tse-tung," *Peking Review,* October 11, 1960, pp. 9–10.

31. *FRUS,* 1946, 9:211, 263. For the text of the Military Reorganization Agreement, see Van Slyke, *China White Paper,* 2:622.

32. *CFJP,* March 4, 1946, p. 1; *FRUS,* 1946, 9:501–2, 510.

33. *New York Times,* March 6, 1946, pp. 1:8, 2:4.

34. *New York Times,* March 10, pp. 1:8, 4:1:1; March 11, p. 2:2; March 13, p. 1:5; March 14, p. 2:2; March 23, p. 1:5; and *CFJP,* March 12, 13, 14 (all p. 3).

10. The Road to War (*March–July 1946*)

1. Tung Yen-p'ing, pp. 52, 84, 92, 97, 102, 113, 117, cited in Levine, "Political Integration," pp. 174–79; *FRUS,* 1946, 9:443, 733–34.

2. *New York Times*, March 10, 1946, p. 1:6; March 11, p. 1:1; March 13, p. 9:1; March 16, p. 6:1; March 21, p. 15:1; May 15, p. 12:3; Robert B. Rigg, "Campaign for the Northeast China Railway System," pp. 27–28.

3. Tang Tsou, p. 417; Levine, "Political Integration," p. 183; *FRUS*, 1946,9:156.

4. *HHJP*, March 19, in *CPR* (Chungking), 1946, 7:6; *CFJP*, March 19, 1946, p. 1; Van Slyke, *China White Paper*, 1:144.

5. *New York Times*, February 17, 1946, p. 1:4; *FRUS*, 1946, 9:444; Lauterbach, pp. 313–14. Gillem's attitude is revealed in his reports in *FRUS*, 1946, vol. 9.

6. Michael Lindsay, "Post Mortem on American Mediation in China," pp. 206–7.

7. Frank and Shaw, p. 600; Shaw, pp. 9–14

8. *New York Times*, May 15, 1946, p. 12:3.

9. *CPR* (Tientsin), 1946, 37:1; TASS dispatch of April 6, *CFJP*, April 7, 1946, p. 1.

10. History, Peiping Executive Headquarters, 1st quarter, 1946, section 4, *Conflict and Control Groups and CCG Field Teams*, Part A, 2, in Peiping Headquarters Group, box 3562.

11. *FRUS*, 1946, 9:502, 542.

12. *Ibid.*, pp. 535–36, 543.

13. *Ibid.*, pp. 564, 567–68, 579.

14. *Ibid.*, pp. 587, 591, 593, 597.

15. *Ibid.*, pp. 596, 742.

16. *Ibid.*, pp. 712, 719–20, 726; Kehoe, p. 234.

17. *FRUS*, 1946, 9:719–20; *HHJP*, April 12, in *CPR* (Chungking), 1946, 28:3; CFJP, April 12, 1946, p. 1, April 19, p. 1; and *New York Times*, April 23, p. 1:7, April 24, p. 17:1.

18. Cited in *New York Times*, April 22, 1946, p. 7:3.

19. *New York Times*, April 20, 1946, p. 1:1.

20. *FRUS*, 1946, 9:814, 826, 833, 845, 876.

21. This account, which credits Yenan with the decision to defend Ssupingchieh, is a departure from all previous descriptions of this battle. For analyses by western historians see Rigg, p. 254; O. Edmund Clubb, "Manchuria in the Balance, 1945–46," in *Pacific Historical Review*, (1957), 26:377, and Ray Huang, "Some Observations on Manchuria in the Balance, Early 1946," in *Pacific Historical Review* (1958), 27:162. In recent years Chinese polemicists have blamed the defeat at Ssupingchieh on P'eng Chen (allegedly Liu Shao-ch'i's agent in the Northeast) and Lin Piao, following the political line current in Peking. For accounts blaming P'eng see *Current Background*, no. 894, pp. 16–18, and no. 896, pp. 10–12, 23–25. For an account blaming Lin see *Survey of the PRC Press*, 74–79, no. 781 (July 22, 1974), pp. 3–4.

22. Huang, "Some Observations," pp. 163, 164.

23. Rigg, pp. 190–91, 254; O. Edmund Clubb, *Twentieth Century China*, p. 270; History, Peiping Executive Headquarters, 2nd quarter, 1946, section 1, *Situation: General History of the China Area*, p. 36, in Peiping Headquarters Group box 3561; *New York Times*, April 30, 1946, p. 13:3.

24. This exchange of telegrams between Lin Piao and Mao comes from Nationalist reports of documents allegedly provided by a defector from Lin's headquarters (see John R. Beal, *Marshall in China*, p. 67). Here and elsewhere I have used material provided by the Nationalists where that material runs counter to Nationalist propaganda. In this case the alleged documents tend to diminish the degree of Soviet aid to the CCP, which is the opposite of what the Nationalists wanted everyone to believe.

25. Beal, p. 67; *CFJP*, May 13, 1946, p. 1, May 19, p. 1.

26. Mao Tse-tung, *SW* (Peking), 4:87, 88; Tanaka Kyoko, pp. 84–87.

27. *New York Times*, May 13, 1946, p. 1:3; Rigg, p. 191.

28. *FRUS*, 1946, 9:889, 931; *CPR* (Peking), 1946, 54:2; *New York Times*, May 29, 1946, p. 9:6.

29. *FRUS*, 1946, 9:880 ff.

30. Marshall's efforts are recorded in *ibid.*, pp. 902, 912, 914–15, 926. Chou's willingness to accommodate Marshall is demonstrated by one incident in which Chou apparently concealed from Yenan a proposal to give the American chairmen control over the truce teams, which Chou knew would antagonize the Party leadership (see *ibid.* pp. 899, 914–15, 928, 967, 970).

31. *CFJP*, June 1, 1946, p. 1, June 5, p. 1.

32. *FRUS*, 1946, 9:976, 978, 982, 1009–11, 1113; Frank and Shaw, pp. 603–6; Shaw, p. 13–14.

33. *FRUS*, 1946, 9:1313–14.

34. Frank and Shaw, p. 612; A. Dee Willis, "Peïping Executive Headquarters, 1946–1947," p. 80.

35. *New York Times*, July 31, 1946, p. 6:3. This point was made to the author by Henry I. Shaw in an interview in October 1973.

36. U.S. Congress, Senate, Committee on Armed Services and Foreign Relations, *Inquiry into Military Situation in the Far East and Facts Surrounding Relief of Douglas MacArthur from his Assignments in that Area.* Hearings, 82nd Congress, 1st Session, 1950, p. 543; *FRUS*, 1946, 9:1353–1494; 10:1; *CFJP*, August 14, 1946, translated in History, Peiping Executive Headquarters, 3rd quarter, 1946, section 12, *Communist Party Views*, pp. 1 ff., Peiping Headquarters Group, box 3562.

37. Walter S. Robertson, interview with Willis, January 2, 1969, in Willis, p. 85.

Conclusion

1. The phrase comes from the title of Esherick, *Lost Chance in China.* The view is also reflected in Service, *The Amerasia Papers*, Barbara Tuchman, "If Mao Had Come to Washington in 1945," and Donald Zagoria, "Choices in the Postwar World."

2. For the best summary of this thesis see Donald Zagoria, "Mao's Role in the Sino-Soviet Conflict." A. Doak Barnett, *China and the Major Powers in East Asia* (Washington, D.C.: Brookings Institution, 1977), also presents this view (pp. 63–64) and presents a list of books and articles to back it up (p. 352, n. 119).

3. Stuart Schram, "The Cultural Revolution in Historical Perspective," in Schram, ed., *Authority, Participation and Cultural Change in China* (Cambridge: Cambridge University Press, 1973), p. 25.

4. There is a double irony in that Mao may have replayed this scenario two decades later. The attacks on foreign influence which accompanied the Cultural Revolution apparently created a political climate which made Mao's and Chou's opening to the United States more difficult in the late 1960s and early 1970s (see Sutter, *China-Watch*, pp. 72–82, 90–102).

5. For a provocative discussion of this theme see Michel Oksenberg, "Mao's Foreign Policy of 'Self-Reliance.' "

6. "CPC Central Committee Directive on Diplomatic Work," p. 8.

7. Barrett, p. 72.

Bibliography

Unpublished U.S. Government Sources

The records of the U.S. Forces, China Theater, are located at the National Records Center, Suitland, Maryland. These include: the correspondence of the Commanding Generals, Stilwell and Wedemeyer (Record Group [RG] 332); the Army Field Command (RG 338); the G-2 Intelligence Section (RGs 165 and 319); the Office of War Information (RG 208); and the war diaries and reports of the Marines in north China. The records of the Peiping Executive Headquarters and of the field teams which operated under the PEH are also at the National Records Center.

The Office of Strategic Services (OSS) Research and Analysis reports are contained in the Modern Military Records Division of the National Archives. This Division also has some of the raw OSS reports from Yenan released by the CIA in 1973.

The Center of Military History, formerly the Office of the Chief of Military History, has three unpublished manuscripts: "History of the China Theater," "History of the China-Burma-India Theater," and "History of the Executive Headquarters, Peiping, China." The center also has the original papers of the Yenan Observer Group, entitled "History of the Yenan Observer Group" or "Dixie Mission Papers." Microfilm of these papers is available from the Modern Military Records Division of the National Archives.

The Historical Division of the U.S. Marine Corps contains various letters and interviews collected in preparing the official Marine Corps histories, as well as *The North China Marine,* a newspaper published in Tientsin in 1945 and 1946.

The personal papers of Admiral Daniel E. Barbey are at the Operational Archives Branch of the Center for Naval History.

Published U.S. Government Documents

Marshall's Mission to China, December 1945 to January 1947: The Report and Appended Documents. 2 vols.; Arlington, Va.: University Publications, 1976.

U.S. Congress. Senate. Committee on Foreign Relations. *Investigation of Far Eastern Policy.* Mimeographed transcript. 79th Cong., 1st Sess. December 5, 6, 7, and 10, 1945.

U.S. Congress. Senate. Committee on Foreign Relations. *Report on the United States and Communist China in 1949 and 1950: The Question of Rapprochement and Recognition.* Washington, D.C.: Government Printing Office, 1973.

U.S. Congress. Senate. Committee on the Judiciary. *The Amerasia Papers: A Clue to the Catastrophe of China.* 91st Cong., 1st Sess. 2 vols.; Washington, D.C.: Government Printing Office, 1970.

U.S. Congress. Senate. Committees on Armed Services and on Foreign Relations. *Hearings on Military Situation in the Far East.* 5 parts. 82nd Cong., 1st Sess. Washington, D.C.: Government Printing Office, 1951.

U.S. Congress. Senate. Subcommittee of the Committee on Foreign Relations. *Hearings on State Department Employee Loyalty Investigation.* 81st Cong., 2nd Sess. Washington, D.C.: Government Printing Office, 1950.

U.S. Congress. Senate. Subcommittee of the Committee on the Judiciary. *Hearings on Institute of Pacific Relations.* 15 parts. 82nd Cong., 1st and 2nd Sess. Washington, D.C.: Government Printing Office, 1951–52.

U.S. Department of State. *Foreign Relations of the United States: Diplomatic Papers.* 1942, *China;* 1943, *China;* 1944, vol. 6, *China;* 1945, vol. 7, *The Far East: China;* 1946, vols. 9 and 10, *The Far East: China.* Washington, D.C.: Government Printing Office, 1956–72.

Newspapers and Periodicals

Amerasia (New York).

Chieh Fang Jih Pao (Liberation Daily) (Yenan) was the official organ of the CCP during the war and after.

Ch'ün Chung (The Masses) was a Communist periodical also published in Chungking.

Current Background. Hong Kong: American Consulate General.

Hsin Hua Jih Pao (New China Daily) (Chungking) was the principal Party paper in the Nationalist capital. After January 1945, key articles and editorials from *Hsin Hua Jih Pao* and from the other Chungking papers (*Chung Yang Jih Pao, Ta Kung Pao,* etc.), were translated and published in a daily news summary, *Chinese Press Review* (Chungking: Office of War Information, 1945–46). After the war this service was extended to Peiping, Tientsin, Nanking, and other cities. *Chinese Press Review* for various cities and dates, 1945–49, is available on microfilm.

New York Times.
Peking Review.
Selections from China Mainland Magazines. Hong Kong: American Consulate General.
Survey of the China Mainland Press. Hong Kong: American Consulate General.
Survey of the China Mainland Press (Supplement). Hong Kong: American Consulate General.

Chinese-Language Sources

Ch'i Wu. *I ke Ke ming Ken-chü-ti ti Ch'eng-chang* (Growth of a Revolutionary Base). Peking: Jen-min Ch'u-pan-she, 1958.

Chou Erh-fu. *Tung-pei heng-luan-mien* (Cross-section of Manchuria). Harbin, 1946.

Chou Li-p'o. *Nan Hsia Chi* (Diary of the Move South). Kuang-hua shu-tien, February 1948.

Feng Tzu-chao, ed. *Chung-kuo K'ang-chan Shih* (History of the Chinese war of resistance). Shanghai, 1946.

Hsin Chung-kuo ti Shu-kuang (Dawn of New China). Chung-kuo Ch'u-pan-she, 1946.

Hsing Huo Liao Yüan (A Single Spark Can Start a Prairie Fire). 10 vols. Peking: Jen-min Wen-hsueh Ch'u-pan-she, 1958.

Hsu Kuan-san. "Liu Shao-ch'i yü Mao Tse-tung" (Liu Shao-ch'i and Mao Tse-tung), Hong Kong: *Ming-pao Yueh-k'an*, July 1966.

—— "Tang ti Ta Chien-chu-shih" (The Party's Great Architect). Hong Kong: *Jen-Wu yü Ssu-hsiang*, no. 40.

Hu Hsi-k'uei. "Shih-chü Pien-hua ho Wo-ti Fang-chen" (Changes in the Present Situation and Our Plan). Taipei: Report, Bureau of Investigation, August 30, 1945.

Hu Hua, et al., eds. *Chung-kuo Hsin-min-chu chu-i Ke-ming Shih* (History of the Chinese New Democratic Revolution). Peking, 1952.

Hu Hua. *Chung-kuo ko-ming Shih Chiang-i* (Lectures on the History of the Chinese Revolution). Peking, 1962.

Hung-ch'i p'iao-p'iao (Red Flag Flying). 17 vols. Peking, 1957–66.

K'ang-jih Chan-cheng Shih-ch'i ti Chung-kuo Jen-min Chieh-fang Chün (The PLA in the Anti-Japanese War). Peking: Jen-min Ch'u-pan-she, July 1953.

Liu Pai-yü. *Shih-tai ti Yin-hsiang* (Impressions of an Age). Harbin: Kuang-hua Shu-tien, 1948.

Ma Han-ping. *Wang Chen Nan-cheng Chi* (Record of Wang Chen's Southern Expedition). Chung-kuo Ch'u-pan-she, January 1947.

Mao Tse-tung Chi (The Works of Mao Tse-tung), edited by Takeuchi Minoru et al. Tokyo, 1970—.

T'ang Yun, ed. *Tung-pei Wen-t'i Chen-hsiang* (The Truth about Northeast Problems). Shih-tai Ch'u-pan-she, n.d.

Tung-pei Wen-ti (Northeast Problems). Tung-pei Shu-tien, April 1946.

Wang Chien-ming. *Chung-kuo Kung-ch'an-tang Shih K'ao* (Draft History of the Chinese Communist Party). Taipei: Cheng Chung Book Company, 1965.

Wei Tung-pei ti Ho-p'ing Min-chu erh Tou-cheng (Struggle for Peace and Democracy in the Northeast). Ta-chung Wen-hua Ho-tso-she, 1946.

Yeh Hu-sheng. *Jen-min ti Sheng-li* (People's Victory). Peking: Kung-jen, 1956.

Yushodo Bookstore Microfilms. "Checklist to Yu-kuan Chung-kuo Kung-ch'an-tang Tzu-liao" (Materials Concerning the CCP). Tokyo, 1970.

—— *Yu-kuan Chung-kuo Kung-ch'an-tang* (Materials on the CCP). 20 reels. Tokyo, 1970.

Books

Band, Claire, and William Band. *Dragon Fangs: Two Years with Chinese Communists*. New Haven: Yale University Press, 1948.

Barbey, Daniel E. *MacArthur's Amphibious Navy: Seventh Amphibious Force Operations, 1943–1945*. Annapolis: Naval Institute Press, 1969.

Barrett, David D. *Dixie Mission: The United States Army Observer Group in Yenan, 1944*. Berkeley: University of California Press, 1970.

Beal, John R. *Marshall in China*. Garden City, N.Y.: Doubleday, 1970.

Belden, Jack. *China Shakes the World*. New York: Harper, 1949.

Beloff, Max. *Soviet Policy in the Far East, 1944–1951*. London: Oxford University Press, 1953.

Bianco, Lucien. *Origins of the Chinese Revolution, 1915–1949*. Stanford: Stanford University Press, 1967.

Bisson, T. A. *Yenan in June 1937: Talks with the Communist Leaders*. Berkeley: University of California Press, 1973.

Boyle, John H. *China and Japan at War, 1937–1945: The Politics of Collaboration*. Stanford: Stanford University Press, 1972.

Brandt, Conrad. *Stalin's Failure in China*. New York: Norton, 1958.

Brandt, Conrad, Benjamin Schwartz, and John K. Fairbank. *A Documentary History of Chinese Communism*. Cambridge: Harvard University Press, 1959.

Buhite, Russell. *Patrick J. Hurley and American Relations with China*. Ithaca: Cornell University Press, 1973.

Butow, Robert J. C. *Japan's Decision to Surrender.* Stanford: Stanford University Press, 1954.

Carlson, Evans Fordyce. *The Chinese Army: Its Organization and Military Efficiency.* New York: Institute of Pacific Relations, 1940.

—— *Twin Stars of China: A Behind the Scenes Story of China's Valiant Struggle for Existence by a U.S. Marine Who Lived and Moved with the People.* New York: Dodd, Mead, 1940.

Chang, Carsun. *The Third Force in China.* New York: Bookman Associates, 1952.

Chang Kuo-t'ao. *The Autobiography of Chang Kuo-t'ao.* Vol. 2. *The Rise of the Chinese Communist Party, 1928–1938.* Lawrence: University of Kansas Press, 1972.

Chassin, Lionel Max. *The Communist Conquest of China.* Cambridge: Harvard University Press, 1965.

Ch'en, Jerome. *Mao and the Chinese Revolution.* London: Oxford University Press, 1967.

Ch'en Shao-yü (Wang Ming). *China: Cultural Revolution or Counterrevolutionary Coup?* Moscow: Novosti Press, 1969.

Chiang Kai-shek. *China's Destiny and Chinese Economic Theory.* Translated by Philip J. Jaffe. New York: Roy, 1947.

Chiang Kai-shek (Chiang Chung-cheng). *Soviet Russia in China, A Summing Up At Seventy.* New York: Farrar, Straus and Giroux, 1965.

China Handbook, 1937–1945. Rev. and enl. with 1946 supplement. Chinese Ministry of Information, comp. New York: Macmillan, 1947.

Chinese Delegation to the United Nations. *China Presents Her Case to the United Nations.* New York: 1949.

China Yearbook. London: George Routledge, 1912–39.

Chu Teh. *On the Battlefronts of the Liberated Areas.* Peking: Foreign Language Press, 1952.

Clubb, O. Edmund. *China and Russia: The Great Game.* New York: Columbia University Press, 1971.

—— *Twentieth Century China.* New York: Columbia University Press, 1964.

Cohen, Warren. *America's Response to China.* New York: Wiley, 1971.

Compton, Boyd, ed. *Mao's China: Party Reform Documents, 1942–1944.* Seattle: University of Washington Press, 1966.

Dallin, David J. *Soviet Russia and the Far East.* New Haven: Yale University Press, 1948.

Davies, John Paton, Jr. *Dragon by the Tail.* New York: Norton, 1972.

Dedijer, Vladimir. *Tito Speaks.* New York: Weidenfeld and Nicolson, 1953.

Dubinsky, A. M. *The Far East in the Second World War.* Moscow: Nauka, 1972.

Eighth National Congress of the CCP. Peking, 1957.

Epstein, Israel. *The Unfinished Revolution in China.* Boston: Little, Brown, 1947.

Feis, Herbert. *Between War and Peace: The Postdam Conference.* Princeton: Princeton University Press, 1960.

—— *The China Tangle: The American Effort in China from Pearl Harbor to the Marshall Mission.* New York: Atheneum, 1965.

—— *Churchill, Roosevelt and Stalin.* Princeton, N.J.: Princeton University Press, 1967.

——*Contest over Japan.* New York: Norton, 1967.

—— *From Trust to Terror: The Onset of the Cold War, 1945–1950.* New York: Norton, 1970.

Fischer, Louis. *The Road to Yalta: Soviet Foreign Relations, 1941–1945.* New York: Harper and Row, 1972.

Fitzgerald, C. P. *The Birth of Communist China.* Harmondsworth, England: Penguin, 1964.

Forman, Harrison. *Report from Red China.* New York: Whittlesey House, 1945.

Frank, Benis M., and Henry I. Shaw, Jr. *History of U.S. Marine Corps in World War II.* Vol. 5. *Victory and Occupation.* Washington, D.C.: U.S. Marine Corps Historical Branch, 1968.

Gaddis, John Lewis. *The United States and the Origins of the Cold War, 1941–1947.* New York: Columbia University Press, 1972.

Garthoff, Raymond L., ed. *Sino-Soviet Military Relations.* New York: Praeger, 1966.

Gati, Charles. *Caging the Bear: Containment and the Cold War.* Indianapolis and New York: Bobbs-Merrill, 1974.

Gelder, George Stuart, ed. *The Chinese Communists.* London: Gollancz, 1946.

Gittings, John. *The Role of the Chinese Army.* New York: Oxford University Press, 1967.

—— *The World and China, 1922–1972.* London: Eyre Methuen, 1974.

Griffith, Samuel B. *The Chinese People's Liberation Army.* London: Weidenfeld and Nicolson, 1968.

Guillermaz, Jacques. *A History of the Chinese Communist Party, 1921–1949.* New York: Random House, 1972.

Harrison, James P. *The Long March to Power: A History of the Chinese Communist Party, 1921–72.* New York: Praeger, 1972.

Hinton, William. *Fanshen: A Documentary of Revolution in a Chinese Village.* New York: Random House, 1966.

Ho Kan-chih. *A History of the Modern Chinese Revolution.* Peking: Foreign Language Press, 1960.

Hsu Kai-yu. *Chou En-lai: China's Grey Eminence.* Garden City, N.Y.: Doubleday, 1968.

Hsüeh Chün-tu, ed. *The Chinese Communist Movement, 1921–1949: An Annotated Bibliography of Selected Materials in the Chinese Collection of the Hoover Institution.* 2 vols. Stanford, Calif.: Stanford University, 1960.

Hu Ch'iao-mu. *Thirty Years of the CCP.* Peking: Foreign Language Press, 1952.

Isaacs, Harold. *No Peace for Asia*. Cambridge: MIT Press, 1967.

Johnson, Chalmers A. *Peasant Nationalism and Communist Power: The Emergence of Revolutionary China, 1937–1945*. Stanford: Stanford University Press, 1962.

Jones, Francis Clifford. *Manchuria since 1931*. Herfordshire, England: Broadwater Press, 1949.

Kataoka, Tetsuya. *Resistance and Revolution in China*. Berkeley: University of California Press, 1974.

Klein, Donald W., and Anne B. Clark. *A Biographic Dictionary of Chinese Communism, 1921–1965*. 2 vols. Harvard East Asian Series, 57. Cambridge: Harvard University Press, 1971.

Kolko, Gabriel. *The Politics of War*. New York: Random House, 1968.

Kolko, Joyce, and Gabriel Kolko. *The Limits of Power, 1945–1954*. New York: Harper and Row, 1972.

Kuo Warren. *Analytical History of the Chinese Communist Party*. Vol. 4. Taipei: Institute of International Relations, 1971.

Latham, Earl. *The Communist Controversy in Washington: From the New Deal to McCarthy*. Cambridge: Harvard University Press, 1966.

Lauterbach, Richard. *Danger from the East*. New York: Harper, 1947.

Liang Chin-tung. *General Stilwell in China, 1942–1944: The Full Story*. New York: St. John's University Press, 1972.

Liao Kai-lung. *From Yenan to Peking*. Peking: Foreign Language Press, 1954.

Liu, F. F. *A Military History of Modern China, 1929–1949*. Princeton: Princeton University Press, 1956.

Liu Shao-ch'i. *On the Party*. Peking: Foreign Language Press, 1952.

Lohbeck, Don. *Patrick J. Hurley*. Chicago: Regnery, 1956.

McLane, Charles B. *Soviet Policy and the Chinese Communists, 1931–1946*. New York: Columbia University Press, 1958.

Mao Tse-tung. *Selected Works*. 4 vols. London: Lawrence and Wishart, 1956.

—— *Selected Works of Mao Tse-tung*. 4 vols. Peking: Foreign Language Press, 1961–65.

Matloff, Maurice. *Strategic Planning for Coalition Warfare, 1943–1944*. Washington, D.C.: Department of the Army, Historical Division, 1959.

Melby, John F. *The Mandate of Heaven*. Garden City, N.Y.: Doubleday, 1971.

Miles, Milton E. *A Different Kind of War*. New York: Doubleday, 1967.

Moorad, George. *Lost Peace in China*. New York: Dutton, 1949.

Morgenthau, Henry, Jr. *Morgenthau Diary, China*. 2 vols. U.S. Senate, 89th Congress, 1st Sess. Committee on the Judiciary, Subcommittee to Investigate the Administration of the Internal Security Laws. Washington, D.C.: Government Printing Office, 1965.

Morton, Lewis. *U.S. Army in World War II: The War in the Pacific: Strategy and Command: The First Two Years*. Washington, D.C.: Government Printing Office, 1961.

North, Robert C. *Moscow and Chinese Communists.* 2nd ed. Stanford: Stanford University Press, 1963.

Pauley, Edwin Wendell. *Report on Japanese Assets in Manchuria to the President of the United States.* Washington, D.C.: Government Printing Office, 1946.

Payne, Robert. *Chinese Diaries, 1941–1946.* New York: Weybright and Talley, 1970.

Peck, Graham. *Two Kinds of Time.* Boston: Houghton Mifflin, 1950.

Rigg, Robert B. *Red China's Fighting Hordes.* Harrisburg, Pa.: Military Service Publishing Company, 1951.

Rinden, Robert, and Roxanne Witke. *The Red Flag Waves: A Guide to the Hung-ch'i p'iao-p'iao Collection.* Berkeley: University of California Press, 1968.

Romanus, Charles F., and Riley Sunderland. *Stilwell's Command Problems. U.S. Army in World War II: The China-Burma-India Theater,* vol. 9, part 2. Washington, D.C.: Department of the Army, Historical Division, 1953.

—— *Stilwell's Mission to China. U.S. Army in World War II: The China-Burma-India Theater,* vol. 9, part 1. Washington, D.C.: Department of the Army, Historical Division, 1953.

—— *Time Runs Out in CBI. U.S. Army in World War II: The China-Burma-India Theater,* vol. 9, part 3. Washington, D.C.: Department of the Army, Historical Division, 1953.

Rosinger, Lawrence K. *China's Wartime Politics, 1937–1944.* Princeton: Princeton University Press, 1944.

Rue, John E. *Mao Tse-tung in Opposition, 1927–1935.* Stanford: Stanford University Press, 1966.

Schaller, Michael. *The U.S. Crusade in China, 1938–1945.* New York: Columbia University Press, 1978.

Schram, Stuart R. *Mao Tse-tung.* Harmondsworth, England: Penguin, 1966.

—— *The Political Thought of Mao Tse-tung.* New York: Praeger, 1969.

Schram, Stuart R., ed. *Chairman Mao Talks to the People: Talks and Letters, 1956–1971.* New York: Pantheon Books, 1974.

Schwartz, Benjamin I. *Chinese Communism and the Rise of Mao.* Cambridge: Harvard University Press, 1964.

Selden, Mark. *The Yenan Way in Revolutionary China.* Cambridge: Harvard University Press, 1972.

Service, John S. *The Amerasia Papers: Some Problems in the History of U.S.–China Relations.* Berkeley: University of California Press, 1971.

—— *Lost Chance in China: The World War II Despatches of John S. Service.* edited by Joseph Esherick. New York: Random House, 1974.

Shaw, Henry I. *The United States Marines in North China, 1945–1949.* Washington, D.C., 1962.

Sherwood, Robert E. *Roosevelt and Hopkins.* New York: Grosset and Dunlap, 1948.

Shewmaker, Kenneth. *Americans and Chinese Communists, 1927–1945: A Persuading Encounter.* Ithaca: Cornell University Press, 1971.

Smedley, Agnes. *Battle Hymn of China.* New York: Knopf, 1943.

—— *China Fights Back: An American Woman with the Eighth Route Army.* London: Vanguard, 1938.

—— *The Great Road: The Life and Times of Chu Teh.* New York: Monthly Review Press, 1956.

Snell, John L., ed. *The Meaning of Yalta.* Baton Rouge: Louisiana State University Press, 1970.

Snow, Edgar. *The Other Side of the River.* New York: Random House, 1961.

—— *Random Notes on Red China, 1936–1945.* Cambridge: Harvard University Press, 1968.

—— *Red Star over China.* London: Gollancz, 1937; New York: Grove Press, 1968.

Stein, Gunther. *The Challenge of Red China.* New York: Whittlesey House, 1945.

Strong, Anna Louise. *The Chinese Conquer China.* New York: Doubleday, 1949.

Stuart, John Leighton. *Fifty Years in China.* New York: Random House, 1954.

Sutter, Robert G. *China Watch: Toward Sino-American Reconciliation.* Baltimore: Johns Hopkins University Press, 1978.

Thornton, Richard C. *China: The Struggle for Power, 1917–1972.* Bloomington: Indiana University Press, 1973.

Tsou, Tang. *America's Failure in China, 1941–1950.* Chicago: University of Chicago Press, 1963.

Tuchman, Barbara. *Notes from China.* New York: Collier, 1972.

—— *Stilwell and the American Experience in China, 1911–1945.* New York: Macmillan, 1971.

Ulam, Adam B. *Expansion and Coexistence: The History of Soviet Foreign Policy, 1917–1967.* New York: Praeger, 1968.

Union Research Institute, eds. *The Case of P'eng Teh-huai.* Hong Kong: Union Research Institute, 1968.

—— *The Collected Works of Liu Shao-ch'i.* 3 vols. Hong Kong: Union Research Institute, 1968.

Van Slyke, Lyman P. *Enemies and Friends: The United Front in Chinese Communist History.* Stanford: Stanford University Press, 1967.

Van Slyke, Lyman P., ed. *The China White Paper.* 2 vols. Stanford: Stanford University Press, 1967.

—— *The Chinese Communist Movement: A Report of the United States War Department, July 1945.* Stanford: Stanford University Press, 1968.

Varg, Paul A. *The Closing of the Door.* Lansing: Michigan State University Press, 1973.

Vladimirov, Pyotr P. *The Special Region of China, 1942–1945.* Bombay: Allied, 1974.

Wales, Nym [Helen Foster Snow]. *Inside Red China*. Garden City, N.Y.: Doubleday, 1939.

—— *My Yenan Notebooks*. Madison, Conn.: 1961.

Wedemeyer, Albert. *Wedemeyer Reports!* New York: Holt, 1958.

White, Theodore H., ed. *The Stilwell Papers*. New York: Sloane, 1948.

White, Theodore H., and Jacoby, Annalee. *Thunder Out of China*. New York: Sloane, 1961.

Whiting, Allen S. *China Crosses the Yalu*. Stanford, Calif.: Stanford University Press, 1960.

—— *Soviet Policies in China, 1917–1924*. Stanford: Stanford University Press, 1953.

Whitson, William. *The Chinese High Command: A History of Communist Military Politics, 1927–71*. New York: Praeger, 1973.

—— *Civil War in China, 1946–1950*. 2 vols. Washington, D.C.: Office of the Chief of Military History, 1967.

Whitson, William, ed. *Military Campaigns in China, 1924–50*. Washington, D.C.: Office of the Chief of Military History, 1966.

Wu Chen-tsai, ed. *Collected Documents on the First Sino-American Conference on Mainland China*. Taipei: Institute of International Relations, 1969.

Young, Arthur N. *China and the Helping Hand, 1937–1945*. Cambridge: Harvard University Press, 1963.

Articles

"The Bankruptcy of China's Devotee of Parliamentarianism." *Peking Review* (Sept. 1, 1967), no. 36, pp. 8–11.

Benton, Gregor. "The 'Second Wang Ming Line' (1935–38)." *China Quarterly* (March 1975), no. 61, pp. 61–94.

Clubb, O. Edmund. "Manchuria in the Balance, 1945–1946." *Pacific Historical Review* (November, 1957), 26:377–89.

Cohen, Warren. "The Development of Chinese Communist Policy toward the United States, 1922–1945." *Orbis* (Spring/Summer 1967), 11:219–37, 551–69.

"CPC Central Committee Directive on Diplomatic Work." *Problemy Dal'nego Vostoka* (*Problems of the Far East*), (March 24, 1972), no. 1, in *JPRS* (October 12, 1972), no. 57230.

Heinzig, Dieter. "The Otto Braun Memoirs and Mao's Rise to Power." *China Quarterly* (April–June 1971) no. 46, pp. 274–88.

Hersey, John. "Letter from Peiping." *New Yorker* (May 4, 1946), 22:70–78.

Hsu Kwan-san. "Liu Shao-ch'i and Mao Tse-tung, 1922–1947." *Chinese Law and Government* (Summer–Fall 1970), 3(2–3):206–250.

Huang, Ray. "Some Observations on Manchuria in the Balance, Early 1946." *Pacific Historical Review* (May 1958), 27:159–69.

Klein, Donald W. "The Management of Foreign Affairs in Communist China." In John M. H. Lindbeck, ed., *China: Management of a Revolutionary Society.* Seattle: University of Washington Press, 1971.

Levine, Steven. "Soviet-American Rivalry in Manchuria and the Cold War." In Hsueh Chun-tu, ed., *Dimensions of Chinese Foreign Policy.* New York: Praeger, 1977.

Liang, Chin-tung. "The Sino-Soviet Treaty of Friendship and Alliance of 1945: The Inside Story." In Paul K. T. Sih, ed., *Nationalist China During the Sino-Japanese War, 1937–1945,* pp. 373–97. Hicksville, N.Y.: Exposition Press, 1977.

Lin Piao. "The Victory of the Chinese People's Revolutionary War Is the Victory of the Thought of Mao Tse-tung." *Peking Review* (October 11, 1960), pp. 9–10.

Lindsay, Michael. "China, 1937–1945." In D. M. Condit et al., eds., *Challenge and Response in Internal Conflict; vol. 1, The Experience in Asia,* chap. 6. Washington, D.C.: American University Press, 1968.

—— "China: Report of a Visit." *International Affairs* (London) (January 1950), 26:22–31.

—— "Military Strength in China—a Summary of OB Based on News Dispatches." *Far Eastern Survey* (April 9, 1947), 16:80–82.

—— "The North China Front: A Study of Chinese Guerrillas in Action." *Amerasia* (March 31, 1944), 8:100–110 and *ibid.* (April 14, 1944), 8:117–25.

—— "Post-Mortem on American Mediation in China." *International Journal* (Toronto) (Summer 1947), 2:200–212.

Melby, John F. "The Origins of the Cold War in China." *Pacific Affairs* (Spring 1968), pp. 19–33.

Okabe, Tatsumi. "The Cold War and China." In Yonosuke Nagai and Akira Iriye, eds., *The Origins of the Cold War in Asia,* pp. 224–51. New York: Columbia University Press, 1977.

Peck, James. "The Roots of Rhetoric: The Professional Ideology of America's China Watchers." *Bulletin of Concerned Asian Scholars* (October 1969), 2:59–69.

Rigg, Robert B. "Campaign for the Northeast China Railway System, 1946–1947." *Military Review* (December 1947), 27:27–34.

Schlesinger, Arthur, Jr. "Origins of the Cold War." *Foreign Affairs* (October 1967), 46(1):22–52.

Schram, Stuart R. "Mao Tse-tung and Liu Shao-ch'i, 1939–1969." *Asian Survey* (April 1972), 12(4):275–93.

Shilin, Alan I. "Occupation at Tsingtao." *Marine Corps Gazette* (January 1946), 30(1):35.

Snow, Edgar. "Chinese Communists and World Affairs: An Interview with Mao Tse-tung." *Amerasia* (August 1937), 1:263–69.

Strong, Anna Louise. "Reminiscences on Interview with Chairman Mao on the Paper Tiger." *China Reconstructs* (November 1966), 15:4–8.

Teiwes, Frederick C. "The Origins of Rectification: Inner-Party Purges and Education before Liberation." *China Quarterly* (January 1976), no. 65, pp. 15–53.

Tuchman, Barbara W. "If Mao Had Come to Washington in 1945." *Foreign Affairs* (October 1972), 51(1):44–64, and in Barbara Tuchman, *Notes from China*. New York: Macmillan 1972.

Zagoria, Donald. "Choices in the Postwar World (2): Containment and China." In Charles Gati, ed., *Caging the Bear: Containment and the Cold War.*, pp. 109–27. Indianapolis and New York: Bobbs-Merrill, 1974.

—— "Mao's Role in the Sino-Soviet Conflict." *Pacific Affairs* (Summer 1974), 47(2):139–53.

Manuscripts

Bauer, Boyd, H. "General Claire Lee Chennault and China, 1937–1958." Ph.D. dissertation, American University, 1973.

DeGroot, Peter T. "Myth and Reality in American Policy toward China: Patrick J. Hurley's Missions, 1944–1945." Ph.D. dissertation, Kent State University, 1974.

Goldstein, Steven M. "Chinese Communist Perspectives in International Affairs." Ph.D. dissertation, Columbia University, 1972.

Kehoe, Robert Richard. "The Cease-Fire in China, 1946: The Operations of the Peiping Executive Headquarters and the Truce Teams during the Marshall Mission." Ph.D. dissertation, American University, 1970.

Lee, Ngok. "The Chinese Communist Bases in North China, 1938–1943." Ph.D. dissertation, University of London, 1968.

Levine, Steven. "Political Integration in Manchuria, 1945–1949." Ph.D. dissertation, Harvard University, 1972.

Liang Chin-tung. "The Sino-Soviet Treaty of Friendship and Alliance of 1945: The Inside Story."

Oksenberg, Michel. "Mao's Foreign Policy of 'Self-Reliance.' " Paper presented to the University Seminar on Modern East Asia: China. Columbia University, March 1970.

Pepper, Suzanne. "The Politics of Civil War: China 1945–1949." Ph.D. dissertation, University of California (Berkeley), 1972.

Willis, A. Dee. "Peiping Executive Headquarters, 1946–47." Senior thesis, Vanderbilt University, 1970.

Index

Studies of the East Asian Institute

The Ladder of Success in Imperial China, by Ping-ti Ho. New York: Columbia University Press, 1962.

The Chinese Inflation, 1937–1949, by Shun-hsin Chou. New York: Columbia University Press, 1963.

Reformer in Modern China: Chang Chien, 1853–1926, by Samuel Chu. New York: Columbia University Press, 1965.

Research in Japanese Sources: A Guide, by Herschel Webb with the assistance of Marleigh Ryan. New York: Columbia University Press, 1965.

Society and Education in Japan, by Herbert Passin. New York: Teachers College Press, Columbia University, 1965.

Agricultural Production and Economic Development in Japan, 1873–1922, by James I. Nakamura. Princeton: Princeton University Press, 1966.

Japan's First Modern Novel: Ukigumo of Futabatei Shimei, by Marleigh Ryan. New York: Columbia University Press, 1967.

The Korean Communist Movement, 1918–1948, by Dae-Sook Suh. Princeton: Princeton University Press, 1967.

The First Vietnam Crisis, by Melvin Gurtov. New York: Columbia University Press, 1967.

Cadres, Bureaucracy, and Political Power in Communist China, by A. Doak Barnett. New York: Columbia University Press, 1967.

The Japanese Imperial Institution in the Tokugawa Period, by Herschel Webb. New York: Columbia University Press, 1968.

Higher Education and Business Recruitment in Japan, by Koya Azumi. New York: Teachers College Press, Columbia University, 1969.

The Communists and Chinese Peasant Rebellions: A Study in the Rewriting of Chinese History, by James P. Harrison, Jr. New York: Atheneum, 1969.

How the Conservatives Rule Japan, by Nathaniel B. Thayer. Princeton: Princeton University Press, 1969.

Aspects of Chinese Education, by C. T. Hu. New York: Teachers College Press, Columbia University, 1969.

Documents of Korean Communism, 1918–1948, by Dae-Sook Suh. Princeton: Princeton University Press, 1970.

Japanese Education: A Bibliography of Materials in the English Language, by Herbert Passin. New York: Teachers College Press, Columbia University, 1970.

Economic Development and the Labor Market in Japan, by Koji Taira. New York: Columbia University Press, 1970.

The Japanese Oligarchy and the Russo-Japanese War, by Shumpei Okamoto. New York: Columbia University Press, 1970.

Imperial Restoration in Medieval Japan, by H. Paul Varley. New York: Columbia University Press, 1971.

Japan's Postwar Defense Policy, 1947–1968, by Martin E. Weinstein. New York: Columbia University Press, 1971.

Election Campaigning Japanese Style, by Gerald L. Curtis. New York: Columbia University Press, 1971.

China and Russia: The "Great Game," by O. Edmund Clubb. New York: Columbia University Press, 1971.

Money and Monetary Policy in Communist China, by Katherine Huang Hsiao. New York: Columbia University Press, 1971.

The District Magistrate in Late Imperial China, by John R. Watt. New York: Columbia University Press, 1972.

Law and Policy in China's Foreign Relations: A Study of Attitudes and Practice, by James C. Hsiung. New York: Columbia University Press, 1972.

Pearl Harbor as History: Japanese-American Relations, 1931–1941, edited by Dorothy Borg and Shumpei Okamoto, with the assistance of Dale K. A. Finlayson. New York: Columbia University Press, 1973.

Japanese Culture: A Short History, by H. Paul Varley. New York: Praeger, 1973.

Doctors in Politics: The Political Life of the Japan Medical Association, by William E. Steslicke. New York: Praeger, 1973.

Japan's Foreign Policy, 1868–1941: A Research Guide, edited by James William Morley. New York: Columbia University Press, 1973.

The Japan Teachers Union: A Radical Interest Group in Japanese Politics, by Donald Ray Thurston. Princeton: Princeton University Press, 1973.

Palace and Politics in Prewar Japan, by David Anson Titus. New York: Columbia University Press, 1974.

The Idea of China: Essays in Geographic Myth and Theory, by Andrew March. Devon, England: David and Charles, 1974.

Origins of the Cultural Revolution, by Roderick MacFarquhar. New York: Columbia University Press, 1974.

Shiba Kokan: Artist, Innovator, and Pioneer in the Westernization of Japan, by Calvin L. French. Tokyo: Weatherhill, 1974.

Embassy at War, by Harold Joyce Noble. Edited with an introduction by Frank Baldwin, Jr. Seattle: University of Washington Press, 1975.

Rebels and Bureaucrats: China's December 9ers, by John Israel and Donald W. Klein. Berkeley: University of California Press, 1975.

House United, House Divided: The Chinese Family in Taiwan, by Myron L. Cohen. New York: Columbia University Press, 1976.

Insei: Abdicated Sovereigns in the Politics of Late Heian Japan, by G. Cameron Hurst. New York: Columbia University Press, 1976.

Deterrent Diplomacy, edited by James W. Morley. New York: Columbia University Press, 1976.

Cadres, Commanders and Commissars: The Training of the Chinese Communist Leadership, 1920–45, by Jane L. Price. Boulder, Colorado: Westview Press, 1976.

Sun Yat-sen: Frustrated Patriot, by C. Martin Wilbur. New York: Columbia University Press, 1976.

Japanese International Negotiating Style, by Michael Blaker. New York: Columbia University Press, 1977.

Contemporary Japanese Budget Politics, by John Creighton Campbell. Berkeley: University of California Press, 1977.

The Medieval Chinese Oligarchy, by David Johnson. Boulder, Colorado: Westview Press, 1977.

Escape from Predicament: Neo-Confucianism and China's Evolving Political Culture, by Thomas A. Metzger. New York: Columbia University Press, 1977.

The Arms of Kiangnan: Modernization in the Chinese Ordnance Industry, 1860–1895, by Thomas L. Kennedy. Boulder, Colorado: Westview Press, 1978.

Patterns of Japanese Policymaking: Experiences from Higher Education, by T. J. Pempel. Boulder, Colorado: Westview Press, 1978.

The Chinese Connection, by Warren Cohen. New York: Columbia University Press, 1978.

Militarism in Modern China: The Career of Wu P'ei-fu, 1916–1939, by Odoric Y. K. Wou. Folkestone, England: Wm. Dawson & Sons, 1978.

A Chinese Pioneer Family: The Lins of Wu-feng, by Johanna Meskill. Princeton: Princeton University Press, 1979.

Perspectives on a Changing China: Essays in Honor of Professor C. Martin Wilbur, edited by Joshua A. Fogel and William T. Rowe. Boulder, Colorado: Westview Press, 1979.

The Memoirs of Li Tsung-jen, by T. K. Tong and Li Tsung-jen. Boulder, Colorado: Westview Press, 1979.

Yenan and the Great Powers: The Origins of Chinese Communist Foreign Policy, 1944–1946, by James Reardon-Anderson. New York: Columbia University Press, 1979.